PHILOSOPHY OF ACTION

Other interview books from Automatic Press ♦ $\frac{V}{I}$-P

Formal Philosophy
edited by Vincent F. Hendricks & John Symons
November 2005

Masses of Formal Philosophy
edited by Vincent F. Hendricks & John Symons
October 2006

Political Questions: 5 Questions for Political Philosophers
edited by Morten Ebbe Juul Nielsen
December 2006

Philosophy of Technology: 5 Questions
edited by Jan-Kyrre Berg Olsen & Evan Selinger
February 2007

Game Theory: 5 Questions
edited by Vincent F. Hendricks & Pelle Guldborg Hansen
April 2007

Philosophy of Mathematics: 5 Questions
edited by Vincent F. Hendricks & Hannes Leitgeb
January 2008

Philosophy of Computing and Information: 5 Questions
edited by Luciano Floridi
Sepetmber 2008

Philosophy of the Social Sciences: 5 Questions
edited by Diego Ríos & Christoph Schmidt-Petri
September 2008

Epistemology: 5 Questions
edited by Vincent F. Hendricks & Duncan Pritchard
September 2008

Complexity: 5 Questions
Carlos Gershenson
November 2008

Mind and Consciousness: 5 Questions
edited by Patrick Grim
January 2009

See all published and forthcoming books in the 5 Questions series at
www.vince-inc.com/automatic.html

PHILOSOPHY OF ACTION
5 QUESTIONS

edited by

Jesús A. Aguilar
Andrei A. Buckareff

Automatic Press ♦ $\frac{V}{I}$P

Automatic Press ♦ $\frac{V}{I}$P

Information on this title: www.vince-inc.com/automatic.html

© Automatic Press / VIP 2009

This publication is in copyright. Subject to statuary exception
and to the provisions of relevant collective licensing agreements,
no reproduction of any part may take place without
the written permission of the publisher.

First published 2009

Printed in the United States of America
and the United Kingdom

ISBN-10   87-92130-08-9   paperback
ISBN-13   978-87-92130-08-2   paperback

The publisher has no responsibilities for
the persistence or accuracy of URLs for external or
third party Internet Web sites referred to in this publication
and does not guarantee that any content on such
Web sites is, or will remain, accurate or appropriate.

Typeset in $\LaTeX 2_\varepsilon$
Graphic design by Vincent F. Hendricks

Contents

Preface	iii
Acknowledgements	v
1 John Bishop	1
2 Michael E. Bratman	17
3 Randolph Clarke	25
4 John Martin Fischer	31
5 Stewart Goetz	45
6 Patricia Greenspan	59
7 Ishtiyaque Haji	69
8 Bennett Helm	87
9 Ted Honderich	99
10 Jennifer Hornsby	119
11 Joshua Knobe	129
12 Storrs McCall	141
13 Hugh J. McCann	155
14 Michael McKenna	165
15 Alfred R. Mele	183
16 Timothy O'Connor	195
17 Derk Pereboom	203

18 Thomas Pink	221
19 Joëlle Proust	233
20 Abraham Roth	247
21 Galen Strawson	253
22 Raimo Tuomela	261
23 Manuel Vargas	273
24 George Wilson	283
About the Editors	293
About Philosophy of Action: 5 Questions	295
Index	296

Preface

The philosophy of action is a broad field. Some characterize the field narrowly, treating it as a sub-area in the philosophy of mind or, if one's concerns are chiefly normative, as providing the foundations of moral psychology. But this strikes us a mistake. Broadly characterized, the philosophy of action encompasses a host of problems about the nature and scope of human action and agency, including, but not limited to, intention and intentional action, the ontology of action, reason-explanations of action, motivation and practical reason, free will and moral responsibility, mental agency, social action, controlling attitudes, *akrasia* and *enkrasia*, and many other issues. Depending upon the topic someone working in the philosophy of action is working on, her work can be characterized as epistemology, metaphysics, philosophy of mind, moral philosophy, philosophy of religion, or philosophy of social science, among other areas. Moreover, the work of philosophers of action overlaps in exciting ways with the work of non-philosophers working on human action and agency, including jurists, neuroscientists, psychologists, and others.

Rather than characterize the philosophy of action as a subfield of any other areas in philosophy, it seems best to regard the philosophy of action as an area in philosophy in its own right. The vague boundaries of the field should not count against treating it as a distinct area any more than the vague boundaries of any of the other established areas of philosophy should count against treating them as distinct (e.g., philosophy of mind overlaps with the philosophy of language, epistemology, and metaphysics—yet it is regarded as a distinct area).

This volume brings together some of the leading figures in the philosophy of action. Some of them have published research on virtually every major problem in the field, while others have devoted their careers to examining a narrow set of topics. Regardless of the scope of their research into the nature of human action and agency, all of the philosophers who have contributed to this volume have made a significant impact on the field. There is as much diversity in the views articulated by these authors as there are ways of conceiving of the field and what issues are important in the field. But they all agree that examining the nature and scope of human action and agency is a worthwhile endeavor that can help us shed light on many other philosophical and existential problems—e.g., the nature of personhood, what makes for a good life, etc.

We asked the contributors to the volume five questions. Some of them answered all five questions directly. Others took the liberty of modifying the questions somewhat. Still others elected to only answer some but not all of the questions. Finally, a few wrote short essays that address the issues raised in the questions, offering nice summaries of their research, its importance, and what they see as some of the most important issues about human action and agency they are addressing or hope to address in the future.

For readers with no background in the philosophy of action the chapters of this volume should serve as a nice introduction to the breadth of issues and the current state of play in much of the philosophy of action. These readers will have the opportunity to become acquainted for the first time with leading contemporary philosophers of action, their views, and motivations. In this way the present volume provides a nice jumping off point to explore topics in the philosophy of action and the work of key players in this exciting field. More experienced readers working on action and agency should find this volume as enjoyable and illuminating as we have. Not only will they appreciate the refreshing reformulation of established views within the philosophy of action but very likely will be exposed to novel ideas and approaches often ignored given the breath of this burgeoning philosophical field. In this sense, it is our hope that this volume will motivate others to explore the philosophy of action, and for those working on a sub-field in the philosophy of action to recognize the value of researching topics they may have ignored until now.

Jesús H. Aguilar & Andrei A. Buckareff
Rochester, NY & Poughkeepsie, NY
January 2009

Acknowledgements

We would like to thank Claus Feestersen and Rasmus Rendsvig when encountering Latex-related problems. Also we would like to thank our publisher **Automatic Press** ♦ ⋎̱P, in particular senior publishing editor V.J. Menshy, for continuing to take on these 'rather unusual academic' projects. We are also very grateful to Vincent F. Hendricks and Evan Selinger for their enthusiastic support of our work on this volume. Additional thanks are due to our respective institutions, Rochester Institute of Technology and Marist College, for encouraging our research endeavors, including our editorial work on this and other volumes. Our families and friends are owed a debt of gratitude for their patience with us while working on this volume. Finally, we are especially grateful to the contributors to this volume for making this volume not a mere possibility, but a reality

Jesús H. Aguilar & Andrei A. Buckareff
Rochester, NY & Poughkeepsie, NY
January 2009

1
John Bishop

Professor of Philosophy
University of Auckland, New Zealand

---

1. Why were you initially drawn to theorizing about action and agency?

Human beings are parts of the Universe with a (limited) capacity for understanding the nature of the Universe. It is sometimes said – grandiosely, and probably not correctly – that in humanity the Universe becomes self-conscious. Certainly, though, *humans* attain a degree of self-consciousness, with human existence itself being one aspect of the Universe that humans themselves have a (limited) capacity to understand. And one feature of human existence we have a (limited) capacity to understand is our own (limited) capacity for understanding. I have long found compelling the (Lockean, Humean, Kantian) idea that inquiry into human understanding – and its limits – is philosophically fundamental to all inquiry.

So human understanding often takes the human for its object: but does it then sometimes require a different method and explanatory "logic" from that which it employs generally? I first encountered this question in the context of the Hempel-Dray debate over whether explanations in history conform to the "covering law" model widely thought applicable to scientific explanations,[1] and this was the source of my initial interest in theorizing about action and agency. For, it is human *action* specifically that seems outside the scope of (purely) natural scientific explanation, since what counts as action does so because a certain kind of explanation in terms of the agent's reasons is proper to it (the Anscombe

---

[1] See C.G.Hempel, "The Function of General Laws in History," in *Aspects of Scientific Explanation and other essays in the Philosophy of Science* (New York: Free Press, 1965) and William Dray, *Laws and Explanation in History* (Westport, CT.: Greenwood Press, 1957).

thesis[2]), and this kind of "intentional" explanation implicates normative considerations in ways that distinguish it from natural scientific explanation (as shown by Davidson[3]). I came to theorize about action, then, *via* an interest in understanding the nature of intentional explanation. This interest rested on an intellectual tension between recognising the distinctness of intentional explanations and finding myself with a strong commitment to the idea that what such explanations explain must belong to one, somehow unified, natural reality. It puzzled me why the (presumed) unity of reality did not seem to be matched by the unity of science. And I found it unsatisfactory to resolve this tension by making anti-realist or eliminativist moves with respect to intentional explanation.[4]

I found eliminativism and anti-realism unsatisfactory because of the link between the notion of action and moral responsibility – and this link was a further motivation for my theorizing about agency. Persons are morally responsible only for what comes about (at least in part) through their agency. So to abandon realist commitment to actions (as importantly distinct from "mere" behavior, anyway) is systematically to remove one of the necessary conditions for moral responsibility as usually understood. From an ethical perspective, then, the difference between actions, for which – given further conditions – agents may be responsible, and mere behavior, for which they may not, is taken to be a *real* difference. Wittgenstein's famous question – "What is left over if I subtract the fact that my arm goes up from the fact that I raise my arm?"[5] – may seem of merely academic interest when taken baldly as the starting point for theorizing about action. Yet its importance does, of course, rest securely on the vital question whether our practice of holding persons morally responsible is well-founded. I was – and remain – convinced that this practice *is* well founded, in the sense that there is a real, natural distinction between outcomes

---

[2] G.E.M.Anscombe, *Intention* (Oxford: Blackwell, 1957)

[3] For a summary of Donald Davidson's account of intentional explanation see "Problems in the Explanation of Action" in *Problems of Rationality* (Oxford: Oxford University Press, 2004).

[4] For anti-realism about intentional explanation, see, for example, Daniel.C.Dennett, *The Intentional Stance* (Cambridge, MA: M.I.T. Press, 1987); for eliminativism, Paul Churchland, "Eliminative Materialism and the Propositional Attitudes," *Journal of Philosophy* 78 (1981), reprinted in W.G.Lycan, ed., *Mind and Cognition: a Reader* (Oxford: Blackwell, 1989).

[5] Ludwig Wittgenstein, *Philosophical Investigations*, 3rd edn, trans. G.E.M.Anscombe (Oxford: Blackwell, 1972), §621, p.161^e

for which persons are responsible and outcomes for which they are not. Whether wider practices that rest on attributions of moral responsibility – such as retributive punishment – are justified is, of course, a further important question.

It thus became a theme of my work to defend the compatibility of our natural scientific perspective on human behavior with our ethical perspective, understood as requiring realist commitment to actions as necessary for moral responsibility. In *Natural Agency*, I described this as the stance of *reconciliatory naturalism*, and I argued that its defence requires us to deal with the skeptical *problem of natural agency* – that is, with doubts about whether actions, understood as exercises of control in some sense originated by the agent, can be understood as constituted by events and states of affairs within the natural causal order, as the prevailing natural scientific metaphysics interprets it.[6] More on this shortly.

Pertinent to the present question, though, is my motivation for favoring a reconciliatory naturalist stance – for the view that human existence must belong to one, ultimately unified, natural reality. Here is what I said twenty years ago:

> It is tempting to hail this assumption [of the truth of reconciliatory naturalism] as straightforward common sense. But I suspect that it actually rests finally on a value judgment: that, somehow, it is *better* for reconciliatory naturalism to be true than for it to turn out either that our belief in [the reality of] agency is mistaken, or that, as agents, we belong mysteriously beyond the natural universe that is open to scientific inquiry. (In my own case the roots of this value judgment, I realise with a shock of surprise, lie in attitudes best described as religious.)[7]

So I did then acknowledge that my theorizing about action had a religious motivation. But there was bad faith in my claiming that this acknowledgment gave me "a shock of surprise": I made that claim, I fear, because I felt that, as a good philosopher, I *ought* to be taken aback by uncovering religious motivations for my philosophizing! In more recent work, I have (I think) overcome the confusions underlying this fault by defending a modest fideism

---

[6] John Bishop, *Natural agency: an essay on the causal theory of action* (Cambridge University Press, 1989), pp 5-9

[7] *Natural agency*, p. 5

of the kind advocated by William James. According to this view, practical commitment to the truth of beliefs with "passional" (= non-evidential) causes is permissible, provided their truth is not *counter*-evidential and provided that both what is believed and the non-evidential motivation for believing it pass muster ethically.[8] That it would be good for reconciliatory naturalism to be true, while not of course counting as any kind of evidence that it *is* true, might nevertheless justify *taking* it to be true – though only if our best assessment of the relevant arguments and evidence leaves its truth open.

But what *is* the religious basis for the judgment that real moral responsibility ought to be compatible with belonging wholly to the natural causal order? The theistic tradition to which I belong (Christianity, though in the respects I here mention neither Judaism nor Islam differ) is committed to these two claims about human persons – first, we are creatures; and second, we are creatures who are (sometimes) properly held morally responsible, both by God and by our fellows. Now, I maintain that a robust acceptance of our creatureliness requires recognizing that we are *wholly* within the natural causal order. Evidently, this claim is contestable: many philosophical theists are fond of libertarian views of the self, and some of these accept (though others hope to resist) the implied non-naturalism about the self – i.e., that the self acts from outside the natural causal order as understood on a scientific metaphysics.[9] As well as finding philosophical fault with such a view, I also find it spiritually problematic. I see in it a device for resisting wholehearted acceptance of the ultimate dependency of our creatureliness. But at the same time I maintain that in our crea-

---

[8] See my *Believing by faith; an essay in the epistemology and ethics of religious belief* (Oxford: Clarendon Press, 2007). I here offer a developed interpretation of the justification of faith James attempted in his famous, though ill-titled, lecture, "The Will to Believe," (*The Will to Believe and Other Essays in Popular Philosophy, and Human Immortality* (New York: Dover, 1956), 1-31).

[9] For an example of a philosopher who affirms the ontological irreducibility of agent-causation yet hopes to save naturalism by appeal to emergentism, see Timothy O'Connor, *Persons and Causes: the Metaphysics of Free Will* (Oxford: Oxford University Press, 2002). Robert Kane, *The Significance of Free Will* (Oxford: Oxford University Press, 1996) seeks to defend a naturalist libertarianism without commitment to agent-causation. For my own discussion of the issues here, see "Prospects for a Naturalist Libertarianism: O'Connor's *Persons and Causes,*" *Philosophy and Phenomenological Research* 66 (2003), 228-243.

tureliness we are yet genuinely agents with the capacity – albeit a conditioned capacity – to exercise some real control of our own. So reconciliatory naturalism strikes me as getting right, relative to the values of theistic religious traditions, the balance between our dependency and our power to act. And that motivates me to try to defend it philosophically. Of course, my judgment on matters spiritual here might be mistaken – and might come to be corrected by theological/spiritual discussion with my co-believers. But this judgment is also vulnerable to *philosophical* correction: if reconciliatory naturalism runs into serious philosophical difficulty, that could exclude it as an option, and force a reassessment of my current spiritual endorsement of it. But just for that reason passional, religiously based, commitment to reconciliatory naturalism provides a strong motivation for attempting to develop and defend a theory of human agency that achieves the required reconciliation between our ethical and our natural scientific perspectives on ourselves.

2. What do you consider to be your own most important contribution(s) to theorizing about agency, and why?

What have I regarded as important in theorizing about action and agency? I prefer this variation on the set question, because I can answer it confidently, whereas I have little confidence in judging the importance of my actual contributions, nor the extent to which those contributions count as "mine." If I have made contributions, they probably do not go much beyond reorganizing the work of others. Indeed, the question, "In what sense, and to what extent, does *anything* that I have done count as 'mine'?," provides a refreshingly existential point of entry into theorizing about action. It is striking that agents (I do not mean myself!) who are indisputably creative and original sometimes disclaim ownership of their contributions, reporting a sense of being the vehicles of active power rather than its original exercisers. Is this a pleasing, but falsifying, modesty – or does it answer to some metaphysically essential feature of what it is to be a finite originative agent, whether highly, moderately, or mundanely creative? I suspect the latter – but let me return to my substitute question: what have I held to be important in action theory?

First, I have regarded it as vital to show why theorizing about action matters. Worthwhile theorizing about action must connect with some clearly important philosophical problem or problems.

Now, there is a family of philosophical problems posed by skepticism about how things could possibly be the way we seem committed to taking them to be. A certain kind of theorizing about action addresses one such sceptical problem, namely the question how genuine responsible agency can possibly belong within the natural causal order. As Davidson remarks in "Intending," a Causal Theory of Action (CTA) "is enough ... to explain the possibility of autonomous action in a world of causality":[10] in my terms, it is enough to show reconciliatory naturalism to be reasonable. For, if, as a CTA maintains, actions consist in behavior with suitable mental causes, then, provided mentality can be understood as part of the natural order, so too can agency. My own focus in action theory has accordingly been on trying to articulate and defend an adequate CTA.

But what is the source of skepticism about natural agency? Here there is a link with the debate over "free will and determinism." At root, this debate is neither about freedom nor about determinism, but rather about the possibility of genuine agency within the natural causal order, be it deterministic or otherwise. Our concept of an action is of an agent bringing about or "originating" an event through the exercise of that agent's own control. This notion, I believe, is *conceptually* irreducible – and I earned an inconvenient early reputation for myself as an agent-causationist by arguing as much. Agent-causationism, however, is properly an *ontological* thesis to the effect that what constitutes action in the real world must be, or at least include, an irreducible relation between the agent and some event or state of affairs. If agent-causationism is correct, then, if we are right to think that the natural scientific worldview admits causal relations only amongst events (or perhaps also amongst states of affairs), natural agency is impossible and reconciliatory naturalism excluded. I believe that agent-causationist intuitions underlie standard arguments for incompatibilism (such as van Imwagen's "Consequence Argument"[11]). This is shown, first, by the fact that, with some adjustment, such argu-

---

[10] Donald Davidson, *Essays on Actions and Events* (Oxford: Clarendon Press, 1980), p. 88

[11] "If determinism is true, then our acts are the consequences of the laws of nature and of nature and events in the remote past. But it is not up to us what went on before we were born, and neither is it up to us what the laws of nature are. Therefore, the consequences of these things (including our present acts) are not up to us." Peter van Inwagen, *An Essay on Free Will* (Oxford: Claredon Press, 1983), p.56

ments generalize to the conclusion that exercises of agent-control are impossible under indeterminism as well as determinism, and, second, by the fact that such arguments beg the question against the truth of a CTA. For, if a CTA is correct, then events over which I have no control can causally condition later events that are intrinsic to my exercise of agency, given that the causal path is of the right kind.[12] So here, then, are two further important features of theorizing about agency on my account: such theorizing should (a) aim to understand how intuitions about agency are implicated at the heart of the perennial debate over free will and determinism; and (b) make the vital distinction between the *conceptual* question whether action may be defined as behavior with suitable mental causes, and the *ontological* question whether such causal relations can constitute what realizes actions. One may admit that agent-causation is conceptually irreducible without at all endorsing the agent-causationist's claim that a world containing actions must contain irreducible relations between agents and events or states of affairs, items in an ontological category foreign to, and indeed repudiated by, a modern natural scientific worldview.

Agent-causationist skepticism about natural agency is not easily overcome: and I have thought it important to identify and evaluate all the arguments that may be given for the view that the ontological reduction posited by CTA cannot succeed. One argument in particular has engaged my attention – namely, the argument that the fact that mental states or events can "deviantly" cause and rationalize behavior shows that non-deviant intentional action must involve ontically irreducible agent-causation. Given his recognition that CTA, if successful, will resolve the skeptical problem of natural agency, I found surprising Davidson's pessimism about resolving the problem of casual deviance, so vividly posed by his own example of the nervous climber in "Freedom to Act."[13] Other defenders of CTA have also tended to sideline this problem: there has been a widespread view that specifying "the right kind

---

[12] For my own extended discussion of the Consequence Argument, see *Natural Agency*, pp 53-60.

[13] For Davidson's pessimism about resolving the problem of causal deviance, see "Freedom to Act" (1973) (*Essays on Actions and Events*, p.80), "Intending" (1978) (p.87, footnote 3), and a comment in his Introduction to *Essays on Actions and Events*, p. xiii. In "Problems in the Explanation of Action" (1987), Davidson reports that he "remain[s] convinced that the concepts of event, cause and intention are inadequate to account for intentional action" (*Problems of Rationality*, p.106).

of way" in which mental events have to cause behavior for there to be genuine, non-deviant, intentional action is a matter of minor detail safely left "to the *aficionados* of deviance theory."[14] I think this view is mistaken: Roderick Chisholm was right to see in the possibility of deviant counterexamples a major challenge to a CTA-analysis of action, and hence a potential argument in favour of agent-causationism.[15] Berent Enç identifies what he takes to be a more central difficulty for CTA than the "somewhat technical problem"[16] posed by causal deviance: namely, the concern that an account of action as constituted wholly by event-causal relationships seems to leave *the active agent* out of the picture.[17] That may indeed be the more basic concern. But the problem of excluding deviance is *expressive of* that concern, since the allegation that CTA cannot exclude deviance is a specific way of claiming that it fails to account for the agent's own activity. I have thus supposed that quite a lot rests on whether or not an ontological CTA-analysis that excludes deviant counterexamples can be provided, and have made an attempt to defend just such an analysis, building on the work especially of Christopher Peacocke and David Lewis.[18]

Agent-causationists often suspect that any CTA will be flawed by circularity or vicious regress – and I have thought it important to try to rebut this suspicion. Clearly there are mental actions, and mental actions (in particular, forming intentions, making practical inferences) are typically implicated in the causal antecedents of overt bodily actions. But a CTA-analysis of intentional action need not *require* that an action's causal antecedents include anything

---

[14] See Paul Snowdon, "The Will and the Way," *Times Literary Supplement*, 9th February, 1990

[15] Roderick Chisholm, "Freedom and Action," in K.Lehrer, ed., Freedom and Determinism (New York: Random House, 1966), 11-44

[16] Berent Enç, *How We Act: Causes, Reasons and Intentions* (Oxford: Oxford University Press, 2003), p.3

[17] Enç quotes J. David Velleman's claim that CTA cannot capture what it is for an agent to be active: 'reasons cause an intention, and an intention causes bodily movements, but [in this picture] nobody – that is no person – does anything' (J.D.Velleman, "What Happens When Someone Acts?," *Mind*, 101, 1992, p.461, quoted by Enç, *op. cit.*, p.134).

[18] See *Natural Agency*, Chapter 5. The work of Peacocke's on which I draw is to be found in his *Holistic Explanation: Action, Space, Interpretation* (Oxford: Clarendon Press, 1979), and that of Lewis in his "Veridical Hallucination and Prosthetic Vision," *Australasian Journal of Philosophy*, 58 (1980), 239-49 – though in this paper, of course, the relevant elaboration of causal non-deviance is applied to the case of perception.

that must itself be counted ontologically as an action (the trap that earlier "volitionist" versions fell into) – even if those causal antecedents do have to include intentions, rather than just beliefs and desires. Furthermore, intentional mental actions involved in practical reasoning can be shown to fit a CTA-analysis themselves, provided appeal may be made to higher-order intentions which belong to agents just in virtue of their having the capacity for intentional agency.[19]

Finally, and related, obviously, to the wider topic of mental action, I have thought it important to get clear about what might be right in the thesis of doxastic voluntarism – that is, to understand the nature and limits of our agency as related to beliefs. I regard it as vitally important to recognize the distinction between *the state* that consists of having the attitude towards a proposition that it is true ('holding it true that p') and *the mental action* of using the truth of a proposition as a premise in reasoning ('taking it to be true that p').[20] Such mental actions are basic actions – exercises of direct control – whereas we can have only limited indirect control over what propositional attitudes we have.

I do, of course, recognize that there are further interesting topics in the philosophy of action – for example, the question of how actions are to be individuated, the question of how to understand the relationship between actions and omissions, and the question of how to understand the 'could have done otherwise' condition that seems necessary for free – or even just for genuine – action.[21] But it is the topics I have mentioned above that have seemed to me to have the greatest importance – at least for anyone who

---

[19] See my "Naturalising mental action," in G.Holmström-Hintikka and R.Tuomela, eds., *Contemporary Action Theory, Volume 1: Individual Action*, Dordrecht, Kluwer, 251-266, 1997. The kind of higher-order intentions I have in mind are such things as the intention to form intentions consistently with one's all-things-considered judgments about what it's best to do (what Davidson calls "the principle of continence," *Essays on Actions and Events*, p. 41).

[20] A significant influence on my thinking here was L. Jonathan Cohen's, *An Essay on Belief and Acceptance* (Oxford: Clarendon Press, 1992). For a discussion of this distinction, see my *Believing by Faith*, pp 33-41.

[21] On this last question, I have argued that it is important to distinguish between 'could have done otherwise' construed as a condition of control and 'could have done otherwise' construed as positing the possibility, in the circumstances, of an alternative outcome. This, I think, is the key to understanding the significance of Harry Frankfurt's counterfactual intervener cases. See *Natural Agency*, pp 23-4.

approaches the philosophy of action with the aim of supporting the "grand project" of reconciliatory naturalism.

3. What other sub-disciplines in philosophy and other disciplines stand to benefit most from philosophical work on the nature of action and agency, and how might such engagement be accomplished?

Action theory that takes the problem of natural agency as its point of orientation has an obvious association with ethics, which I take to be the motivationally basic philosophical discipline. We need to determine not just the proper content of morality (how we should live), but also why we should think the world is such that there could be real point in the project of living in accordance with morality. Action theory as such cannot answer that question. But it can deal with doubts about whether the conditions for moral responsibility can possibly be realized (which they must be if the moral project is to have point), and so contribute to determining in what ways (if at all) we need to transcend a natural scientific understanding of ourselves in order to recognize the applicability of moral ideals to our lives.

That connection with ethics is at a high level of generality. There are very many specific connections between action theory and other philosophical sub-disciplines, and I will mention just two. First, reflecting on what is needed for the defence of a CTA may mutually illuminate methodological debates about reduction in the Philosophy of Mind generally. To defend CTA one needs to give a 'CTA-analysis' that provides necessary *and sufficient* conditions for the occurrence of an action (an agent's exercise of control) that do not employ even implicitly agent-causal notions, and is, in that sense, reductive of use of such notions. Such an analysis is not a meaning analysis – indeed, it may not even need to hold across *all* possible worlds, though it will need to hold across all worlds with the same ontology as naturalism takes the actual world to have. How is this related to what is needed to defend physicalism in the philosophy of mind? Does considering the causalist reduction of action help with the critique of attempts at "non-reductivist" materialism, and at emphasizing "supervenience" rather than reduction? 'Ontological analysis' has the flavour of oxymoron to it: but might it be the key to what philosophy can achieve, being distinct from both conceptual or linguistic analysis, and also from any kind of natural scientific analysis?

Second, there is a specific connection between action theory and epistemology, and, in particular, the epistemology of religious commitment and the defence of some suitably moderate version of fideism. (Unlike my first example, this is a connection on which I have worked myself.) Reflecting on mental action proves helpful in discerning what may sensibly be meant by the notion of 'believing by faith'. Such reflection shows that we have a capacity to commit ourselves in practice to the truth of propositions independently of our holding them true on the basis of supporting evidence. Being in the state of holding a proposition true does, of course, strongly dispose us to take that proposition to be true when salient in practical reasoning (belief would not be what it is without this general connexion): yet *doxastic venture* is a real possibility. We may take to be true when we come to act propositions that we recognise we hold true through "passional," non-evidential, causes. That is what 'believing by faith' comes to (as opposed to any self-inducing of the state of holding a faith-proposition true). Whether we ought to make such faith-ventures, and, if so, under what conditions, are, of course, further questions.[22]

But what about connections with disciplines beyond Philosophy? For those, we need to reflect generally on how philosophical action theory is related to empirical research into agency. Can, and should, there be engagement between the philosophy of action and the natural science(s) of agency? The problem of giving a CTA-analysis that excludes causal deviance provides a good example of how to demarcate philosophical from empirical action theory. Noting that what is sought is an account of what *ontologically* realizes agency, it seems apt to suggest that specifying the right kind of antecedent causal path for non-deviant intentional action can safely be left to empirical inquiry.[23] But why bother, then, with any armchair philosophizing at all? We have to see that

---

[22] The term 'passional' (to refer to causes of belief other than what counts for the believer as evidence for its truth) is, of course, due to William James. The account of doxastic venture in my *Believing by Faith* (see especially pp 33-41 and pp 113-119) is intended as a development of James's 'justification of faith' which avoids the common objection that James defends wishful thinking. (William James, "The Will to Believe," in *The Will to Believe and Other Essays in Popular Philosophy, and Human Immortality* (New York: Dover, 1956), 1-31.). I offer a critical examination of arguments in favour of the permissibility of faith-venture (under certain conditions) in Chapters 8 and 9 of *Believing by Faith*.

[23] Alvin Goldman is one philosopher who makes this suggestion. See his *A Theory of Human Action* (Englewood Cliffs, N.J.: Prentice-Hall, 1970), p.62.

what motivates the philosophizing here (as often) is the challenge of (philosophical) skepticism, represented in this instance by the agent-causationists. They insist that agency is *not* naturally realizable, not, anyway in a natural world that admits causality only of the event-causal kind, and one of their arguments is the argument from the possibility of causal deviance. The challenge of this argument can hardly be met by the mere assertion that empirical science can furnish what the sceptic claims, partly on the strength of this very argument, to be impossible.

So, evolutionary biology and psychology may furnish developmental accounts of animal and human agency. And physiology and neurophysiology may provide accounts of what happens when someone acts. A reconciliatory naturalist, such as myself, will see such accounts as applicable to agency of the kind we appeal to as a condition of moral responsibility in our ethical perspective on ourselves. But entitlement to such a view must be philosophically earned by engaging with those who hold that there are good reasons for concluding that what these empirical disciplines explain cannot possibly extend to the kind of agency that could be a vehicle of moral responsibility. Dealing with such skeptical doubts by defending the possibility of natural agency is something only philosophy can do. Yet engagement with empirical scientific studies of agency may be helpful, even essential, in carrying out the specifically philosophical task here. Philosophy of action cannot abdicate in favor of scientific studies of agency, but it should not regard reflecting on them as simply irrelevant.

4. What do you regard as the most neglected issues in contemporary work on action and agency that deserve more attention?

One set of issues that *I* have neglected yet regard as deserving more attention concerns group agency. I do know of distinguished work on this topic,[24] but retain the impression that this area remains relatively neglected by philosophers in "analytical" philos-

---

[24] Raimo Tuomela has been particularly active in this area. See Volume 2 (on Social Action) of the collection *Contemporary Action Theory*, co-edited with Ghita Holmstrom-Hintikka (Dordrecht: Kluwer, 1997), and his solo-authored works *Co-operation: A Philosophical Study* (Dordrecht: Kluwer, 2000), *The Philosophy of Social Practices: A Collective Acceptance View* (New York: Cambridge University Press, 2002) and *The Philosophy of Sociality: The Shared Point of View* (Oxford: Oxford University Press, 2007).

ophy of action. That human corporations and groups may perform actions is evident: but how should the ontology of group action be understood? Can groups act other than in and through the agency of individuals who are their representatives? Is group agency always something *constructed* through legal or customary conventions – or can there be natural, as well as conventional, group actions? Can there be higher levels of agency that *emerge* out of individual relationships and interactions – for example, in teams, in institutions? (I have even wondered whether an alternative to classical theism might result from treating the Scriptural claim that God is love metaphysically seriously – not by identifying God with an abstract universal, but rather by regarding the divine, and divine activity, as emerging from concrete loving relationships.[25] In any case, Trinitarians need to consider whether divine action always reduces to the activity of one of the Persons, or whether it can belong to the "social" Trinity as such – so the topic of group agency has a place in orthodox as well as revisionist Christian theology.)

In my answer to question 2, I suggested a possible *existential* point of entry to the philosophy of action – namely, the question to what extent any of my actions are truly mine. The answer that emerges from the naturalistic view of agency I favor is that none of my actions are *deeply* mine, since every exercise of my control is conditioned by factors over which I neither have nor had any control of my own. Yet I can exercise my own control, nonetheless. This "compatibilist" answer [26] seems to me usefully to expose what is intellectually lacking in egocentrism – by contrast with the competing libertarian understanding of action (which in my view cannot ultimately escape viewing the agent as a mini-creator *ex nihilo*). These thoughts belong to a set of existential and ethical issues about how we view ourselves and others as agents which are always in the background of philosophical action theory but which might usefully receive more foreground attention. A genuinely compassionate ethics of our responses to actions (praise and blame, punishment and reward) may then be seen to rest importantly on settling foundational questions in action theory.

---

[25] See my "Can There Be Alternative Concepts of God?," *Noûs* 32 (1998), 174-188.

[26] This answer is not merely compatibilist in the usual sense - i.e., of taking genuine agency to be realizable under determinism: it is *hyper*comptabilist in holding that genuine agency is realizable in the natural causal order, whether that causal order is determinist or indeterminist.

5. What are the most important open problems in philosophical theorizing about action and agency, and what are the prospects for progress?

Since my own focus has been on defending CTA in order to rebut skepticism about natural agency, I will confine my answer to what I regard as open problems for this project.

First, there is the question whether any CTA analysis can succeed. And, of course, I am concerned to know whether a proposal such as my own does indeed provide necessary and sufficient conditions for an ontological CTA analysis – namely the proposal that

> basic intentional action may be analysed as matching behavior that is sensitively caused by the agent's basic intention, and in a context where any feedback to central mental processes returns to the agent's, rather than to anyone else's brain.[27]

Second, there is the question whether this CTA-analysis can sensibly be applied to mental actions, given that this seems possible only if appeal may be made to higher-order intentions – something that some philosophers contest.

And, third, there is the question whether skilled activity, on the one hand, and "arational," "futile" or purely volitional actions, on the other, provide decisive counterexamples to the causal theory of action.[28]

I believe that prospects for progress in dealing with all of these questions rest on closer engagement with developing scientific studies of agency. I believe it will turn out that scientific theories will produce an account of the active capacities of animals that extends to the human animal. Skepticism about whether such active capacities could count as capacities for the kind of action for which agents could be morally responsible will then be able to be met by means of a CTA-analysis of the kind I have proposed (though some refinements may well be needed). But, evidently, a naturalist account of intentions will be presupposed. To achieve this it is, I think, necessary to extrapolate from the (arguably foundational) notion of an intention (as a *conscious* setting of oneself to act

---

[27] *Natural Agency*, p.171
[28] Both the second and the third question noted here engage with challenges to a CTA-analysis raised by the work of David-Hillel Ruben, *Action and its Explanation* (Oxford: Clarendon Press, 2003).

towards a given end) so that its functional component is retained and its phenomenological component abandoned. It will then – or so reconciliatory naturalists like myself will hope – become clear how the enhancement of unproblematically natural active capacities can itself be naturalistically achieved without any need to appeal to irreducible agent-causation from outside the causal order as the natural sciences understand it.

2
Michael E. Bratman

Durfee Professor in the School of Humanities & Sciences and Professor of Philosophy

Stanford University, USA

Reflections on the Philosophy of Action[1]

We are both knowers and doers. In each case our minds are appropriately connected to the world. Or so it seems. These commonsense remarks are the background of three central areas of philosophy: epistemology, philosophy of mind, and philosophy of action. In all three cases the issues are conceptual, metaphysical and normative. We seek concepts adequate to an understanding of the phenomena; we seek to understand in what these phenomena consist; and we seek to understand relevant norms – both theoretical and practical – and their relation to matters conceptual and metaphysical. The problems throughout are deep and of great importance in our understanding of who we are; and these problems across these different areas of philosophy interact in complex ways. But I think it is clear that the western philosophical tradition has – with some notable exceptions – tended to focus more intensely on knowledge and mind than on action and agency. One powerful source of the attraction and excitement of the philosophy of action to me is that the target of its inquiries – our nature as agents – is gripping within self-reflection and of fundamental importance within a wide range of human concerns (some of which I mention below). A second source of the attraction to me of the philosophy of action is the sense that, as compared with our philosophical understanding of knowledge and mind, this is less well understood – though equally fundamental – territory, and so territory that is more susceptible to our seeing things in new and newly fecund ways.

---

[1] Thanks to Manuel Vargas for helpful comments on an earlier draft.

What is it to be an agent, and not just an object in the natural, causal order? What is it to act? to act intentionally? to act for a reason? What is it for the agent to be the source of the activity, for the activity not just to be the outcome of an event-causal process? What kind of knowledge do we have of our own agency? How is the idea of a normative reason – a reason that is relevant to the justification of action – connected to the concepts and metaphysics of agency and action? to the phenomenon of motivation of action? to the explanation of action? How is the bearing of rationality on these practical domains – as we say, practical rationality – related to the bearing of rationality on the domains of knowledge and belief – as we say, theoretical rationality? We think that some agents govern their own lives; but what is that? How do these matters look when we turn from the actions and agency of individual human agents to the actions of agency of groups – to our singing the duet, or – to move from small to large – to "we the people"? These, anyway, are some (I do not say all) of the deep, difficult, and complexly inter-related questions that are central to the philosophical study of human agency.

In the background is another question, one that returns to issues about the relation between the practical and the theoretical, to the relation between action and knowledge. The idea of *will* – roughly, of choice or decision – seems distinctively relevant to our understanding of agency, and in a way that distinguishes acting from knowing. Choosing or deciding to believe in most cases seems problematic in ways that we begin to get at in our talk of wishful thinking. But choosing or deciding to act and so acting accordingly seems a central case of agency. But what is this idea of will, and what in the world (if anything) does it point to?

One aspect of this idea that is a part of a certain amount of common talk is the thought that a choice or decision in some sense breaks the causal, deterministic chain from the past to the future. I myself find that this "incompatibilist" thought – at least, as a thought about what is essential to choice or decision – looses its grip when we reflect on how breaking that chain could matter to the metaphysics of the forms of agency we care about. On reflection, what seems to me most important about the will – about choice, decision, and the like – is not whether it is outside the causal order (how would that help us live our lives?), but that these will-like phenomena settle practical questions in ways that impose distinctive structure on our downstream practical thinking and acting. Creatures with what we might as well call "a will" are creatures with the psychological structures and capacities that are involved in imposing this structure on thought and action.

What structure, and why bother? Here I think both the concept and the phenomenon of planning, and associated norms, are fundamental. Intentions are elements of typically partial and almost-always at least partly future-directed plans. Plans and planning play fundamental coordinating roles in our temporally extended and social lives, especially given our cognitive limitations. That is why we bother with plans. Choice and decision are standard ways we have for arriving at such plan-like states of mind. To understand what the will is we need to understand what it does; and to understand what it does we need to understand how such planning functions in our temporally extended and social agency. Our understanding of that does not depend on seeing the will as outside the natural, causal order. But it does depend on understanding the distinctive roles of planning structures in our practical thinking and action. And that is a matter both of understanding how those structures function, and, relatedly, what the relevant norms (norms, for example, of consistency of intentions and means-end coherence of plans) are that apply to and sometimes guide this functioning. Or so I have over the years argued, in developing what I have called the planning theory of intention and our agency – a theory that can be thought of as a modest theory of the will.

In a way, the planning theory is a response to a debate that didn't quite happen. Philosophy of action as we know it was formed on the crucible of the interactions – primarily in the 1960s – between Anscombe and Davidson about intention and agency. They agreed about the individuation of action – about the idea that normally when I B by A-ing I perform one action, multiply describable. They disagreed about whether the explanation of action by appeal to the agent's reasons for so acting was a kind of causal explanation. And they also disagreed about Anscombe's claim that in acting intentionally one necessarily has a distinctive kind of non-observational knowledge of what one is doing. The disagreement about reasons and causal explanations shaped much of what we know as the philosophy of action. Davidson's enormously influential desire-belief causal model of intentional agency – a model that sees purposiveness, rather than a distinctive mode of self-knowledge, as at the heart of agency – is one of the main fruits of this debate. In contrast, the disagreement about self-knowledge in intentional agency stayed for awhile on the back burners, though – due in part to work of David Velleman – it has lately returned to center stage (together with implications for our understanding of the relation between practical and theoretical rationality). But there was also an underlying agreement – or anyway, a truce – about the very idea of intending to act. For different reasons, neither saw this idea as getting at something fundamental, though in later work Davidson did seek a conservative correction in this skepticism. But in a different tradition of research on agency – associated in particular with Hector Neri-Castañeda – the concept and phenomenon of intending to act were seen as fundamental. In particular, intending was seen not just as an output of practical reasoning (which is how Davidson eventually came to think about intending) but as a fundamental element in the inputs to practical reasoning. (A central example is reasoning from intending an end to intending means, though this is not an example highlighted by Castañeda.) The question of how to draw on the insights both of the Davidsonian desire-belief model and of the focus on intending as a basic phenomenon tended to be ignored, though it was brought to the fore in Gilbert Harman's groundbreaking 1976 essay, "Practical Reasoning". The planning theory was my response to this incompletely articulated debate.

And it is a response that has implications for many of the issues noted above that are at the heart of the philosophy of action. One example is that it supports a view of intending as importantly different from believing. Intending p will play different roles in downstream planning, means-end reasoning, and action than will believing p (though here I disagree, in different ways, with both Harman and Velleman). As I see it, this also helps us avoid collapsing the norms on intending that are central to our planning agency to theoretical norms, and thereby helps support an important distinction between theoretical and practical rationality. This is tied to recent debates about the nature and ground of what John Broome calls rational requirements – for example, rational requirements of consistency of belief, and of intention. And one outstanding question here is whether the planning theory can put us in a better position to assess and respond to recent challenges from Joseph Raz and Niko Kolodny to the normative force of such rational requirements.

I also think that the planning theory can make significant contributions to our understanding of basic human capacities for self-governance and sociality – capacities that seem central to what it is to be a human being. I think, first, that when we highlight these planning structures as deeply embedded in the kind of agent we are, we can make progress in understanding what it is for an agent to govern her own life – what self-governance is. This is in part because, or so I think, the possibility of appealing to planning structures helps us answer a deep question that is in the background of our thinking about self-governance: what psychological structures are such that when they guide thought and action the agent directs and governs? (I call this the question of the agential authority of those psychological structures.) And this is in part because of the central roles of planning structures in constituting and supporting major forms of cross-temporal organization of our practical thought and action, and so organization of our temporally extended agency. Appeal to these planning structures gives us a way of understanding the role of the will in self-governance without seeing the will as outside the natural, causal order.

I also think the planning theory helps us better understand the kind of shared agency illustrated by cases like that of our singing the duet, or Margaret Gilbert's example of our walking together – cases of what I call modest sociality. A central problem here is how to understand the distinctive way you and I are related when – to use Gilbert's example – we walk together, and how this differs from the way in which you and a stranger are related to each other when you are both merely walking down the same street at the same time without bumping into each other. Broadly speaking, the game-theoretic tradition aims to understand our special relation to each other when we walk together as a matter of a kind of equilibrium in a context of common knowledge. But this seems ill-suited to make the contrast between you and me when we walk together, on the one hand, and, on the other hand, you and the stranger merely walking down the same street at the same time without bumping into each other. An alternative view, associated with Gilbert's work, is to see what is special as certain mutual, reciprocal obligations between us and entitlements of each to hold the other accountable for failing to play her role. In contrast, the planning theory gives us the conceptual, metaphysical, and normative resources to chart a path in the territory between these two approaches: our modest sociality is not just a matter of equilibrium given common knowledge; but it need not (though it usually does) involve mutual obligations and entitlements. Very roughly, what is distinctive of our shared agency are certain structures of interrelated intentions of the participants; and we understand such intentions within the planning theory.

The conjecture, then, is that basic planning capacities are at the bottom of two fundamental human practical capacities: our capacities both for self-governance and for certain forms of sociality. Whether these planning theoretic approaches to self-governance and to modest sociality will be successful is a matter for further research. But it does seem to me at least a potential advantage of the planning theory that it promises to help us characterize important features of human agency that may well turn out to be central to these further basic capacities for self-governance and modest sociality.

An underlying idea is that a central target of our reflections in the philosophy of action are basic structures – basic capacities and modes of thought – characteristic of (what we can call) the will and thereby of our agency. We get at these structures by studying how they function in particular cases of practical thinking and intentional action, and by studying the norms that apply to such functioning. But it is these general structures of agency – structures that help constitute and support our temporally extended and social lives – that are our primary target. And the conjecture is that these planning structures help us understand other basic human practical capacities – including, in particular, capacities for self-governance and sociality.

Questions about how to understand our agency – about the needed concepts, the underlying metaphysics, and the associated norms – are at the foundation of our understanding of who we are both as individuals and as participants in sociality. Our answers to these questions will impact our approach and answers to a wide range of issues. The concepts and phenomena of agency and intention – both individual and shared – are at the heart of an enormous range of targets of human reflection. There are countless examples from moral philosophy (there is, of course, the very idea of moral responsibility and accountability; and think also about the distinction between intending and expecting that is built into the principle of double effect), from literature and the arts (think of the ideas of authorial intent, and of artistic collaboration), from social scientific studies (which tend to presuppose certain models of individual agency and practical rationality), from law (think of appeals to intent in the criminal law, and to the very idea of a conspiracy), from artificial intelligence (what exactly are we looking for an artificial version of?), and from efforts to understand the interaction between neuroscience and our self-understanding as agents, both in our commonsense and in domains of accountability, such as the law.

For example, if the planning theory can help us answer the question about agential authority noted earlier – what psychological structures are such that when they guide the agent governs? – then perhaps we can make better sense of how a neuroscience of mind and behavior, one that traffics solely in an event causal order, can be compatible with the reality of agency, of agents as the source of actions. And we can ask whether this can be part of the effort to understand the compatibility of such a science with fundamental norms of accountability. A related question is whether this helps us better understand current debates, both in philosophy (deriving from Anscombe's work) and in psychology (for example, some of the skeptical views of Daniel Wegner), of the scope and limits of our knowledge of our own agency.

At another extreme, we can ask whether, and to what extent, our understanding of what I have called modest sociality can help us to understand larger forms of social agency. Prominent examples here include the social activities central to a legal system and/or to democratic politics. Is it fruitful to think of law, and/or democracy, as a distinctive kind of shared activity? (Scott Shapiro has recently been exploring the first question, about law, and Anna Stilz has been exploring the second query, about democracy.)

I am a "let many flowers bloom" sort of philosopher: I doubt we can know in advance which specific research projects will lead to important results. Indeed, in philosophy it is hard to know how significant the results are even once one has arrived at them – these judgments of significance can require years of further reflection on the part of the philosophical community. But it does seem clear to me that our understanding of our agency, both individual and shared, is as fundamental as things get in philosophy. And I am hopeful that a modest theory of the will such as that sketched in the planning theory can help us better understand how to think about our agency and about related matters of practical rationality, self-governance, sociality, and the location of our agency in the natural order.

3
Randolph Clarke

Professor of Philosophy
Florida State University, USA

---

1. Why were you initially drawn to theorizing about action and agency?

During my first semester of graduate school, I took a seminar on agency, free will, and responsibility taught by Tim Scanlon, and I've been intrigued by these issues ever since. I went on to write my dissertation on free will, and most of my subsequent philosophical writing has been on topics such as deliberation, action, the explanation of action, free will, and moral responsibility.

I'd explain my interest in these topics as follows. Many of the things we do, we do intentionally–making a decision, saying something, opening a door. These actions differ in important ways from things that, in some sense, we do, but not intentionally, such as maintaining a constant body temperature or dreaming. When we act intentionally, we exercise a distinctive kind of control over what we do. That we exercise this sort of agency is surely one of the most important facts about us.

What is our agency? To some extent, it resembles the agency of many nonhuman animals–apes, cats, dolphins. But certainly our capacities for deliberation, planning, and rational action exceed those of any of these other creatures. And it seems that we typically exercise free will when we act, and that we're generally responsible for what we then do.

There are deep problems about how this could really be so. One of the most fundamental of these stems from fact that our actions seem to be occurrences in the wider course of events that constitutes history, and thus seem to have their origins prior to and outside of us. It is hard, then, to see how they can truly be up to us. Thomas Nagel gives this problem an eloquent, if rather pessimistic, expression:

> Something in the idea of agency is incompatible with actions being events, or people being things. But as the external determinants of what someone has done are gradually exposed, in their effect on consequences, character, and choice itself, it becomes gradually clear that actions are events and people things. Eventually nothing remains which can be ascribed to the responsible self, and we are left with nothing but a portion of the larger sequence of events, which can be deplored or celebrated, but not blamed or praised.[1]

A fundamental aim of my work on agency has been to understand the extent to which our activity can really be what it seems to be, and whether, to some extent, our ordinary conception of it must be acknowledged to be mistaken. I'm not as pessimistic as Nagel seems to be. I don't think that the idea of *agency* is incompatible with actions being events, or with people being things. But it's a harder problem to see how genuinely free and responsible action is possible. I do think some revision of our everyday understanding of our responsibility for what we do may be required.

2. What do you consider to be your own most important contribution(s) to theorizing about action and agency, and why?

I think what I've written on free will is my most important contribution to philosophical work on agency. We can understand free will simply as what it takes to act freely. There are more basic kinds of agency that don't involve acting freely, but we tend to think that we generally do act freely, and that our doing so is the ground of our responsibility for what we do. What such free agency might amount to is something that has greatly interested me.

It's commonly thought that whenever someone acts freely, whatever she does on that occasion, she could have done otherwise. Alternatives were open to her, and she determined which she would pursue. She had a choice about what she would do; what she did was up to her. When she acted, she was a source or origin of her action.

---

[1] Thomas Nagel, "Moral Luck," in *Mortal Questions*, pp. 24-38, at p. 37. Cambridge: Cambridge University Press, 1979.

There are several different questions that we can pursue about free action. We can inquire whether we really act with the sort of freedom that we tend to think we have. Or, holding that question in wait, we can first inquire whether it's even possible for any agent to act with such freedom. Or we can examine various accounts of what free will is to determine whether they make sense, whether what they require for freedom is genuinely possible, and whether, if we have all they require, that will suffice for our having the freedom we think we have. This last approach is the one that I've pursued, particularly with regard to what are called libertarian accounts.

These views take free will to be incompatible with determinism, and they aim to set out requirements, including a requirement of indeterminism, satisfaction of which would suffice for someone's having free will. The thesis of determinism holds that, given the laws of nature, how the world is at any point in time completely determines how it is at any later point in time. Determinism implies, for example, that given the laws, the way the world was at some time in the distant past, long before you were born, completely determines whether or not you perform a certain action right now. It's a widely held view, and one to which I'm sympathetic, that if determinism is true, then we can't have the sort of freedom we generally think we have.

But it's difficult to see how indeterminism of any sort could help. A free action is up to the agent; the agent exercises control in so acting. But an event that is undetermined can seem to be a random occurrence, not under anyone's control. And there are difficulties in seeing how an undetermined occurrence could be, for example, a choice made for reasons and one that is fully rational, since whatever reasons the agent had, the choice wouldn't be determined by those reasons.

I've aimed to provide a sympathetic and balanced assessment of various sorts of libertarian theories. While I think many of the standard objections to these views are off the mark, I've argued that there's no type of libertarian account that adequately characterizes free action, on the supposition that indeterminism is required. What I think must be concluded is that either free will is, after all, compatible with determinism, or it is impossible.[2]

Philosophy can sometimes seem to be a curious enterprise. A lot

---

[2] My most comprehensive treatment of these issues is in my *Libertarian Accounts of Free Will* (New York: Oxford University Press, 2003).

of time can be spent on the details of a theory that, one concludes, is unacceptable. But there can be important lessons to learn along the way. It can be enlightening to see that, and why, some familiar objections to the view are mistaken, and which objections are in fact forceful. The theory in question might have firm believers, and it can take a lot of argument to persuade them to abandon it. I think my work on libertarian theories of free will has contributed in some of these ways to a better understanding of such views.

3. What other sub-disciplines in philosophy and non-disciplines stand to benefit the most from philosophical work on the nature of action and agency, and how might such engagement be accomplished?

There is a great deal of work in ethics that concerns agency and moral responsibility. Some conception of agency is crucial to theorizing about what behavior is admirable, or obligatory, or attributable to persons as a basis for moral assessment of those individuals, or as a ground for liability to sanctions. And there is work in philosophy of mind, such as that concerned with the nature of belief, desire, and intention, and with causation of and by mental events, that is of clear importance to action theory.

Philosophers working on action theory and those working in these other areas have much to learn from each other. This isn't at all a one-way thing; all the parties stand to benefit. Sometimes we approach what seem to be the same issues from quite different perspectives, asking quite different questions. Reading each others' work, and seeing the differences in what our interests are with respect to agency, can broaden our understanding of this phenomenon. Conferences on agency that bring together philosophers from these several sub-disciplines can also be very productive, and there have been several good meetings of this sort in recent years.

There is also a wealth of work being done in psychology and cognitive science on agency. I've learned a great deal about the functional organization of action production–for example, the roles of motor representations and perceptual feedback–from reading this material. On the other hand, I'm unconvinced of some the startling claims made by some of these researchers, such as that our decisions are always made before we are aware of them, or that conscious intentions never cause our behavior. (One of my colleagues, Alfred Mele, has argued persuasively that the data simply don't support such conclusions.) Again, I think conferences that bring together researchers who approach agency from a variety of different perspectives can be very fruitful.

4. What do you regard as the most neglected issues in contemporary work on action and agency that deserve more attention?

I don't think there are any issues about agency that are badly neglected by contemporary theorists. But there's one topic in particular that I'd like to see given more attention.

As I indicated above, I'm inclined to think that the type of free agency we tend to think we have is something that in fact we lack. But even if that's so, it might not imply that we lack responsibility for what we do, for responsibility might not require that type of freedom. Whether we then really are responsible for our actions depends crucially on what the nature of moral responsibility is.

There are several different conceptions of this: that being responsible is being an appropriate target of reactive attitudes such as resentment or gratitude; that it's a matter of being someone to whom it's appropriate to demand an account of why something was done; that it's a matter of one's behavior's being a basis for moral appraisal of oneself; that it's a matter of having some mark–positive or negative–on one's moral record; that it's a matter of deserving certain types of reactions, such as reward or punishment, in response to what one has done. Whether moral responsibility is something we in fact have, and whether we might have it even if it should turn out that determinism is true, clearly depend on which of these things moral responsibility is. Various writers presume one or another of these basic conceptions of moral responsibility, but the issue is seldom given extensive treatment. It might make for progress if more work were done on this fundamental question.

5. What are the most important open problems in philosophical theorizing about action and agency, and what are the prospects for progress?

As I've just indicated, it seems to me an important open question whether we really are morally responsible for what we do, and, if so, what this amounts to. I think the prospects for progress are good, but it should be realized that progress in philosophy seldom consists in convergence on a common answer to a question such as this. We come to understand a theory better, we learn that what was thought to be a difficulty for it can be resolved, or that it has a problem not previously foreseen. As problems for a theory mount, that view can become much less attractive and some competing theory can begin to look more appealing. I think we can make progress of these sorts with regard to moral responsibility, as we have with other issues related to agency. But philosophers will never all agree about any such major issues. That's not because we're especially quarrelsome individuals; it reflects the nature of the problems we address.

4
John Martin Fischer

Professor of Philosophy
University of California Riverside, USA

---

1. Why were you initially drawn to theorizing about action and agency?

As I grew up in a Jewish family and regularly attended "Sunday school," I initially was troubled by the Problem of Evil. I had never met my grandfather, because he was killed in a concentration camp, and I remember wondering how difficult it must have been for my father to have moved precipitously to a new country and never to have seen his father again. As I thought more about religious and (in a preliminary way, I suppose) theological issues, I became increasingly interested in the role of human freedom: its place in the Free Will Defense (against the Problem of Evil), and also the relationship between God's omniscience and human freedom.

When I was an undergraduate at Stanford in the 1970s (which, as far as I can tell, were the real '60s–whatever is alleged to have happened in the '60s seems to have happened in the '70s!)–I had broadened the scope of my concerns to include various issues pertaining to the relationship between science and human free will (and moral responsibility). I wondered how we could be free and morally responsible, if science could in the end predict and explain all our behavior. Against this backdrop, I took an upper-division undergraduate class entitled "Action Theory," taught by Michael Bratman. I loved the class, and I was especially fascinated by the work of Harry Frankfurt, in particular, "Alternate Possibilities and Moral Responsibility."[1] From that moment on (my senior year at Stanford) I was hooked: since then I have been fascinated

---

[1] Harry G. Frankfrut, "Alternate Possibilities and Moral Responsibility," *Journal of Philosophy* 66 (1969), pp. 829-39.

by Frankfurt's work and, more generally, the relationship between causal determinism, human freedom, and moral responsibility.

2. What do you consider to be your own most important contribution(s) to theorizing about action and agenc, and why?

I have sought to build on what I take to be the insights of John Locke and Harry Frankfurt to construct what I have called an "actual-sequence" account of moral responsibility. On this sort of account, moral responsibility is a matter of how the actual sequence unfolds, rather than the availability of alternative possibilities. My general project is to present and defend a systematic theory of moral responsibility, according to which the sort of freedom that involves access to alternative possibilities is *not* necessary for moral responsibility for *anything*–choices, character traits, actions, and the consequences of actions. This applies to all individuals and all times. So it might be the case that no one has ever had genuine metaphysical access to alternative possibilities, and yet we are (at least many of us) morally responsible (at least for important chunks of our behavior).

In *An Essay Concerning Human Understanding* (Book II, Chapter 21, Section 10), John Locke discussed a man who was in a room the door to which was, unbeknownst to him, locked. The man decided to stay in the room for his own reasons, and thus Locke said that he voluntarily stayed in the room, although he could not have left the room. This example is the "prototype" for the Frankfurt examples. In his 1969 paper (referred to above), Frankfurt essentially put the locked door inside the agent's head, as he imagined that some counterfactual intervener (as I have dubbed him) could monitor an agent's mind and ensure that the agent act as he actually does, even if he were inclined to behave differently (or even choose to do otherwise). At least Locke's man could have attempted to do otherwise, could have chosen to leave the room, and so forth; in contrast, Frankfurt's agent chooses and acts freely, although he couldn't have even "willed" or chosen otherwise. Or so it seemed to Frankfurt, and it has always seemed to me.

One of my major projects has been to defend a rather simple, intuitive idea about the Frankfurt examples. I call it the "moral of the stories"–that what matters to moral responsibility is how the actual sequence unfolds, rather than the genuine availability (at any point) of alternative possibilities. As part of my defense of an actual sequence approach to moral responsibility, I have pointed out that the sorts of alternative possibilities typically identified by the proponents of (PAP) are too insubstantial and flimsy to plausibly ground attributions of moral responsibility: they are "mere flickers of freedom', not sufficiently "robust" to ground ascriptions of moral responsibility. My argument here is that anyone who is inclined to adopt a view of moral responsibility that requires genuine access to alternative possibilities must construe those alternatives as involving (at least) voluntariness, in the absence of which they are mere flickers of freedom and too thin to support moral responsibility. To suppose that adding an alternative possibility in which there is no voluntariness to an actual sequence in which there is no moral responsibility to get–presto!–moral responsibility is to believe in a kind of alchemy. And when (PAP) is revised accordingly (requiring robust alternative possibilities), the Frankfurt-examples can be seen to provide a powerful challenge to (PAP).[2]

Given that one can defend the contention that moral responsibility does not require genuine metaphysical access to alternative possibilities, it is still an open question whether (say) God's foreknowledge and causal determinism are compatible with moral responsibility. I (together with Mark Ravizza) have presented a systematic and comprehensive theory of moral responsibility, according to which moral responsibility is compatible with God's foreknowedge and causal determinism. In developing the theory, I (and my co-author) exploit a crucial lesson from the Frankfurt-type examples: there are two kinds of control, regulative control (which requires genuine access to alternative possibilities) and guidance control, which does not require such access to alternative possibilities. Although typically we assume that the two kinds of control go together, they can be prized apart (especially in Frankfurt scenarios). My contention is that guidance control, and not regulative control, is the "freedom-relevant" condition (to be added to the epistemic condition) for moral responsibility.[3]

---

[2] John Martin Fischer, "Responsibility and Alternative Possibilities," (adapted from Chapter 7 of *The Metaphysics of Free Will: An Essay on Control* [Oxford: Blackwell Publishers, 1994), in D. Widerker and M. McKenna (eds), *Moral Responsibility and Alternative Possibilities: Essays on the Importance of Alternative Possibilities* (Ashgate, 2003), pp. 27-52; reprinted in John Martin Fischer, *My Way: Essays on Moral Responsibility* (New York: Oxford University Press, 2006), pp. 38-62.

[3] John Martin Fischer and Mark Ravizza, *Responsibility and Control: A*

Further, I contend that one can present an elegant and comprehensive account of guidance control that exhibits such control to be entirely compatible with causal determinism (and God's foreknowledge). My approach starts with the ingredients of "mechanism ownership" (the actual-sequence mechanism's being the agent's own) and "reasons-responsiveness" of that mechanism and presents an account of guidance control of action. On this approach, an agent exhibits guidance control of an action insofar as the action issues from his own, moderately reasons-responsive mechanism. I then develop a comprehensive account of moral responsibility–for omissions, consequences-particulars, consequence-universals, and character traits–that builds on the basic analysis of guidance control of action. The same core elements of the analysis are employed in natural ways in the comprehensive account of moral responsibility.

All compatibilists must hold that not all causally deterministic chains are created equal. The traditional compatibilist holds that some sorts of causally deterministic chains "compel" the agent in such a way that the agent cannot do otherwise, whereas other such chains are completely consistent with genuine freedom to choose and otherwise. In contrast, I am inclined to accept the Consequence Argument (so-called by Peter Van Inwagen) to the effect that causal determinism would rule out such freedom (regulative control). I am also inclined to believe that God's foreknowledge would rule out such freedom. But I take it that the Frankfurt examples help to show that we do not need access to alternative possibilities in order to be morally responsible for our behavior. Thus, because I believe that guidance control is all the freedom we need for moral responsibility, I am a "semi-compatibilist"; I am a compatibilist about casual determinism (and God's foreknowledge) and guidance control/moral responsibility, quite apart from whether causal determinism (or God's foreknowledge) is consistent with access to alternative possibilities.

The semicompatibilist shares with the traditional compatibilist the view that not all causally deterministic chains are created equal. For the semicompatibilist, however, this does not entail that we sometimes have regulative control in a deterministic world; rather, it entails that we sometimes have guidance control in such a world. An important project then is to seek to explain in a

---

Theory of Moral Responsibility (Cambridge: Cambridge University Press, 1998).

systematic way just which causally deterministic sequences rule out moral responsibility, and which sequences are consistent with it (and, indeed, help to confer responsibility). Some compatibilists are content with providing lists of stock examples of lack of moral responsibility, or perhaps with relying on intuitions about a range of cases; in contrast, I (with my co-author, Mark Ravizza) have attempted to provide a general and systematic account of the distinction (in terms of guidance control).

So, two important projects have been to try to defend the notion that we don't need genuine access to alternative possibilities (regulative control), in or to be morally responsible, and, also, to present an attractive, comprehensive, and compatibilistic account of guidance control (what I take to be the freedom-relevant component of moral responsibility). I believe additionally that there are basic "pictures" behind the regulative control model and the guidance control model of moral responsibility. The picture that underlies the regulative control model is the "make-a-difference" idea; here it is thought that what is important in our morally responsible behavior is our making a difference (of a certain sort) to the world. Here the idea is we make a relevant kind of difference by *selecting* our path from a number of genuinely available paths into the future. On this view, the value of being morally responsible agents—and the value of acting in such a way as to be morally responsible—is the value of making a difference through selection of one among various open options.

Clearly, the picture that lies behind the guidance control model must be different. On my view, what we care about in behaving so as to be morally responsible is *not* making a difference, but *making a statement* of a certain distinctive kind. The picture here is not *selection*, but *self-expression*. Thus, the value of so acting that one is morally responsible—and we *do* place a value on being morally responsible agents rather than mere automata or animals that are driven solely by instinct—is the value of aesthetic activity: the value of producing a certain sort of narrative. I have argued that when we act freely (exhibit guidance control), it is as if we write a sentence in the narrative of our lives, and that it is in virtue of so acting—exhibiting the relevant kind of freedom—that we transform our lives into lives that have a special, narrative dimension of value.

3. What other sub-disciplines in philosophy and non- disciplines stand to benefit the most from philosophical work on the nature of action and agency, and how might such engagement be accomplished?

Obviously, I believe that many areas in philosophy of religion overlap with questions about agency and free will. Clearly, areas of moral philosophy (and, in particular, ethics) also overlap considerably with such questions. It should also be evident that views in philosophy of law and legal theory–especially theories in the criminal law–depend heavily on views about agency and freedom. In particular, discussions of the nature of intention, coercion, addiction, various mental disorders, and psychopathy will have important implications for views in the criminal law.

In my view, many neuroscientists could benefit from engagement with the philosophical work on agency, free will, and moral responsibility. Although there is much of potential interest in neurorscience, and I have learned a great deal from some of it (for instance, work by Adina Roskies), I nevertheless believe that many neuroscientists have "klunky" and unsophisticated views about the philosophical issues. For example, many neuroscientists seem entirely to dismiss–or even be unaware of–compatibilism; that is, they appear to infer from their conclusion that the brain works deterministically (if they do in fact conclude this from the evidence) that there is no room left for free will. But this is obviously problematic, as it leaves out a range of compatbilistic views, including semicompatibilism.

4. What do you regard as the most neglected issues in contemporary work on action and agency that deserve more attention?

Surprisingly, there is very little explicit discussion of the relationship between different accounts or conceptions of the laws of nature and causation, on the one hand, and agency and freedom, on the other. Of course, there has been much work in metaphysics and philosophy of science on the laws of nature and causation; but especially given the central role of these notions in debates about free will, I am somewhat surprised that there is so little discussion of the implications of different conceptions of (say) the laws of nature or causation for freedom and moral responsibility.

Further, whereas there have been lively discussions recently in metaphysics about persistence of objects and persons over time, with debates about endurantism versus perdurantism and related issues about whether to conceive of objects three-dimensionally or four-dimensionally, there has been very little discussion of the relationships between these ideas and views about free will and moral responsibility. And yet there are presumably important connections here, especially between different conceptions of the nature and persistence of persons and moral responsibility.

Another area in which lots of work has recently been done is philosophy of time, in which views such as "presentism" and "eternalism" have been discussed. There has been some preliminary exploration of the relationship between particular views on time, claims about the supervenience of truth on being, and various views about free will; but I believe that much more remains to be done here. I believe it is especially promising to seek to gain illumination of some of the debates about God's omniscience and human freedom by reference to views about the nature of time and supervenience of truth on being. It is interesting to me that much of the "contemporary" work on God and free will (although certainly by no means all of it) was done in the 1960's through 1980's, prior to the more recent work on "presentism" and "eternalism" and their relationships to tense, truth, and being. I think it would be worthwhile to examine that literature on God's omniscience and human freedom in light of the more recent work in the philosophy of time (and related issues in metaphysics).

There has been much work seeking to bring to bear empirical analysis on questions about agency, free will, and moral responsibility. This work runs the gamut from neuroscience to social science studies to "polls". I certainly am open to the possibility that some of this work will help–even significantly–to illuminate philosophical issues about agency, freedom, and responsibility. But what seems to me to be under-theorized is the question–or better questions–of *how exactly* this work is supposed to bear on philosophical questions. More precisely, I believe that we don't have a very good understanding of the *philosophical significance* of at least some–if not much–of the empirical work. So, for example, if we glean from a "poll"–however carefully crafted–that a certain number or percentage of people in a certain context say that a causally determined action cannot be a free action, what exactly are we to make of this? We already know that what people say in reply to such questions is exquisitely sensitive to factors about the context and, in particular, to the specific wording of the question. Further, it is just unclear what to make of the putative information we get from such polls.

It is perhaps worth pausing to think about this a bit more. An analytic philosopher might say something like, "Most people would say such-and-such about the case in question," and she may use this alleged truth as support for her position. Then I suppose that carefully crafted polls of carefully selected audiences might well be helpful in getting at whether the philosopher's evidence for her point really provides any reason to adopt it. But typically I wouldn't be inclined to rely on such evidence at all. Typically, at least, I would seek to capture an intuitive point, or a point I think would be intuitively attractive, perhaps upon sustained reflection of a certain sort. Then I would attempt to show how acceptance of the point–articulated in a certain way–can be defended. Perhaps the defense would consist in showing that the claim helps to solve some philosophical puzzle or problem, or that it follows from a package of positions that seems to solve such a problem, or it in some way illuminates a philosophical question or conundrum. If the point–articulated in a certain way–is in this way helpful, and it can be seen to be appealing upon reflection, then it is reasonable to take it seriously, quite apart from what the polls say!

It is as if I'm saying: I commend this view to you. Look, it makes some sense, and it can help to solve certain problems, or perhaps to clarify them–or even to show why they are problems. I'm presenting a view or structured package of views, and I'm commending them to my philosophical audience as helpful or illuminating; I do not really care whether a group of people–perhaps without attending to the philosophical resonance of the views or without sustained and comprehensive reflection–would vote "yes"!

No doubt I have presented a somewhat over-simplified sketch of my own sort of methodological predilections, and presumably I have also only given a caricature of the sort of work that seeks to chart the actual views of the "folk". Perhaps my main point here is that, in spite of the increasingly voluminous empirical data being developed by "experimental philosophy," its precise role and philosophical significance is under-developed. Of course, this is not to say that it doesn't have a role to play; rather, my point is simply that we need better to understand this role.

I am particularly interested in two areas of intersection of empirical work with more traditional work on free will and moral responsibility. "Situationism"–the view that situational cues are much more significant than enduring traits of character in explaining our behavior–has been thought to call into question "reasons-responsiveness" views of freedom and moral responsibility. This is in part because the literature giving rise to the doctrine of situationism threatens the views that we typically know our reasons for action and that such (transparent) reasons typically motivate us (or cause our actions).[4] I think it is unclear how strong a conclusion of this sort can be derived from the empirical literature, and I am also uncertain as to how it bears on reasons-responsiveness accounts of control. This is a subject for future work.

Adina Roskies has made a fascinating suggestion–or perhaps a suggestion that I can be excused for finding fascinating. That is, she has suggested that certain work in neuroscience can help with the "individuation-problem" for the behavior-producing mechanisms in the Fischer/Ravizza account of guidance control (and moral responsibility). Roskies has suggested that at least some progress toward giving a fruitful and non-arbitrary account of mechanism-individuation might be made, given some results about the actual neurophysiology that underlies the operation of the processes that issue in choices and that initiate human behavior.[5] This is–of course–intriguing but programmatic stuff, and (in my view) worth attention in the future. In John Fischer's ideal world, neuroscientists of the future would identify a certain family of neurophysiological precesses that underlie all and only those mechanisms that are plausibly thought to involve guidance control; I suppose that I would be pleased if it simply turned out that the notion of guidance control could (to a certain extent) help to frame and shape some of the empirical inquiries in social science and neuroscience.

Another surprisingly neglected area of inquiry pertains to the notion of "sourcehood". There is much discussion of the sort of control that involves alternative possibilities, and the relationship between such control and (say) the doctrine of causal determinism. But there is less focus on "sourcehood" and whether (say) causal determination of behavior is compatible with the agent's being the source of the behavior (in the sense relevant to moral responsibility). Whereas we have some intuitive grasp of the notion of sourcehood, this important idea is somewhat under-theorized.

Also, we speak of being "fully responsible" and being "partly re-

---

[4] See, for example, John Doris, *Lack of Character: Personality and Moral Behavior* (Cambridge: Cambridge University Press, 2002).
[5] Adina Roskies, "Can Neuroscience Resolve Issues About Free Will?", delivered at the University of Indiana, Bloomington, Conference on Agency and Responsibility, September 2007.

sponsible" for behavior or upshots of behavior, but what exactly is it to be "fully" or "partly" or "partially" responsible? To be fully morally responsible is not necessarily the same as being "solely" morally responsible, and there are various distinct ways we could be "partially" morally responsible. I take it that two people who jointly build a bomb can be partially responsible for the devastation it causes in virtue of contributing some necessary part of the bomb; one can be partially responsible in virtue of contributing part of the product of teamwork. Sometimes people speak of adolescents or significantly retarded or impaired human beings as being "partially morally responsible"; in the case of adolescents, this is a developmental point. It is also suggested that abusive parents can be "partially morally responsible" for the behavior of their children; if this is so, it seems that the sense in which the parents are partially responsible is different from both the "teamwork" or "joint agency" sense and also the developmental sense. It is interesting to ask whether the parents' partial responsibility for the child's behavior in some way diminishes the child's allotment of responsibility for the behavior in question. Also, are "Leave-It-To-Beaver" parents partially responsible for their children's good behavior, and does this diminish the child's responsibility of his praiseworthy behavior?

5. What are the most important open problems in philosophical theorizing about action and agency, and what are the prospects for progress?

I would include most, if not all, of the areas I mentioned in my answer to the previous question. But certainly the under-theorized questions have no monopoly on the category of "unresolved". I would say that the two most pressing and important challenges posed by the doctrine of causal determinism for our freedom and moral responsibility are the worry about alternative possibilities and the worry about sourcehood, and it turns out these two challenges involve some of the most salient unresolved issues in contemporary discussions. In my view, then, the first major unresolved issue is the question of whether moral responsibility requires the sort of control that involves genuine metaphysical access to alternative possibilities ("regulative control", in my terminology). The second significant unresolved issue is whether causal determinism is consistent with the sort of "sourcehood" required for moral responsibility,

There are various "routes" to the denial of (PAP) and thus to the conclusion that moral responsibility does not require regulative control. One route, as discussed above, is via reflection on the Frankfurt examples, with their signature structure of preemptive overdetermination. Above I pointed out that I have argued that even if there are ineliminable residual alternative possibilities in the Frankfurt-examples, they may not be sufficiently robust to ground attributions of moral responsibility; they are, as I have put it, "mere flickers of freedom".

There is however a powerful reply to my argument that has been employed by such philosophers as Robert Kane, Carl Ginet, and David Widerker: the dilemma defense of PAP.[6] The dilemma defense essentially invites us to consider either the possibility that causal determinism obtains in the Frankfurt cases, or not. If it does obtain, then it would seem to be question-begging to conclude from a consideration of the examples that the agents are morally responsible in them. After all, what is at stake in the debate is whether causal determinism is consistent with moral responsibility! If causal determinism does not obtain, then it would seem that the counterfactual intervener is not in a position to squelch *all* robust alternatives. After all, the counterfactual intervener cannot tell simply by looking at any feature of the actual past that the agent in question will definitely choose and act in a certain way; thus, it will be open to the agent at least to begin to choose otherwise. And an alternative possibility of this sort is surely robust, even if small; although in certain areas of life it is arguable that size matters, not here; what is relevant is not size, but oomph. Whereas I have attempted to respond (in various ways) to the dilemma defense, it remains (lamentably) an open question whether I have–or *anyone* has–succeeded in offering a satisfactory response.

Although this view is highly controversial, I am attracted to the idea that God's foreknowledge is a good "model" of a Frankfurt case. Given certain assumptions about God, He does not causally intervene in the relevant agent's choice and behavior, and yet His mere presence (and foreknowledge) ensures that the agent could

---

[6] Robert Kane, *The Significance of Free Will* (New York: Oxford University Press, 1996), pp. 142-45; David Widerker, "Libertarianism and Frankfurt's Attack on the Principle of Alternative Possibilities," *Philosophical Review* 104 (1995), pp. 247-61; and Carl Ginet, In Defense of the Principle of Alternative Possibilities: Why I Don't Find Frankfurt's Argument Convincing," *Philosophical Perspectives* 10 (1996), pp. 403-17.

not have chosen or done otherwise. (Of course, this is the view of the "theological fatalist" or incompatibilist about God's foreknowledge and human freedom, and there are various ways of calling the view into question.) If we accept that God's foreknowledge is a kind of Frankfurt case, and if we accept incompatibilism (as well as the contention that God does not directly cause human choices and behavior), then we could reply to the indeterministic horn of the dilemma defense. Also, there may be other ways of responding to the indeterministic horn, based on versions of the Frankfurt cases defended by philosophers such as Pereboom, Hunt, and McKenna. Additionally, I have offered some suggestions for responding to the deterministic horn, although I am not sanguine about the prospect of my suggestions' being universally and warmly embraced (with the subsequent singing–in unison–of "Kumbaya").

While some compatibilists still wish to maintain that there is an important sort of freedom or "ability" to do otherwise that is compatible with causal determinism, I think this is implausible. It is much less clear, however, that such freedom is not required for moral responsibility. In addition to applying even more ingenuity and creativity to the construction of–and analysis of–Frankfurt cases, progress here might be made by emphasizing that there are various routes to the denial of PAP. Suppose one finds it plausible that the denial of PAP is indeed the moral of the Frankfurt stories, but one also is wiling to admit that one has no knockdown argument for this conclusion. At this point one can point out that the denial of PAP can gain some additional credence by noting that there are other powerful methods of arguing against PAP; one very attractive strategy follows Peter Strawson and has been given forceful expression by Jay Wallace, and another appealing strategy–or perhaps congeries of strategies–has been sketched by Daniel Dennett.[7] After all, there may be more than one way to skin the cat, and, to switch the metaphor, the Frankfurt examples are not necessarily the only tool in our arsenal.

A final note on progress. Progress can be achieved within the context of a reasonable philosophical methodology that does not set the bar too high. More specifically, one should not expect–or even hope–to change the mind of a committed proponent of an

---

[7] R. Jay Wallace, *Responsibility and the Moral Sentiments* (Cambridge, Ma.: Harvard University Press, 1994); and Daniel Dennett, *Freedom Evolves* (New York: Viking, 2003).

opposing position. Rather, one should (as Van Inwagen has also argued) aim one's arguments at reasonable and fair-minded "agnostics". Progress can be conceptualized as increasing the level of appeal of the doctrine in question to an audience of antecedent agnostics. Also, if we are a bit more liberal about progress, we can see progress in argumentation that helps people see the force of philosophical questions, that brings out hitherto under-appreciated difficulties, and that helps to identify important theoretical connections.

Finally, one can see progress as decreased distance from one's goal, or as increased distance from one's starting point. Progress will certainly be easier to attain if we think of it as increased distance from the beginning, and we are much more likely to enjoy the journey.[8]

---

[8] Thanks to Andrei Buckareff for his helpful comments.

5
Stewart Goetz

Professor of Philosophy
Ursinus College, USA

Noncausal Libertarianism and the Principle of Alternative Possibilities

David Charles, my tutor in philosophy at Oriel College, Oxford, introduced me to action theory. Over the course of numerous tutorials, my belief that we have libertarian free will began to take shape. David recommended that I take a look at the work of Roderick Chisholm, and I subsequently immersed myself in *Person and Object*[1] and "Freedom and Action."[2] Though I discovered a kindred spirit in Chisholm, I was puzzled by his view that agents are causes. My belief in libertarianism arose out of my first-person experience as an agent, and the fundamental data provided by that experience simply did not include my agent-causing an undertaking or some functionally equivalent mental event. Chisholm, however, had whetted my intellectual appetite. My project for the years ahead would be to articulate what I came to think of as a noncausal theory of agency.

From the very beginning, the work on this project was not easy. Most philosophers disputed what I regarded as fundamental data.[3]

---

[1] Roderick Chisholm, *Person and Object* (La Salle, IL: Open Court Publishing Company, 1976).
[2] Roderick Chisholm, "Freedom and Action," in *Freedom and Determinism*, ed. by Keith Lehrer (New York: Random House, 1966), pp. 11-44.
[3] Many, if not most, philosophers claimed that my first-person experience of libertarian freedom was shared by non-philosophers (ordinary people). Cf. Thomas Nagel's *The View from Nowhere* (Oxford: Oxford University Press, 1986), p. 114; and Saul Smilansky's *Free Will and Illusion* (Oxford: Clarendon Press, 2000), pp. 3-4, 26. Some philosophers, however, dispute this claim. See Eddy Nahmias, Stephen G. Morris, Thomas Nadelhoffer, and Jason Turner, "Is Incompatibilism Intuitive?," *Philosophy and Phenomenological Research* 73: (2006), pp. 28-53.

The few who were libertarians thought that 'libertarianism' was synonymous with 'agent causation.' The idea that we could have libertarian freedom without agent causation was for them literally self-contradictory. In this environment, I had a very difficult time making any intellectual progress. I thought that I had some interesting ideas (the principal one of which was that choices are explained teleologically, not causally) that could be developed into a coherent and plausible noncausal view of libertarian freedom, but no one, including libertarians, took these ideas seriously.

Then one afternoon, everything changed. The grand master himself, Roderick Chisholm, arrived for a campus visit (I was now in a philosophy doctoral program at Notre Dame) and delivered the first of a series of three lectures. I remember sitting in a packed room and listening as Chisholm talked about things agential in nature, but without mentioning agent causation. Questions and answers followed his talk. One of my mentors raised his hand and proceeded to ask a question about agent causation that I believed was designed for no other purpose than to put the final nail in my intellectual coffin. I waited anxiously for Chisholm's response and when it came I experienced one of those rare moments when all seems right with the world. "I no longer believe in agent causation," answered Chisholm. The mentor who had asked the question was, to put it mildly, dumbfounded. I turned to look at another of my mentors who was sitting about six seats away. He slowly turned toward me and our eyes met. His look was one I shall never forget. As Chisholm continued his answer, he explained how he thought one might have libertarian freedom without agent causation. His explanation was no more intellectually satisfying for me than was the idea of agent causation. But I didn't care at that point. All I knew that afternoon was that there was intellectual life for me.

The following day, Chisholm invited the second of the mentors just mentioned and me to his hotel room for a friendly chat about libertarianism. I do not know what he thought about my ideas that day. One comment of his, however, still sticks in my mind: "I invented agent causation to solve a problem that I now believe can be solved without it." "You *invented* agent causation?" I recall mumbling to myself. "*Invented* it?" I left that face-to-face meeting, which was the only one I would ever have with Chisholm, with those words echoing over and over in my mind.

What was the problem that Chisholm initially thought could not be solved without agent causation? It was fundamentally a dilemma about the need for and nature of an explanation of an event. On the one hand, he had believed that an event that is not causally determined is inexplicable and, therefore, a random occurrence. On the other hand, he had thought that if a free action is caused, its cause would have to be another event. Moreover, if an event were caused by another event, it would be part of a deterministic causal chain and, therefore, could not be a free action. In order to pass through the horns of this dilemma, Chisholm claimed he had invented the idea of agent causation. Not only are there event-causes, but there are also agent-causes. And because these agent-causes are not event-causes, they cannot (or at least they need not) themselves be caused to cause the events that they cause. Hence, libertarian freedom is possible without free actions being inexplicable, random occurrences.

It was an intriguing idea, and one that I was to discover was not literally invented by Chisholm. At least it seemed to me that he did not invent it. Because of Chisholm's own work on Thomas Reid, I was learning that Reid was an agent causationist. Whatever the correct history was of Chisholm's coming up with the idea of agent causation, I remained convinced that it was possible to have libertarian freedom without agent causation.

As I have already indicated, I believe that a choice is an uncaused event that is explained teleologically by a reason or purpose. The idea in a nutshell is as follows: As self-conscious subjects we possess the power to choose, where the power to choose is ontologically a fundamental and irreducible mental property of an agent. The exercising of that power by the agent is a primitive or simple event in the sense that it has no event parts (it lacks an internal causal structure) and is intrinsically active and, thereby, essentially uncaused. An agent has a single power to choose and whenever he exercises it at a time t he is free at that time to exercise it in a different way. In other words, when an agent is free to make either choice C1 or C2 at t, it is not the case that he has one power to choose whose exercising is C1 and a second power to choose whose exercising is C2. There is one, and only one, power to choose that can be exercised in only one of two or more incompatible ways.

Given that the concept of an exercising of the power to choose is the concept of an essentially uncaused event, an agent who is aware of an instance of this concept need not conduct a search to make sure that his exercising of his power to choose is not caused (deterministically or indeterministically) by either internal goings-on in his mind or events outside his mind. His knowledge that his choice is uncaused is not a conclusion at which he arrives after conducting an investigation. An agent knows straight off that his choice is uncaused by being aware of exercising his power to choose. The exercising of his power to choose is a mental event over which he has direct or intrinsic control. Because an agent cannot be caused to exercise his power to choose, he never finds himself a patient with respect to his choices. He might undergo the twitch of an eyelid or a leg, or have his eyelid or leg forcibly closed or moved respectively by others, but he never has a twitch of a choice or is forced to choose by others. Not even the proverbial gun at his head can literally force him to make a choice.

Though an agent's choice cannot be explained causally, it is explained teleologically by a reason. A reason for choosing to act is a *purpose*, where a purpose is a conceptual entity, an *ens rationis* or intentional object, which is about or directed at the future. When an agent chooses to act, he does so *in order to* accomplish or bring about a purpose. In general, a teleological explanation of a choice to perform an action involves an agent (1) conceiving of or representing in the content of a propositional attitude such as a belief or a desire the *future* as including a state of affairs that is a purpose to be brought about or produced for the sake of its goodness; (2) conceiving of or representing the means to the realization or bringing about of this end, where the means begin with the agent performing an action; and (3) making a choice to perform that action in order to bring about that purpose. Borrowing a term of art from discussions of the nature of propositional attitudes, teleological and causal explanations have different *directions of fit*.[4] While a teleological explanation is future-to-present in character, a causal explanation is past-to-present in nature. Hence, to propose a causal explanation of a choice is fundamentally to misunderstand and/or misrepresent the correct explanatory direction of fit for a choice.

In order to do adequate justice to this direction of fit, one must not only include the idea that a reason is a conceptual entity that is about or directed at the future, but also add that it is optative in mood. To illustrate the optative conceptual nature of a reason, consider briefly Robert Kane's example of a businesswoman (call her 'B') who is on her way to an important meeting and witnesses

---

[4] For the idea of direction of fit, see John Searle's *Intentionality* (Cambridge: Cambridge University Press, 1983).

an attack on another individual.[5] Let us assume that B chooses to return to help the victim. She believes that the victim's well-being is in jeopardy and that her returning to help the victim is morally right. In light of this belief, her reason or purpose for acting is *that she do what is morally right* (which, in terms of the first person, is *that I do what is morally right*), and the teleological explanatory relation is expressed by saying that she chooses to return to help the victim *in order to* achieve or bring about the purpose that she do what is morally right. If S had chosen to continue on to the meeting because of her desire that she further her career, the content of her reason for choosing would have been *that she further her career* (which, in terms of the first person, is *that I further my career*). She would have chosen *in order to* achieve or bring about the purpose that she advance her career.

An example of Jonathan Dancy's helps clarify the optative conceptual nature of a reason.[6] Assume I am aware that a particular woman is ill and that I send for a doctor. Dancy maintains that it is the woman's being ill, an actual state of affairs of the world, that is my reason for sending for the doctor. Contrary to what Dancy asserts, however, it is not the woman's being ill that is my reason for sending for the doctor. Rather, my reason is the purpose that the woman be well, which is grounded in the content of a propositional attitude such as my desire that she be well (which represents a future, non-actual state of affairs). Therefore, if I choose to send for the doctor, I do so in order to achieve or bring about the purpose that the woman be well. Thus, while a reason is not a desire or a belief, its optative character stems from its being *grounded in* the content of a desire or belief that represents a future state of affairs as good and something to be brought about by a more temporally proximate chosen action of the person who has the desire or belief.

The close link between a choice and the purpose for making it requires that the following point be emphasized: A choice *qua* propositional attitude (as an event) does not derive its active nature from the reason that explains it. While choices are explained by purposes, those purposes do not transform what is non-active in nature into that which is active. Choices are intrinsically active.

---

[5] Robert Kane, "Responsibility, Luck, and Chance: Reflections on Free Will and Indeterminism," *Journal of Philosophy* 96 (1999): 225.

[6] Jonathan Dancy, *Practical Reality* (Oxford: Oxford University Press, 2000), p. 114.

When an agent is free to choose, he always has two or more reasons that recommend incompatible actions to him. In the case of businesswoman B, she had a reason to return to help the victim and a reason to continue on to her meeting, where the second course of action was incompatible with the first. One should not conclude from this point about incompatible actions and the point that a choice is essentially uncaused that the idea of a determined mental action is nonsensical. One should not conclude this because the concept of determinism is broader than that of causal determinism. For example, Peter van Inwagen defines 'determinism' as "the thesis that there is at any instant exactly one physically possible future,"[7] and Richard Taylor asserts that determinism is the principle that "there are antecedent conditions . . . given which [something] could not be other than it is."[8] If one is a little more permissive than van Inwagen and allows for the possibility of a nonphysical as well as a physical future, then the concept of determinism expressed by van Inwagen is that at a particular moment there is one and only one possible future. Unless one is committed to the view that all explanation is causal explanation, it is possible that there are other forms of explanation that can guarantee that there is at a moment one and only one possible future. Given that there is both causal and teleological explanation, there is the possibility for teleological determinism. In a case of teleological determinism, an agent has a reason R1 to act one way and neither a reason R2 not to act in that way nor a reason R3 to act in some other incompatible way, and given this psychological makeup he proceeds deterministically to form an intention to act for R1. Deterministically forming an intention to act is not choosing to act. Choosing is sufficient for forming an intention but forming an intention is not sufficient for choosing.

My development of noncausal libertarianism is by and large distinctive among contemporary philosophers.[9] I believe that the most important contribution it makes to theorizing about agency is that it makes clear that the most fundamental divide among

---

[7] Peter van Inwagen, *An Essay on Free Will* (Oxford: Clarendon Press, 1983), p. 3.

[8] Richard Taylor, *Metaphysics*, 3rd ed. (Englewood Cliffs, NJ: Prentice Hall, 1983), p. 34.

[9] Hugh McCann and Carl Ginet have developed different versions of noncausal libertarianism. See McCann's *The Works of Agency* (Ithaca: Cornell University Press, 1998) and Ginet's *On Action* (Cambridge: Cambridge University Press, 1990).

actions theorists is not between libertarians and nonlibertarians but between those who hold that that the explanation of (free) mental action is teleological in nature and those who hold that it is causal. To accord teleology this fundamental explanatory role is politically incorrect given the virtually doctrinal view in contemporary philosophy that any acceptable view of agency must conform to the naturalistic paradigm and its assumption of both the nonexistence of ultimate and irreducible teleological explanation and the causal closure of the physical world (physical effects can have only physical causes).

While agent causationists contest naturalism (they hold that some physical effects have nonnatural mental causes), they accept the naturalistic view that no explanation of an event is adequate without the inclusion of causation. Hence, according to agent causationists, even an agent's choice (or the first event-part of a choice) must have a cause. Thus, in the case of businesswoman B, an agent causationist will insist that her choice to return to help the victim cannot be adequately explained by a reason alone, but must be agent-caused by B. Timothy O'Conner has made this argument and I have limited space in which to summarize it and present the gist of my response to it here.[10]

By O'Connor's lights, there must be something to link the reason for which an agent chooses with that choice:

> Were we . . . simply [to] claim that the [choice] was uncaused [and made for a reason], then noting the fact that the agent had a reason that motivated acting in that way would not suffice to explain it. . . . For in that case, any number of actions may have been equally likely to occur, *and* the agent would not have exercised any sort of *control* over which of these was actually performed.[11]

O'Connor believes that to insure an adequate explanation of an agent's choice and his control of it there must be a *link* be-

---

[10] For a detailed response, see my "A Noncausal Theory of Agency," *Philosophy and Phenomenological Research* 49 (1988): 303-316; "Failed Solutions to a Standard Libertarian Problem," *Philosophical Studies* 90 (1998): 237-244; and "Review of Timothy O'Connor's *Persons and Causes: The Metaphysics of Free Will*"' *Faith and Philosophy* 19 (2002): 116-120.

[11] Timothy O'Connor, "Agent Causation," in *Agents, Causes, and Events*, ed. by Timothy O'Connor (Oxford: Oxford University Press, 1995), p. 191. The emphases are O'Connor's.

tween a reason to choose and the choice made for that reason, and the most reasonable view for a libertarian is to hold that this link is agent-causal in nature. An agent's exercise of active or agent-causal power "provides a necessary link between reason and [choice], without which the reason could not in any significant way explain the [choice]."[12] According to O'Connor, a choice is defined as a complex state of affairs consisting of an agent's bearing a causal relation to a causally simple mental event that is the coming-to-be of an intention to act.[13] A reason will explain the coming-to-be of the intention (and, thereby, a choice) only if the two are coupled together by the agent's agent-causing of the coming-to-be of the intention, where this agent-causal activity must itself be uncaused or have no sufficient causal condition.[14] Thus, on O'Connor's view of the case of businesswoman B, she controllably chose to return to help the victim for the reason that she do what was morally right because she agent-caused the coming-to-be of the intention to return to help the victim, where the content of that intention included reference to the content of the belief that she ought to do what was morally right and the action of returning to help the victim fulfilled that belief.

Does agent causation *do any real explanatory work* with respect to B's choice to return to help the victim that is left undone on my noncausal, teleological view of the reason that explains her choosing? I do not think so. To see why, what one needs to ask is 'What on O'Connor's view *explains* B's agent-causing of the coming-to-be of the intention to return to help the victim?' Presumably, the answer is that it is teleologically explained by the reason for returning to help the victim that teleologically explains B's choosing to return to help the victim. Thus, all that O'Connor's agent causationist account does is *relocate* the ultimate and irreducible teleological connection, which on my noncausal view of agency is between the choice and the reason for which it is made, to the relationship between an agent's exercising of agent-causal power and the reason for which it is made. At this point, O'Connor cannot respond that the reason that explains the exercise of agent-causal power does its explanatory work in virtue of an additional exercise of agent-causal power that causally *links* that reason with the

---

[12]O'Connor, *Persons and Causes: The Metaphysics of Free Will* (Oxford: Oxford University Press, 1995), p. 88.

[13]O'Connor, Agent Causation," p. 198, endnote 15.

[14]Ibid., pp. 186, 187; and Timothy O'Connor, "Why Agent Causation?," *Philosophical Topics* 24 (1996): 146.

exercise of agent-causal power that directly produces the coming-to-be of the intention to act. He cannot claim this because he maintains that an exercising of agent-causal power is essentially uncaused.[15] Moreover, it is doubtful that O'Connor would think it wise to claim this because such a response has all the makings of a vicious infinite regress.

What, then, can O'Connor say? It seems that he must say that B exercises her agent-causal power for the reason that she do what is morally right, and that reason noncausally and teleologically explains her exercise (exerting) of agent-causal power, where "exerting active [agent-causal] power is intrinsically a direct exercise of control ...."[16] Moreover, to insure that an agent has control over his exercise of agent-causal power there need not be a link between the exercise of that power and the reason that explains its exercise. No such link is needed because of the agent's intrinsic control over his exercise of agent-causal power. Leaving out agent causation, this is essentially the noncausal view of agency that I defend. In short, a *tu quoque* response to O'Connor is appropriate: If a reason can directly teleologically explain an agent's essentially uncaused agent-causal activity of causing the coming-to-be of an intention without jeopardizing the agent's control of that exercise of agent-causal power, why cannot it directly teleologically explain the uncaused making of a choice without jeopardizing the agent's exercising of his power to choose? It certainly seems that if the noncausal libertarian's position is inadequate, then so is O'Connor's.[17] Hence, I conclude that agent causation is explanatorily superfluous and there is, as Chisholm came to realize, no reason to invoke (invent) it.

It is hard to read and write about action theory today without in some way entering the lively discussion about the principle of alternative possibilities (PAP), which is the thesis that an agent

---

[15] "A consequence of the agent-causation account . . . is that it is impossible for an agent's causing of his intention to itself be caused." O'Connor, *Persons and Causes: The Metaphysics of Free Will*, p. 81, footnote 25.

[16] O'Connor, *Persons and Causes: The Metaphysics of Free Will*, p. 61.

[17] Most recently, O'Connor notes "the difficult matter facing most agent causationists of how reasons . . . explain the agent's exertion of causal power." "Libertarian Views: Dualist and Agent-Causal Theories," in *The Oxford Handbook of Free Will*, ed. by Robert Kane (Oxford: Oxford University Press, 2002), p. 349. After sympathetically summarizing Richard Taylor's belief that explanations in terms of reasons or purposes are entirely different from explanations in terms of causes, O'Connor claims that he construes "reasons explanations as noncausal." Ibid.

is morally responsible for a choice only if he was free in the libertarian sense to choose otherwise. In recent years, I have published several papers on this topic in which I critique various Frankfurt-style counterexamples that purport to show how an agent can be morally responsible for a choice even though he was not free in the libertarian sense to choose otherwise (determinism is compatible with moral responsibility).[18] Beyond trying to point out the particular flaws in particular Frankfurt-style counterexamples, I believe that my most important contributions to the discussion of PAP are two in number.

First, I believe that my work on libertarian agency has helped to clarify how the concept of a *robust* choice is relevant to PAP. John Fischer has written several important pieces about PAP in which he has made clear that attempts to defend PAP against Frankfurt-style counterexamples must, to be effective, make use of a robust undetermined alternative possibility to what an agent actually chooses to do.[19] According to Fischer, an alternative possibility is robust enough for grounding moral responsibility for the making of an actual choice only if it is the case that the agent would have avoided moral responsibility for his actual choice by bringing about the alternative possibility.[20] Fischer claims (surely correctly) that it is not sufficient for grounding an agent's moral responsibility for his actual choice that it have been possible (in an indeterministic sense) for him to come, say, to have an inclination to do otherwise or to blush (where blushing would be a sign that he would do otherwise). Because coming to have an inclination and blushing are not events over which an agent has the kind of control that is necessary for moral responsibility, it cannot be the case that an agent is morally responsible for a choice that he actually makes because he might have indeterministically come to have an inclination or blushed. Hence, if an agent is morally responsible for an actual choice only if he had an alternative open to him, then it is reasonable to think that the available alternative

---

[18] See my "Alternative Frankfurt-Style Counterexamples to the Principle of Alternative Possibilities," *Pacific Philosophical Quarterly* 83 (2002) 131-147; "Stump on Libertarianism and the Principle of Alternative Possibilities," *Faith and Philosophy* 18 (2001): 93-101; and "Stumping for Widerker," *Faith and Philosophy* 16 (1999): 83-89.

[19] Many of Fischer's papers are collected in his *My Way: Essays on Moral Responsibility* (Oxford: Oxford University Press, 2006).

[20] For example, see Fischer's *The Metaphysics of Free Will: An Essay on Control* (Oxford: Blackwell, 1994), Chapter 7.

was in the most robust sense an alternative choice.

At this point it is only fair to point out that if a libertarian must make use of a robust alternative possibility such as an alternative choice in defending PAP, then someone must also make use of a robust sense of choice in the actual sequence of events in challenging PAP. To illustrate what I have in mind, consider the following summary of Derk Pereboom's Frankfurt-style counterexample:

> Joe is considering whether to claim a tax deduction which he knows is illegal. He also knows, however, that he probably will not be caught and that if he is he can convincingly plead ignorance. Suppose he has a very strong but not overriding desire to advance his self-interest no matter what the cost to others, and no matter whether advancing his self-interest involves illegal activity. Furthermore, Joe is a libertarian free agent. His psychology, however, is such that the only way in this situation he could choose not to engage in tax evasion (choose to pay his taxes) is for moral reasons. He cannot, for example, choose not to engage in tax evasion for no reason at all. It is causally necessary for his choosing not to evade taxes in this situation that a moral reason occur to him with a certain force. Joe can choose that a moral reason occur to him. But a moral reason occurring to him is not causally sufficient for his choosing not to evade paying his taxes. If a moral reason were to occur to him, then Joe could choose (in a libertarian sense) to evade paying his taxes or choose not to evade paying his taxes. In order to ensure, however, that he choose to evade paying his taxes, a neuroscientist implants an electronic device which, were it to sense a moral reason occurring (by hypothesis, Joe chose that it occur), would intervene in Joe's brain to cause him to choose to evade paying his taxes. In actual fact, no moral reason occurs to him, and Joe chooses to evade paying his taxes while the device remains idle.[21]

Pereboom claims that Joe's desire to evade paying his taxes

---

[21] See Derk Pereboom, "Alternative Possibilities and Causal Histories," *Philosophical Perspectives* 14 (2000): 119-137; cf. *Living Without Free Will* (Cambridge: Cambridge University Press, 2001), pp. 18-22.

along with the lack of a moral reason to pay his taxes does not causally determine his choice to evade paying his taxes. But does Joe *choose* to evade paying his taxes? If we work with a robust sense of choice, then he does not. Recall what Pereboom says about the moral reason for Joe to pay his taxes. According to him, this reason is a necessary causal condition of Joe's choosing to pay his taxes. What Pereboom overlooks, however, is that having this moral reason (or some reason for an action other than evading paying his taxes) is also a necessary condition of Joe's *choosing* to evade paying his taxes. Without a reason to act otherwise— to do something other than evade paying his taxes, Joe cannot make a *choice* to evade paying his taxes because making a choice presupposes alternatives from which to choose. With a reason to evade paying his taxes and no moral reason to pay them (no reason to act otherwise), Joe will deterministically form the intention to evade paying his taxes and, ultimately, evade paying his taxes because he does not have a reason to do anything else. This is because if an agent has a reason R1 to do A and does not have either a reason R2 not to do A or a reason R3 to do something else, then by default he will deterministically form an intention to do A (without first choosing to do A) and, *ceteris paribus*, thereby do A. It is his having R2 (or R3) that requires either a choice to do A for R1 or a choice not to do A for R2 (or a choice to do something else for R3). In light, then, of his reason-giving structure, Joe is determined to form the intention to evade paying his taxes without choosing to evade paying them.

My second important contribution to the debate about PAP is contained in an essay in which I respond to Fischer's argument against PAP.[22] In the barest of terms, Fischer has argued that Frankfurt-style counterexamples have helped to achieve a dialectical breakthrough. Up until Frankfurt's groundbreaking argument against PAP, the disagreement between incompatibilists and compatibilists about whether causal determinism excludes the freedom to choose otherwise (alternative possibilities) had reached a stalemate. "Frankfurt-type examples have [had] the important function of *shifting the debate* away from considerations pertinent to the relationship between causal determinism and alterna-

---

[22] See my "Frankfurt-Style Counterexamples and Begging the Question," In *Midwest Studies in Philosophy: Free Will and Moral Responsibility*, vol. 29, ed. by Peter A. French, Howard K. Wettstein, and John Martin Fischer. Oxford: Basil Blackwell, 2005, pp. 83-105.

tive possibilities."²³ Incompatibilists and compatibilists can agree that causal determinism excludes the freedom to choose otherwise, but Frankfurt-style counterexamples have led to the compatibilist conclusion that it is possible for an agent (Jones) to be morally responsible even though he could not choose otherwise. This is "genuine—[and] not illusory—progress."²⁴ And Fischer has argued that this progress has been achieved without begging the question against the libertarian.

In response to Fischer, I have argued that the supposed progress is illusory and that Frankfurt-style counterexamples beg the question against the libertarian. Fischer has since stated that my argument against him is correct. And this leads to what I believe is one of the most important problems now facing philosophical theorizing about action and moral responsibility, namely, can either compatibilists or libertarians present a convincing non-question-begging argument for their views? Over the years, I have grown increasingly doubtful about the possibility of developing such an argument. In the words of Fischer, I believe a "dialectical statement" might very well exist between compatibilists and libertarians about the nature of some human freedom and PAP.²⁵ I certainly do not have such an argument for either libertarianism or PAP. If my doubt is warranted, then perhaps the future of philosophizing about action will extend no further than developing and clarifying a coherent libertarian or non-libertarian view of action with little or no hope of persuading an opponent of that view that it is true.

---

²³ See Fischer's "Frankfurt-Style Compatibilism," in *Contours of Agency: Essays on Themes from Harry Frankfurt*, ed. by Sarah Buss and Lee Overton (Cambridge, MA: MIT Press, 2002), p. 8. The emphasis is Fischer's.
²⁴ Ibid., p. 20.
²⁵ See Fischer's *The Metaphysics of Free Will*, pp. 83-85. I say that a dialectical stalemate might exist between compatibilists and libertarians about the nature of "some human freedom" because a libertarian need not deny that some of our freedom is compatibilist in nature. What a libertarian believes is that not all of our freedom is of this kind.

6
Patricia Greenspan

Professor of Philosophy
University of Maryland, USA

---

1. Why were you initially drawn to theorizing about action and agency?

Like many people, I was initially attracted to free will issues – at first embracing hard determinism, as part of a general rejection of doctrines associated with religion, though exposure to Kant's views in my first philosophy course made me begin to consider nonreligious grounds for an indeterminist conception of free action. Of course, Kant also takes belief in God and immortality as presupposed by moral agency, but I was never much moved by those arguments. On free will, though, I thought seeing my acts as determined would give me a reason to expend less effort on them.

It's hard to articulate this without committing what Mill called the "lazy sophism." I don't mean that I'd necessarily work less hard or the like. If determinism is true, and the causes of my accepting the doctrine and still working hard to accomplish something were in place, then presumably I *would* work hard. Nor will hard work be any less necessary to accomplish my aims. But why should I exert the effort it would take to *get* myself to work hard? This, too, may be needed in order to accomplish my aim, so the argument can keep going back. But on some level, an attitude of "let it happen" would also seem to be justified (at any rate, in noninstrumental terms), if the causes of my expending effort (or not) are already in place. Something at least seems funny here, though it takes some work to spell out coherently: I shouldn't actually do things any differently, if I want to accomplish my aims, but I'd be warranted in adopting a different practical attitude toward what I do (roughly: "let it happen"), if I genuinely took determinism to heart. Or perhaps the point is best put negatively: I'd lose the sense that I need to add something to the pre-existing situation – some new element of effort or the like, not already supplied by it. If this is possible, I think it might very well make a difference to what I'm likely to do, even if it wouldn't affect my means-ends reasoning about what I should do, or *instrumental* practical reasoning – even as applied to what attitude to take toward what I do. If it's not possible (as determinism would seem to imply), that means there's a sense in which I can't take determinism to heart. The implications of a belief in determinism would have to be kept compartmentalized from reasoning about action – essentially, Kant's point.

Of course, this is an argument at most only for *belief* in indeterminist free will, not for its truth. Later, though, in graduate school, what really got me hooked on free will issues was hearing a version of the Humean argument that indeterminism would undermine free will by making action random, arbitrary, merely a matter of chance, or the like. I had many other interests, so free will stayed on the back burner for quite a while, but the challenge of responding to various forms of this argument in the contemporary literature led me to general readings in philosophy of action. I particularly appreciated Davidson's work, on weakness of will and other issues as well as on reasons as causes, both for its clarity and for drawing mainstream attention back to these areas, though I tended to disagree with many of Davidson's views.

For me the basic challenge in this area and others has been finding ways to combine naturalistic inclinations – the sort of outlook that Davidson and others identify with Hume – with views on foundational issues in ethics that are usually associated with the opposite, roughly Kantian, approach. My interests in moral philosophy at around the same time centered on how and to what extent one could combine the understanding of ethics as a human invention with the insistence on a hard or inescapable moral "must." In fact, it's occurred to me that the various subjects I've worked on over the years involve different uses of "must" in application to action – senses in which we might be said to *have to* do something, where what's at issue may or may not be causation. My published work for the most part hasn't been directly concerned with defending a position on free will versus determinism, but rather with exploring topics about motivation and normativity that sometimes are wrongly entangled with the standard free will issue. These include the explanation of cases of psychological compulsion, the rational and moral role of emotions, and in my current work, the nature and normative basis of practical reasons.

In nonmoral cases I've been inclined to debunk any straight claim that one "must" act, in a sense that might be interpreted in terms of "blind" causation by nonrational factors. But I don't take the Humean line that the element of necessity is just in the mind of the observer. Instead, I essentially refer it to something about the agent's view of her practical options. In cases of psychological compulsion, for instance, I take the claim that the agent "has to" act as elliptical for a claim that the "compelled" act is her only tolerable option. She has to act *or* suffer the consequences – some sort of psychological distress that she experiences as overwhelming. But her perception of the threat may well be idiosyncratic and distorted. So the point is not to defend such cases as fully rational, but just to dispel a common picture of them as explained simply by causal necessitation.

I also apply the general strategy of interpreting "must" in terms of intolerable options to normal cases, especially of "pressured" action from emotion. But in relation to Humean arguments on free will issues, it provides another way of looking at the relation between character and action besides the all-too-easy resort to deterministic causation. In terms of the recent literature, I have in mind, say, the case of Luther's famous assertion that he could "do no other" than refuse to recant the 95 theses. What I think is really meant by such claims is not that alternatives are strictly impossible for the agent, but rather that he thinks he'd lose any coherent or tolerable view of himself (or "self-narrative") if he did otherwise.

This way of looking at things is compatible with a causal view, but it doesn't require one. In short, character isn't (or needn't be) a deterministic cause of action, or part of one – nor, if we deny it that role, do we have to take it instead just as summing up the agent's actual pattern of action. It makes certain actions more likely, of course, but rather than just substituting a weaker notion of causation, I'd be inclined to see it as constraining action rationally, in part by imposing difficulties (upfront "costs") on some of our practical options, apparently making them poor choices. I'm sure there are further ways of working it out, but this general idea, of what might be called "constraining rationality" as an alternative to causation, is what initially got me going in philosophy of action.

2. What do you consider to be your own most important contribution(s) to theorizing about action and agency, and why?

I've applied the idea of constraining rationality to acts of a sort that are usually quickly dismissed as results of nonrational factors – unless they're distorted to fit a somewhat bloodless desire/belief model of instrumental rationality. The main example I've dealt with at length is action out of emotion. Here we also have what's now called "*constrained* rationality": emotions are designed as "quick-and-dirty" heuristic responses, suited to cognitively limited agents like us, who often have to act without taking time to access and process all relevant information. We need emotion as a mechanism of "snap" response to partial evidence, and the rationality of an emotional response ought to be assessed in that light. So I argue that emotions are sometimes appropriate, and supply a reason for action, in cases where we wouldn't have adequate evidence for a corresponding evaluative belief.

I have in mind everyday cases of emotion, not "blinding" rage or the like. You rebuke someone, avoid him, deny him a favor, or whatever, because you're angry about something he did. In part this just means that you're under the impression that he deserves it; some sort of retaliation is called for. I treat that evaluation as spelling out the content of your emotion: what your anger "says," in effect, about its object, the person you're angry with. Where anger is appropriate, it therefore seems to give a reason for action – in the sense of a rational ground, or what recent authors refer to as a "normative" reason: not just a motive explaining what you do, but also a consideration you could cite in favor of it.

Now, some might want to say that the emotion just refers to an evaluative judgment or corresponding desire that states your real reason for action. Its rational role is just to make salient some independent consideration, bringing it to consciousness and holding it there by loading it with feeling, or "affect." But it's important to my account that the affective aspect of emotion *reinforces* whatever reason is given by its evaluative content. The fact that anger is an irritating feeling – in itself, but also in persistently reminding you of something you think you ought to do but haven't done yet – adds a further, self-regarding reason for doing something to alleviate or appease the feeling. I don't mean that you're likely to be thinking about improving your own state of feeling when you act out of anger. But you're at least peripherally aware of how the emotion feels, and how retaliatory action might make it better. So anger gives you a further motive.

Even without supplying a further motive, though, the affective element of anger would still supply a normative reason for action, and we may need to add this to the evaluative reason to justify action in some cases, where the emotion isn't fully warranted in the terms that apply to belief, though it's still an appropriate reaction to partial information. I don't mean *morally* appropriate (as I've sometimes been misread as saying), but just rationally – given the heuristic purposes of emotional response. Anger might be appropriate, say, in reaction to what seems to be an intentionally harmful or insulting act, even though fuller information would show it to be based on some sort of misunderstanding.

So I've argued that it's some element of unpleasant emotion that's responsible for the illusion of "must" here, or emotional pressure; and that, besides constraining action, it supplies a reason of the sort that *justify* action. I'm now working on a general conception of practical reasons that supports a deontological moral "must," but without the common notion that reasons as such require action. It will also leave an appropriate space for emotions as sources of moral motivation, without the Humean insistence that reason alone is incapable of motivating. But most important for my purposes, it will allow for an intermediate position on free will issues, by helping to answer arguments against libertarianism from chance, arbitrariness, and the like, that turn on taking alternative choices as irrational.

Since I've also done recent work allowing for cases of moral responsibility without libertarian free will, the overall picture I'm filling out might be seen as a libertarian version of "semi-compatibilism": libertarian with respect to free will, but compatibilist about responsibility – or at any rate, the core elements of responsibility, which suffice for its practical applications. I haven't yet published work that puts the picture together – it's only gradually come into focus – but perhaps it will ultimately be my main contribution to philosophy of action, since as far as I know it's a position no one else holds. All libertarians I'm aware of rest their case on taking free will as a requisite of moral responsibility. The term "semi-compatibilism" was coined by John Fischer to cover his soft determinist view, which acknowledges an incompatibilist sense of free will only to dismiss it immediately as irrelevant to practical reasoning. But this is what the argument I sketched at the outset of this interview would deny, if we focus not just on instrumental practical reasoning about overt action, but also on other sorts of reasoning used to justify practical attitudes. The attitude toward one's action that I think is tied to libertarian free will resembles what Robert Kane calls "ultimate responsibility," but it's importantly limited to *forward-looking* responsibility: the sort we attribute to ourselves when we take responsibility *for* some as-yet-undetermined state of affairs. Being the ultimate *agent* in a chain of causes seems to me to be ultimate enough for purposes of attributing credit or blame to an agent, so I think we can reconstruct backward-looking responsibility in a form that's compatible with determinism.

3. What other sub-disciplines in philosophy and non- disciplines stand to benefit the most from philosophical work on the nature of action and agency, and how might such engagement be accomplished?

There's room for a multi-disciplinary field with the study of motivation as its unifying subject – "conative science," perhaps. While I tend to favor fairly abstract issues in my own work, there are recognized points of contact with psychology, psychiatry, neuroscience, the social sciences, and law, as well as to moral philosophy and philosophy of mind – the various sub-disciplines inside and outside philosophy that concern themselves with rational and moral motivation and the assessment of human agency. I wouldn't get much work done if I tried to canvas the literature in all these areas, though I'm open to input at conferences and the like. However, the emphases and assumptions of experimental work often seem to be at odds with those of philosophers. What I read in psychology and neuroscience lately suggests that these fields could benefit from increased awareness of the subtlety and complexity of work in philosophy of action. They need particularly to be made aware of the inaccuracy, or even absurdity, of some of the claims to philosophic implications of empirical work that I keep encountering: claims to have refuted this or that philosophical view or historical philosopher with an experiment or two.

There's also a tendency within philosophy, though, to accept as established various positions or arguments on the passions or free will or other issues in the area on the basis of an over-simple conception of the alternatives, or of what's entailed by a scientific world view. Before one considers possibilities of "engagement" between different areas, I think an essential first step toward getting out word of serious work in philosophy of action is to give the subject a recognized place in the philosophical curriculum. This isn't aided by making discussions of it too quickly dependent on literature in other areas, as useful as that may be at a more advanced stage. The area needs to be set on its own feet, preferably with dedicated course offerings – rather than always being treated as parasitic on ethics or philosophy of mind, the areas where most of the relevant historical work was carried on – if it's to be made more salient to people in other fields. At a minimum, it should be mentioned by name in connection with relevant readings in introductory courses, so that students know it exists as a recognized field of contemporary research. To allow for dedicated courses, at a level likely to attract students headed toward other areas, we really need suitable introductory texts for the general area. Robert Kane's recent *Contemporary Introduction to Free Will* provides a taste of what's needed, and I've used it successfully in a 200-level course, though it's limited to free will. Anthologies (or those still in print) don't seem adequate; those I've sampled bring together such diverse approaches that the pieces don't connect into a coherent whole. We need something capable of serving as a solid foundation for a general course in philosophy of action that would help make the area more salient to people in relevant fields.

At a more advanced level, sponsoring more cross-disciplinary conferences and blogs, and collecting some of the better contributions to them for publication, might be helpful in encouraging serious engagement between different disciplines. I mean "cross-disciplinary" to contrast with "interdisciplinary," which often involves bringing a thousand unrelated flowers into bloom; what's wanted is work from different disciplines focused on a common topic, conceived specifically enough that diverse treatments are clearly treatments *of* the same thing. Perhaps the easiest way to initiate this is to get participants to address work from other areas on their own subjects of interest – though in immediate terms, that might have to be a bit antagonistic. Personally, I'd love to see something in print that collects philosophers' critiques of recent work outside philosophy purporting to have philosophic implications. But I'm not in favor of making philosophy of action into philosophy *of* the relevant empirical disciplines. We're not in the position of philosophy of physics, say, where the science is developed enough that it's appropriate for philosophers to study the subject mainly *by* studying scientists' work on the subject. Engagement will also be deeper and less one-sided if people in other areas gain some serious background in philosophy of action, which is most likely if the area is brought to their attention as undergraduates.

4. What do you regard as the most neglected issues in contemporary work on action and agency that deserve more attention?

I think that the role of emotions within practical rationality is still largely neglected, even as the general topic of emotion has come into its own outside philosophy of action. The dominant question in the emotions literature has been what emotions are, with the answer shifting between feelings or physiological reactions on the one hand (the views familiar from Descartes and William James) and on the other hand evaluative judgments (the twentieth-century "cognitivist" view held by Bedford and Solomon, among others). But the important question for philosophy of action is how emotions bear on action. Taking emotions as cognitive states is of course one way of assigning them rational bearing on action, but there are others worth considering, and in any case the tendency among cognitivist authors has been simply to assimilate their role to that of judgment. I think they have a distinctive role to play that's gone largely unexplored. Many philosophers cling without question to the old dichotomy between emotions and rationality, even if some of them find reason to favor the emotional side over the rational.

Perhaps one reason why emotions have not been linked in a serious way to philosophy of action is that serious treatment of emotions within ethics has often been tied to approaches stressing the virtues, following Hume and Aristotle – as against the image of a Kantian approach as unwilling to be tainted by contingent emotional influences, or of a utilitarian approach as treating emotions as extrinsic motivators, morally significant only to the extent that they count among the good or bad states resulting from action. Virtue ethics takes character and motives rather than acts as the primary subject of moral evaluation. But emotions motivate acts – and if the work done by Robert Solomon, myself, and other recent authors on the degree of control we have over emotions is taken seriously, emotions can also be assessed *as* acts, or at any rate as resting on acts, insofar as we can control them at least by indirect means. They can be seen as raising free will issues, given the common tendency to take them as causes of action in a stronger sense than the one that seems to apply to unemotional judgment and desire.

In this connection, I'd add that another relatively neglected area is free will *apart from* the question of universal determinism. The intensity of the debate over general theoretical positions on free will has tended to obscure some particular topics that deserve attention in their own right. An example is the explanation of cases of psychological compulsion. These mainly come up in philosophy of action as problems for compatibilist accounts. I agree that they need to be handled in some way that's independent of determinism, so compatibilists have made an important contribution just in disentangling them from common determinist assumptions. But it's not clear that they can be handled adequately by simple application of a general compatibilist theory. Gary Watson discusses issues of compulsion in a set of essays dealing with addiction in *Agency and Accountability*, though his eventual explanation of addiction shifts it out of the category of compulsion. The issue of course has practical implications for medicine and the law, but in purely philosophical terms such cases raise questions of motivation and responsibility that deserve more focused consideration.

Speaking more generally, perhaps one should think of the neglected issue that stands behind both of those I've mentioned in supplementing causation as the explanation of action. Davidson importantly defended treating reasons as causes, but he and others moved all too quickly to thinking that they *must* be causes, and that fitting actions under the causal rubric was enough to explain them. The only recognized alternative seems to be a simple sort of rational explanation involving reference to future aims with no motivational "push from behind." But there are degrees of motivational "push" that need to be distinguished, to handle both normal cases of action from emotion and abnormal cases like compulsion. No doubt there are further examples I haven't thought of.

5. What are the most important open problems in philosophical theorizing about action and agency, and what are the prospects for progress?

I take it that "progress" in philosophy doesn't involve moving toward consensus but rather recognizing significant distinctions and drawing out implications, as needed to decide among competing positions. In those terms enormous progress has been made on the general issue of free will versus determinism in recent years – so much that I'm not sure it can continue at quite the same rate, though that issue will always remain both important and open.

At this point I think that issues of practical rationality are coming into the spotlight in philosophy of action. So far, much of the discussion has been focused on the relation of reasons to an agent's ends or desires, but it's broadening out a bit, and I hope it eventually includes more work on alternatives to the simple desire/belief model of rational motivation. Typically, desire/belief is interpreted as a causal model, though it can be understood without reference to causation. However, since the belief it refers to is understood as spelling out the means to some desired end, it's limited to instrumental rationality. To date I've seen only fragmentary attempts to characterize distinct forms of practical reasoning, following either Aristotle or Kant, and the model is taken for granted as the basis for much work in cognitive science. It's appealing in its simplicity, but cognitivists in ethics question the necessity of desire, and cognitivists about emotion question the inclusion of evaluative states like emotions in the category of desire. Besides making room for different mental states, though, we also ought to look into the *social* aspect of reasons – as I attempt to do in my current work by interpreting reasons in terms of potential criticism. Justification is *to* someone, after all – if only an imagined someone, or an inner critic, in an exchange made intelligible by social interaction. Along with recent work on agency in a social context, it's worth exploring alternatives to the primary focus on the first-person standpoint in understanding practical rationality.

I'd also welcome further work on interpreting practical "ought" – and "wrong" and related moral notions – in terms of reasons. This seems to me to be the way to go in attempting to "demystify" deontological approaches to ethics. Making sense of normativity may require a step beyond naturalism, but reference to reasons is part of our ordinary nonmoral justification of action, so it might be able to yield an approach to ethics that's non-consequentialist but more down-to-earth than current alternatives. Prospects for progress would be good with enough people working on the project, which is essentially that of finding a sensible middle-ground between extremes. In recent years the emphasis has been more on defining and defending sharply opposed alternatives on general issues, but I get the impression from students coming up now that this trend may begin to reverse itself soon. So I have hope.[1]

---

[1] Let me thank Karen Jones for very helpful comments on initial drafts.

7
Ishtiyaque Haji

Professor of Philosophy
University of Calgary, Canada

---

1. Why were you initially drawn to theorizing about action and agency?

I have long been interested in the freedom presuppositions of the truth of various sorts of normative judgment, including judgments of moral responsibility, moral obligation, good and evil, practical rationality, and practical reason. Judgments of moral responsibility concern moral praise and blameworthiness. Such judgments should be distinguished from judgments of moral obligation (or "morally deontic judgments") which have to do with moral right, wrong, and obligation. The judgments that it is morally obligatory for Tim to keep his promise to cut down on coffee, and that it is morally wrong for some not so savvy but powerful political leader to wage war on Iraq, are instances of morally deontic judgments. Axiological judgments are connected with good and evil. Examples include the judgments that Fred takes pleasure in the fact that a cold beer is going down his hatch, and that some possible world is intrinsically better than another. Judgments of practical reason concern our having practical reasons for or against doing something. Practical reasons, roughly, are reasons to have our desires and goals, and to do what might secure these goals. So, for instance, when faced with certain options, we might ask which of them (if any) do we have most reason to do, or, which (if any) does reason forbid that we do, or which (if any) do we have a sufficient reason to do. Finally, judgments of practical rationality (and irrationality) relate to what one perceives one's reasons for action to be. To illustrate, imagine that you (nonculpably) believe that you have most reason to take some pills because you (nonculpably) believe, on good authority, that the pills will alleviate your pain. However, you have decisive reasons *not* to take these pills because ingesting them would prove fatal. It would be rational for you to take the pills although you have no reason to take them.

Regarding this array of judgments, we may raise the following questions which, in large measure, drew me to theorizing about action and agency: what impact does lack of freedom have on appraisals of moral praise- or blameworthiness, moral obligation, practical rationality, practical reason, and so forth? If none of our decisions, choices, or actions is free, does this lack of freedom undermine the truth of the sorts of judgment that we have identified? This issue on the freedom presuppositions of normative assessments cannot be properly explored without a thorough appreciation of various concerns about agency and various challenges in the philosophy of action.

2. What do you consider to be your own most important contribution(s) to theorizing about action and agency, and why?

This is a difficult question. Perhaps I can summarize my response in this way, and then amplify: The freedom presuppositions of different sorts of normative judgment need not coincide. For example, whereas I believe that there is no requirement of alternative possibilities for the truth of judgments of moral responsibility and practical rationality, I think that there is such a requirement for the truth of judgments of moral obligation and practical reason.

Elaborating, on an intuitive and highly attractive picture of free agency, free agents, on various occasions of choice, have more than one path or option genuinely open to them. This picture has it that the paths into the future all branch out from the present—"the future is a garden of forking paths," as John Fischer following Borges says—and it is "up to us" on which pathway we tread;[1] it is "up to us" how we choose and act. So although we may have chosen and acted in one way, we could, given the same past and the laws, have chosen and acted in another way. Many have thought that determinism poses a serious threat to this conception of free agency. Determinism is the view that a complete statement of the non-temporal or genuine facts of the world at a time, together with a complete statement of all the laws of nature, entails all truths.

---

[1] John Martin Fischer, "Compatibilism," in John M. Fischer., Robert Kane, Derk Pereboom, Vargas, Manuel, *Four Views on Free Will* (Oxford: Blackwell Publishing, 2007), p. 46.

Roughly, on this view if all the facts of the world at a time were "plugged into" the laws of nature—whatever these laws turn out to be—the result would be propositions expressing truths about the world, including truths involving human choices and actions. The powerful Consequence Argument seeks to convince us that if determinism is true, there are no alternative pathways for any of us into the future; determinism expunges all alternatives. Peter van Inwagen summarizes this argument as follows: If determinism is true, then our acts are the consequences of the laws of nature and events in the remote past. But it is not up to us what went on before we were born; and neither is it up to us what the laws of nature are. Therefore, the consequences of these things (including our own acts) are not up to us.[2]

Responsibility requires freedom or control; without such control, no one can be responsible for anything that one does. Suppose that this species of control *is* the freedom, or power, or ability to do otherwise. Then it would seem that as determinism precludes our being able to do other than what we do (as the Consequence Argument authoritatively suggests), determinism undermines responsibility.[3] This line of reasoning, though, for the incompatibility of determinism and responsibility has been called into question by various considerations, including so-called "Frankfurt examples." In typical Frankfurt examples, an agent does something on his own—Jones lies, for instance, to prevent embarrassment—despite believing that in so acting he is doing wrong. However, because of some failsafe mechanism or arrangement which plays no role whatsoever in Jones' acting as he did, but that ensures that Jones acted in just this way, Jones could not have done otherwise.[4] Many are inclined to judge that Jones is morally to blame for lying even though he could not have refrained from doing so. After all, he acted in just the way that he would have had the failsafe mechanism been "subtracted from" the scene. Assume that such examples make a telling case for the view that responsibility does not require that we have access to genuine alternatives, as I believe they do; in other words, assume that Frankfurt examples speak against the principle of alternate possibilities: persons are morally

---

[2] Peter van Inwagen, *An Essay on Free Will* (Oxford: Oxford University Press, 1983), p. 16.

[3] Speaking more accurately, there are many variations of the Consequence Argument.

[4] See Harry G. Frankfurt, "Alternate Possibilities and Moral Responsibility," *Journal of Philosophy* 66 (1969): 829-39

responsible for what they have done only if they could have done otherwise.

If we can be responsible—say, blameworthy—for something even if we could not have done otherwise, then, as some might see it, it seems equally plausible that we can have a moral obligation to do something, or that it can be wrong for us to do something, even though we could not have done otherwise. But I think this is a mistake. The truth of obligation judgments, unlike the truth of responsibility judgments, *does* require that we have alternatives. We may, very briefly, sketch the line of reasoning for this asymmetry. Two principles of moral obligation that command widespread intuitive appeal as well as support from promising analyses of the concept of moral obligation (or if we want, "theory-backed" support) are the "ought" implies "can" principle (principle K) and the principle that it is obligatory to do something just in case it is wrong not to do it (principle OW). The "ought" implies "can" principle can be put in this way:

> (K): If it is overall obligatory for one to do something, then one can do it, and if it is (overall) obligatory for one to refrain from doing something, then one can refrain from doing it.

Moral obligation expresses a kind of necessity or requirement. If morality *requires* that you do something, then you can do it. If you can't, for example, save the drowning child because you have been tethered to your seat, or because you have been overcome by paralysis, the "ought" implies "can" principle implies that you don't have a moral obligation to save the child; morality can't require you to do what it is not in your power to do.

We have emphasized that moral responsibility requires control; if you are morally praise- or blameworthy for an action, then you have responsibility-relevant control in performing this action. Similarly, think of the "ought" implies "can" principle as a control principle for moral *obligation*; if you have a moral obligation to perform an action, then you have obligation-relevant control in performing it. If you can't perform an action, then, you can't have control in performing it; so you can't be morally obligated to perform it.

Turning, next, to (OW), (OW) may be stated in this way:

> (OW): It is (overall) obligatory for one to do something if and only if it is (overall) wrong for one to refrain from doing it.

One would think that to say that some action is morally wrong (or morally forbidden) for you is just to say that you morally ought—you have a moral obligation not to do it (or there is a moral requirement that you not do it). But then it would seem that an act is morally obligatory for you—morality *requires* that you do it—if and only if it is morally wrong for you not to do it; this is just what (*OW*) says.

If we accept (*K*) and (*OW*), we may confirm that there is a requirement of alternative possibilities for the truth of judgments of obligation. First, we register that (*K*) and (*OW*) entail that an agent can do moral wrong only if the agent had an alternative; that is, from (*K*) and (*OW*), we may infer that *if it is wrong for one to do something, then one can refrain from doing it.*

Barring persuasive reasons to believe otherwise, if we assume that "ought" implies "can," there is little reason not to assume, too, that "wrong" (and "right") imply "can." Again, think of the "ought" implies "can" principle as a control principle for obligation. Just as praise- and blameworthiness require control, so does obligation and wrongness. The control requirements of blameworthiness, unless we have sound reason to believe the contrary, mirror those of praiseworthiness: both have the same freedom requirements. Similarly, it would seem that the control or freedom requirements of obligation, unless we have strong reason to think otherwise, should also be the very ones of wrong and right.

If we grant that just as "ought" implies "can," "wrong," too, implies "can'," there is a straightforward argument for the conclusion that obligation requires alternative possibilities: If it is obligatory for one to refrain from doing *A*, then it is wrong for one to do *A* (from *OW*). Further, if it is wrong for one to do *A*, then one can do *A* (from the "wrong" implies "can" analogue of (*K*): *if it is wrong for one to do A, then one can do A.*) Therefore, if it is obligatory for one to refrain from doing *A*, then one can do *A*.

There is no similar way to derive the proposition that rightness, likewise, requires alternatives. This is because even if it is agreed that "right" implies "can," there is no principle like (*OW*) that will allow us to infer that "right" implies "can refrain." Nevertheless, it is very plausible that "right" does imply "can refrain." For suppose an agent, Jones, is in a situation in which Jones cannot refrain from pushing an innocent child off the pier to her death. Perhaps Jones is in a "Frankfurt-type" situation in which Jones supposedly freely pushes the child off the pier but could not have refrained from doing so. It is neither wrong nor obligatory for Jones to perform this act in his circumstances because there is a requirement of alternative possibilities for wrongness and obligation. It seems, then, that there are two principal options. An act has a *primary morally deontic status* only if it is morally right, wrong, or obligatory. Either pushing the child off the pier is permissible for Jones or this act lacks a primary morally deontic property altogether, not being morally right, wrong, or obligatory; it is, we can say, "amoral" for Jones. The latter is more plausible than the former. After all, Jones' act is the cold-blooded killing of an innocent child; for that matter, his act could have been any other heinous deed. In Jones' circumstances, if pushing the child to her death were not amoral for Jones, this act would be permissible— that is, *morally right*—for Jones, a result that resists acceptance. Insisting, again, that in the absence of persuasive reason to think otherwise, the freedom requirements of "right" parallel those of "wrong" and "obligation," enables us to circumvent this unpalatable result. Hence, "right," too, implies "can refrain."

We may conclude that the truth of obligation judgments, as opposed to the truth of responsibility judgments, requires alternative possibilities: one has a moral obligation to do something only if one could have done otherwise. If it is genuine alternatives that are at issue (holding "fixed" the past and the laws, one could have done otherwise), then determinism poses a real threat to obligation.[5]

One might wonder about what it is regarding the nature of responsibility judgments and obligation judgments that sheds light on their being asymmetric with respect to the requirement of alternative possibilities. I propose the following. Responsibility judgments are "*agent-focused*" in that, first and foremost, they concern an appraisal of the *agent*, and only derivatively, if at all, an appraisal of what the agent does (or fails to do). When, for instance, we hold an agent blameworthy, we are primarily *faulting the agent* and not what she does. Such judgments disclose the moral worth of an agent with respect to some episode in her life—a person "expresses what she morally stands for" when she is morally responsible for some deed. When blameworthy, one expresses ill will (typically) toward another, and it is the expression of such ill will that (in part) sanctions the judgment that one's moral worth with

---

[5] For elaboration, see my *Deontic Morality and Control* (Cambridge: Cambridge University Press, 2002).

respect to the relevant action has been diminished. On the view that I defend, an expression of such ill will is manifested when one (nonculpably) believes that some act is wrong, and despite this belief, performs the act; in short, when blameworthy, one acts in light of the belief that one is doing moral wrong. Similarly, when one is praiseworthy, one expresses good will (usually) toward another, and it is the expression of such good will that (in part) validates the judgment that one's moral worth vis-à-vis the relevant deed has been augmented. When praiseworthy, one acts on the basis of the belief that one is doing what is obligatory or permissible.

An agent can manifest ill will or good will by an action that she performs—she can disclose what she morally stands for on the particular occasion—even when she lacks, as she would in a Frankfurt situation, alternative possibilities, because such expression does not presuppose the availability of alternative options. If an act from your perspective is morally wrong—if you take yourself to be doing intentional moral wrong—then even if you lack alternatives (and, thus, your act is not in fact morally wrong), you can still express ill will in your conduct; and, similarly, if you take yourself to be doing something that is morally obligatory, even without alternatives, you can still express good will in your conduct.

In contrast, moral appraisals of right, wrong, and obligation—morally deontic appraisals—are pronouncedly *act-focused* insofar as, fundamentally, they concern an assessment of an *action* (or intentional omission) and only secondarily, if at all, an appraisal of the agent. Such act appraisals are *not* tied, in any necessary fashion, to how the agent perceives the situation or with germane motivations or beliefs. An agent, for instance, may act "from" virtue on a certain occasion and (assuming the act is not virtue-deficient or not significantly so), be commendable for so acting, consistently with doing moral wrong on that occasion. Whether an agent's act, then, has a primary morally deontic property (*being morally right*, or *being morally wrong*, or *being morally obligatory*) is *not* essentially connected with, for example, whether the agent performs that action in the belief that it is wrong, or more generally, with the agent's "moral perception" of her act. Act-focused morally deontic appraisals turn primarily on conditions that the act itself must satisfy, and these conditions may not be met despite the agent's believing otherwise or failing to believe that the conditions are not met.

To summarize, agent-focused judgments of moral praise- and blameworthiness are associated essentially with belief in what is morally obligatory or morally wrong, and not with obligation or wrongness *per se*. So, for instance, it is possible both for it to be the case that you can fail to be blameworthy for doing something that is wrong, and that you can be blameworthy for doing something that is not wrong (as along as, from your perspective, you are doing intentional wrong). So I reject the principles that an agent is morally blameworthy for something only if it is morally wrong for that agent to do that thing ($M1$); and that an agent is morally praiseworthy for something only if it is morally obligatory for the agent to do that thing ($M2$).

If responsibility appraisals are different, in kind, from morally deontic appraisals, there is no reason to assume that the conditions requiring satisfaction for one to be apt must be the very conditions requiring satisfaction for the other to be apt. For instance, freedom to do otherwise may well be necessary for the latter sorts of moral appraisal but not for the former sorts. In light of this, there is little preliminary reason to believe that a counterexample against a proposed condition for the appropriateness of one sort of moral appraisal (for instance, Frankfurt examples as proposed counterexamples against the principle of alternative possibilities) will *also* be a counterexample against an analogous condition for the other. So even though Frankfurt examples cast doubt on the principle of alternate possibilities, it is not clear, as some might argue, that they cast doubt on the "ought" implies "can" principle.

3. What other sub-disciplines in philosophy and non- disciplines stand to benefit the most from philosophical work on the nature of action and agency, and how might such engagement be accomplished?

Sub-disciplines in philosophy include free will, philosophical psychology, philosophy of law, normative ethics, metaethics, axiology (roughly, that branch of ethics concerning intrinsic value), and philosophy of education. Some of the more practical subfields, such as medical ethics, neuroethics, and perhaps environmental ethics, would also benefit. Non-philosophical disciplines include psychology, sociology, neuroscience, education, and biology.

Encouraging interdisciplinary work—maybe through relevant collaborations—would be fruitful. For example, some theorists of education propose that one overarching aim of education is to ensure that our children turn into morally responsible agents or autonomous agents. But unless we first understand what it is to be a morally responsible agent, or what it is to be an autonomous agent (these are squarely *philosophical* concerns), such theorists would have an insufficient grasp of these alleged overarching aims. Here, philosophical inquiry would aid people in other disciplines. In the other direction, studies in psychology, may, for instance, help to shed light on phenomena that interest many philosophers, such as, weakness of will or self-deception.

4. What do you regard as the most neglected issues in contemporary work on action and agency that deserve more attention?

There are a number of such issues, but I'll confine attention to one. In my estimation, it would be desirable to have more discussion on the following: What are the freedom presuppositions of judgments regarding practical rationality and practical reasoning? Does the truth of such judgments require that we have the freedom to do otherwise, and is their truth hostage to determinism?

Sharing some of my preliminary thoughts on these concerns, suppose that, on a particular occasion, we have several different genuine alternatives: holding "fixed" the past and the laws, we have different options. And suppose that our ("objective" *pro tanto*) practical reasons to act in some way are stronger—perhaps far more so—than our reasons to act in any other way. Then we have most reason to act in this way; the reasons we have to act in this way outweigh the reasons we have not to act in this way. We may say that acting in this way is *reasons-wise obligatory*; we reasons-wise ought to act in this way. Suppose that, on a different occasion, we have sufficient or enough reason to act in two or more ways, and no better reason to act in any other way. Then we may say that each of these acts is *reasons-wise permissible*. Finally, suppose we have most reason not to act in a certain way. Then we may say that acting in this way is *reasons-wise wrong or forbidden*. If (given suitable circumstances) taking a dose of the medicine will kill you, it is reasons-wise wrong for you to take it; if the medicine affords the best cure, you reasons-wise ought to take it; and if two medicines available to you are equally effective in curing you (and similar in all other pertinent respects), it is reasons-wise permissible for you to take either.

When it is moral obligation that is of concern, we may think of the "ought" implies "can" principle in this way: if you have most moral reason to do A, and, thus, if morality *requires* that you do A, then you can do A. (Understand 'can' in the strong categorical sense of 'can': in a world with the same laws and the past as the actual world, at the pertinent time, you do other than what you do in the actual world). Suppose, now, that you have *most (practical) reason* to do A; as we may say, *reason requires that you do A*, or, alternatively, that *you ought to do A from the point of view of reason*. Then it seems that you *can* do A. You cannot have an "obligation"—it cannot be *necessary*—from the point of view of reason, to do something if you *cannot* do that thing. Imagine that you are in western Canada in Vancouver. Suppose you do not know how to swim, and you do not now believe that there is child drowning in the ocean off the Australian coast. It turns out, though, that there *is* a child who is just about to drown off this coast. Had this child lived, she would have transformed the world from the horrible place it is into a blissful one. How can you *now* have a reason to save this child? For that matter, if the child were drowning because of the Titanic's going down, how can it be that you now have a reason to save this hapless child? And if it is false that, as of now, you can have a reason to save this ill fated child, it is also the case that it is false that, as of now, you can have most reason to save this child.

Indeed, the "ought" implies "can" principle appears to be a more restricted version of the general principle that:

> *Reasons-Wise "Ought" Implies "Can" (KR)*: If one has most reason to do something, A, and, thus, if one reasons-wise ought to do A, then one can do A.

KR's corollary is

> *Reasons-Wise "Ought Not" Implies "Can Refrain From" (KRC)*: If one reasons-wise ought not to do something, A, then one can refrain from doing A.

Further, we should, I believe, accept this principle (*Reason-1*):

> *Reasons-Wise "Ought Not" amounts to Reasons-Wise "Wrong" (Reason-1)*: If one reasons-wise ought not to do A, then it is reasons-wise wrong for one to do A.

From KRC and *Reasons-1*, we derive:

Reasons-Wise Wrongness Requires Alternatives (Reason-2): If it is reasons-wise wrong for one to do A, then one can refrain from doing A.

Reason-2 tells us that there is a requirement of alternative possibilities for *reasons-wise* wrongness (just as there is such a requirement for *moral* wrongness). By constructing an argument analogous to the argument (sketched above) for the view that there is a requirement of alternative possibilities for *moral* obligation, the argument that invokes the principle that if it is morally wrong for one to do something, then one can do that thing, we may conclude that there is a requirement of alternative possibilities for *reasons-wise* obligation. (This argument would invoke the principle that if it is reasons-wise wrong for one to do something, then one can do that thing).

If the truth of judgments of practical reason requires alternatives, but determinism effaces alternatives, then just as determinism threatens the truth of judgments of obligation, so determinism threatens the truth of judgments of practical reason.

What, though, of judgments of practical *rationality* (henceforth, I drop the qualifier *practical*)? It may be proposed that rationality judgments are closely allied with having practical reasons for or against doing something. Assume that when one is rationally at fault for something, one acts irrationally. This may not be quite right. For maybe it is possible, as I think it is, that one is less than fully rational, and so rationally at fault, with respect to what one does without being *irrational*. In the interest of simplicity, though, I ignore this possibility. Similarly, assume that if one is rationally commendable for doing something, one acts rationally. To draw out the alleged connection between rationality judgments and reasons in favor of, or against, doing something, one may now venture the following:

Irrationality Requires Reasons-Wise Wrongness (R1): If one is rationally at fault for doing something, A—if, that is, one is irrational with respect to doing A—then it is reasons-wise wrong for one to do A.

The general thrust of $R1$ is straightforward: despite one's having most reason not to do something, one still does it; so one is irrational—one is rationally at fault—for doing that thing.

Rationality Requires Reasons-Wise Obligatoriness (R2): If one is rationally commendable for doing something,

A—if, that is, one is rational with respect to doing A—then it is reasons-wise obligatory for one to do A.

Again, for simplicity, I am assuming that if one is rational with respect to doing something, then one has most reason to do that thing. (One could argue, for instance, for the alternative principle that one is rational regarding doing something only if one has most reason *or* sufficient reason for doing it.)

The germane parallelism between $R1$ and $R2$ and what we have labeled $M1$ and $M2$ is inescapable: the truth of the "negative" judgments, judgments of moral blameworthiness and irrationality, requires moral wrongness and reasons-wise wrongness respectively. And the truth of the "positive" judgments, judgments of moral praiseworthiness and rationality, requires moral obligation and reasons-wise obligatoriness respectively.

$R1$ and $R2$, though, like $M1$ and $M2$, are both suspect. Rationality, just like moral praiseworthiness, is connected with *what one takes one's reasons for action to be*, or *what one believes these reasons to be*. Similarly, irrationality is first and foremost associated with one's beliefs regarding what one's reasons for action are. If one is rational with respect to doing something, A, one acts on the basis of the (nonculpable) belief that one is doing what is reasons-wise obligatory: one believes that one has most reason (or perhaps sufficient reason) to do A, and one does A. This may be so *even if* one has *no* reason to do A, or one has most reason *not* to do A. Thus, imagine, again, that you (nonculpably) believe that you have most reason to take some pills (pills that are in the experimental stage of development) because you (nonculpably) believe, on the advice of the medical team, that the pills will assuage your pain. But in fact you reasons-wise ought not to take these pills because (unbeknown to the doctors) taking the pills will kill you. It would be rational for you to take the pills although you reasons-wise ought not to take them. And it would be irrational for you not to take the pills because you (nonculpably) believe that you have most reason to take them.

The reason why rationality judgments (just like responsibility judgments) are tied to relevant beliefs—in the case of rationality judgments, beliefs concerning what reasons one has (or fails to have) for acting in various ways (and in the case of responsibility judgments, beliefs concerning what is morally obligatory or wrong)—is, again, forthright: rationality judgments, just like those of moral praise- and blameworthiness, are agent-focused. At issue, fundamentally, is the appropriate normative appraisal of the *agent*, and *not* an apt appraisal of the reasons there are (if any) for the agent to act in some way or another, or of what the agent does. With the relevant agent-appraisal of practical rationality, we are interested in how the agent conducted herself, given her epistemic information.

We may conclude that the truth of rationality judgments, unlike the truth of judgments of practical reason, does not require alternatives. So one cannot argue that determinism threatens rationality judgments because there is a requirement of alternative possibilities for their truth, alternatives that none of us has if determinism is true.

5. What are the most important open problems in philosophical theorizing about action and agency, and what are the prospects for progress?

Again, it is hard to fix on *the* "most important open problems," but here is an "open" issue that I deem significant: Relatively little thought has been invested into whether the truth of judgments regarding good or evil—*axiological judgments*—presupposes acting freely (or with free will). This important topic has not commanded the attention it deserves owing to what is a prevalent assumption that freedom leaves axiological judgments largely unaffected.

There are many different varieties of this species of judgment. Two are of particular interest to me: welfare-ranking judgments (judgments of personal well-being) and world-ranking judgments. Regarding the former, philosophers have long debated about what makes a person's life intrinsically good for that person; what makes a life high in welfare value? Many different answers have been given to this question. Hedonism, for example, is one of them. The hedonist appeals to the view that pleasure is the Good to account for the amount of welfare that an individual enjoys. In contrast, preferentists maintain that what makes a life intrinsically good for a person is that desires of some sort are satisfied rather than frustrated within that life. With respect to the assessment of worlds, the concern is not with individual well-being but, rather, with the intrinsic value of *entire* worlds: when is one possible world intrinsically better than another?

Well, what are the prospects for progress concerning this project? Here, I merely outline a program of investigation—a program that has three primary segments—regarding the execution of which I am cautiously optimistic. First, I believe that just as freedom has an impact on, for example, the truth of judgments of moral responsibility, so freedom has an impact on the truth of judgments of welfare. Toward establishing this view, the following broad strategy looks promising. Every welfare- or world-ranking axiology identifies some items that have their intrinsic values in the most primary, nonderivative way. Think of each such item as an atom of value. Whereas positive atoms (episodes of pleasure on hedonistic views or desire satisfactions on preferentist views, for example) enhance intrinsic value, negative atoms (episodes of displeasure on various hedonistic views or desire frustrations on preferentist views, for instance) mitigate such value. The intrinsic value of a complex thing, such as a life or world, is the sum of the value of its atoms. I think that on credible hedonistic views, or preferentist views, or whole life satisfaction views of welfare (according to which well-being is a function of the happiness experienced over an entire life), free positive atoms that contribute to the value of lives—"life atoms"—are better than otherwise similar unfree atoms, and free negative life atoms are not as bad as otherwise similar unfree atoms. For example, *freely* taking intrinsic pleasure in something is better than an otherwise similar unfree atom, and freely taking intrinsic displeasure in something is not as bad as an otherwise similar unfree atom. So a life with free atoms of value, other things equal, is better in itself for the person than an otherwise similar life containing unfree atoms.[6]

Possibly, there is a connection between something's being good (or bad), whether intrinsically or extrinsically, for a person and practical reason, a connection that bears on whether determinism precludes values. First, certain clarifications are in order. Assume that every episode of intrinsic attitudinal pleasure is intrinsically good, and every episode of intrinsic attitudinal displeasure is intrinsically bad. Assume, further, that the objects of intrinsic attitudinal pleasure and of intrinsic displeasure are states of affairs.

Suppose that *your taking intrinsic pleasure in drinking wine*—that is, *your being pleased in drinking wine*—is intrinsically good for you. If it is true that your being pleased in drinking wine is intrinsically good for you, then, it seems, you have a *pro tanto* reason—maybe a defeasible one—in favor of bringing about the state of affairs *your drinking wine pleases you*. Analogously, if your being displeased in sitting in the sun is intrinsically bad for

---

[6]For some preliminary thoughts on this issue, see my "Freedom, Hedonism, and the Intrinsic Value of Lives," *Philosophical Topics* 32 (2004): 131-51.

you, then you have a reason against bringing about the state of affairs *your taking intrinsic displeasure in sitting in the sun*. In a deterministic world, though, you have no practical reasons—whether defeasible or not—to bring about any such states of affairs. Hence, in such a world, no states of affairs relevantly like *your taking intrinsic pleasure in drinking wine*, or *your taking intrinsic displeasure in sitting in the sun* obtain.[7]

Regarding the second segment of the project in axiology, in addition to freedom's having an influence on the truth of judgments of personal well-being, I believe that freedom has a marked impact on the truth of judgments of worldly value. Arguably, a case can be made for the view that that free positive world atoms—atoms that enhance worldly value—are better than otherwise similar atoms that are unfree, and that free negative world atoms—atoms that assuage worldly value—are not as bad as otherwise similar atoms that are unfree. So, again, a world with free atoms of value, other things equal, is intrinsically better than an otherwise similar world with unfree atoms.[8] Here, including some detail will help to make this part of the project less enigmatic.

Simplifying considerably, imagine that the world-ranking axiology in question recognizes only episodes of intrinsic attitudinal pleasures as positive atoms, and episodes of intrinsic attitudinal displeasures as negative atoms, the value of a world being the sum of the value of these atoms. Next, imagine that an entire world, the Matrix, is a huge, slimy womb in which its occupants are nourished. Every person in this nutrient-rich world begins life as a zygote. Their brains are connected to a sophisticated computer. As

---

[7] "Buck-passers" about value will not accept this conclusion. Buck-passers will probably agree that if your drinking wine is extrinsically good for you, then you have a reason in favor of *your drinking wine*. But they will claim that it is not the fact that your drinking wine is (extrinsically) good for you that gives you this reason; goodness, they claim, does not or could not give us reasons. Rather, they will claim that, perhaps, it is your *deriving or taking pleasure in drinking the wine* that gives you this reason. Others will reject this argument by offering this conditional thesis: If your drinking wine's pleasing you is intrinsically good for you, then you have a (possibly defeasible) reason in favor of bringing about *your drinking wine pleases you* if you can refrain from bringing about *your drinking wine pleases you*. This conditional option would allow for the existence of the relevant values even if alternative possibilities are absent.

[8] See, for example, my "Incompatibilism's Threat to Worldly Value: Source Incompatibilism, Desert, and Pleasure," forthcoming in *Philosophy and Phenomenological Research*.

they mature into individuals who can adopt or assume attitudes, the computer stimulates suitable centers in their brains with the result that each is made to take intrinsic attitudinal pleasure in various objects; none takes intrinsic displeasure in anything. In this way, each occupant of the Matrix lives a make-believe life. Not one of these individuals is aware that he or she is living in the Matrix and is being made to take pleasure in different things. Their pleasures are, intuitively, not free. It would seem that the Matrix is less intrinsically good than an otherwise as close as possible world in which the denizens experience similar pleasures but pleasures that are free.

My interest in worldly value is spurred, by among other things, interest in the attractive moral principle that our moral obligations consist in making the world as good as we can: we morally ought, as of a time, to perform actions that we perform in all the intrinsically best worlds then accessible to us.[9] This moral principle requires a ranking of possible worlds in terms of their intrinsic values. If freedom can have an impact on worldly value, then it stands to reason that freedom can have an impact on moral obligation as well.

A prevalent theme in the recent literature on freedom and responsibility is that lack of free will is not such a bad thing. In the final segment of the tripartite project, I think that a case can be made for the view that living without free will does, contrary to this theme, have serious hitherto unnoticed costs that are associated with the intrinsic value of lives and worlds. (If, to have free will is, in part, to have the freedom to do otherwise, as many incompatibilists believe, then one will incur additional costs: worlds devoid of free will are worlds in which no judgments of practical reason and no judgments of moral obligation are true.)

One central project in moral philosophy is the attempt to identify the Good Life—the attempt to identify the features in virtue of which a person's life is good in itself for that person. Many theories about practical rationality also presuppose the notion of a Good Life. On these views the concept of rationality is to be explained by appeal to the concept of individual well-being. What's rational for you to do is what will most enhance your

---

[9] On this principle, see, for instance, Fred Feldman, *Doing The Best We Can* (Dordrecht: D. Reidel Publishing Company, 1986); Fred Feldman, *Utilitarianism, Hedonism, and Desert* (Cambridge: Cambridge University Press, 1997); and Michael J. Zimmerman, *The Concept of Moral Obligation* (Cambridge: Cambridge University Press, 1996).

well-being (usually weighted for probability). The first segment of the proposed program of investigation that I have sketched—what influence does free will (or its lack) have on personal well-being?—is directly relevant to these fundamental issues. Another central project in moral philosophy is the attempt to explain the concept of obligation in terms of the intrinsic value of worlds. The second segment of the proposed program—what influence does free will (or its lack) have on worldly value?—bears significantly on this project. A project pivotal in the literature on free will is whether being deprived of freedom is such a bad thing. The third segment of the proposed program—what are the implications of the view that, other things equal, freedom enhances welfare value and worldly value for various issues in the free will debate?—speaks to this project.

8
Bennett Helm

Professor of Philosophy
Franklin & Marshall College, USA

My central philosophical concern for many years has been with what it is to be a person. Of course, we persons are agents, indeed agents of a special sort, so understanding personhood has of course led me to think about that special sort of agency. Yet my background in the philosophy of mind leads me to think that any account of this special sort of agency must appeal to psychological capacities that are themselves grounded in an account of the relation between the mind and the body. Here I have in mind not the thought that we must provide a compatibilist account of free will (though I do think that is true) but rather the thought that it is all to easy for philosophers of action to make what turn out to be false presuppositions about the nature of psychological capacities like belief and desire and the role they play in motivation. Conversely, I think, philosophers of mind, focused too narrowly on worries about intentionality and consciousness, have offered accounts of various psychological capacities that are inadequate to understanding the sort of agency characteristic of us persons.

Before I begin, I need to acknowledge my general orientation in philosophy of mind. Mental states and capacities are to be understood in terms of their place within an explanatory framework. Psychological explanation, however, I take to be fundamentally normative, a matter of locating particular phenomena within a broader pattern of rationality. This is a broadly Davidsonian or Dennettian orientation to the mind, according to which, as Davidson says, rationality is the constitutive ideal of the mental.[1] In particular, it implies that intentional actions are to be explained

---

[1] Donald Davidson, 'Mental Events', in: *Essays on Actions and Events* (New York, NY: Clarendon Press, 1980), 223; cf. Daniel C. Dennett, *The Intentional Stance* (Cambridge, MA: MIT Press, 1987).

by showing how what was done is the thing that ought to have been done given the agent's reasons.[2] This will be important in what follows.

1. Direction of Fit and the Problem of Import

I claimed that philosophers of mind have focused too narrowly on intentionality and consciousness and so have failed to provide accounts of mental states and capacities adequate to an understanding of ourselves as persons. Understanding why I think this will lead to one contribution I have made to action theory.

A central concern of philosophers of mind is to understand intentionality—the "aboutness" of mental states, or the fact that they can have representational content. Philosophical orthodoxy has been to understand mental states to be attitudes towards such content, where these attitudes come in two mutually exclusive and exhaustive types. Thus, *cognitive* states like belief have what is known as *mind-to-world direction of fit* insofar as they are sensitive to truth: when confronted with a discrepancy between belief and world, we modify our beliefs to fit the world. By contrast, *conative* states like desire have *world-to-mind direction of fit* insofar as they motivate us to change the world when it does not fit our desires. This notion of direction of fit suggests a kind of rational priority of the world over the mind in the case of mind-to-world direction of fit and of the mind over the world in the case of world-to-mind direction of fit; such rational priority in turn implies that the two directions of fit are mutually exclusive: it cannot simultaneously be true with respect to the same intentional state that the world is rationally prior to the mind and the mind is rationally prior to the world.

In understanding agency, we must be careful to distinguish actions pursued out of genuine desires from what I have called rationally mediated goal-directedness. Thus, systems like chess-playing computers might be said to display goal-directedness insofar as they consistently pursue—and sometimes achieve—an end in light of information about the changing state of the world. Yet desires are to be distinguished from such goal-directedness insofar as a desire normally says something in favor of a particular course of

---

[2] For a cogent defense of this understanding of the explanation of action, see William Dray, 'The Rationale of Actions', chap. V in: *Laws and Explanation in History* (London: Oxford University Press, 1957), 119–155.

action. To *desire* something is to find it *worth* pursuing, to *care* about achieving it, to find it to have *import* to one. We agents differ from chess-playing computers in that *to be an agent is essentially to be a subject of import*, and until we have given a clear account of what such import consists in we have failed to make sense of agency.

Once we bring this notion of import into the picture, we can begin to recognize that the notion of direction of fit itself is problematic. For we can ask: do things have import to us because we desire them, or do we desire them because they have import to us? If we accept the idea of direction of fit, these look like mutually exclusive options, and yet both seem to be true: whether something has import to us is not independent of our desires for it, and yet we can assess our desires for appropriateness in light of whether their objects really do have import to us. The standard understanding of the intentionality of desire in terms of the notion of direction of fit, I claim, considerably impoverishes our understanding of desire—by assimilating it to mere goal-directedness—and so impoverishes our understanding of agency quite generally. It is roughly this thought that leads me to reject the notion of direction of fit and instead provide a holistic account of import.

This has important implications for our understanding of human agency and freedom. For part of what is distinctive about human agency is that we can have and exercise control over what we do on the basis of reasons, through an exercise of our rational capacities. On the face of it, we exercise such rational control by engaging in practical deliberation the outcome of which is a motivation to do what we have come to judge we ought; indeed, this seems to suggest a conceptual connection between such considered practical judgments and motivation. However, to accept the standard understanding of our intentional mental states in terms of the idea of direction of fit seems to require that we abandon any such conceptual connection. For the reasons to which we appeal in practical deliberation are reasons concerning what really is worth doing, reasons that purport to justify our practical judgments; that our practical judgments can get things right or wrong implies that they are cognitive states with mind-to-world direction of fit. Hence practical judgments on this view are distinct in kind from our desires and other motivational states, which have world-to-mind direction of fit. The result is an *inevitable motivational gap* between practical judgment and motivation: our practical judgments can motivate us only indirectly, via (for example) a mediating desire to do what we think we ought, a desire that thereby bridges this gap. This means we should sharply distinguish the *justifying reasons* (or "normative reasons") that ground our practical judgments from the *motivating reasons* that desires provide as causes of (and so explanations for) our actions. Moreover, all of this seems to be confirmed by the phenomena of *weakness of will*, in which our practical judgments fail adequately to motivate us in the face of contrary motives, and *listlessness*, in which our judgments end up having absolutely no effect on our motivation—in which we have lost whatever it is that usually bridges the motivational gap.[3]

The trouble with this understanding of human agency is that it seems to give up on the very sort of rational control that is central to human agency. For in the face of weakness of will or listlessness, when the required bridge over the motivational gap is ineffective, there seems to be nothing we can do to regain that effectiveness except simply to wait and hope that it returns. Yet it is precisely in cases of weakness and listlessness that rational control over our motivations is most needed: if our ability to control our actions can simply come and go without our being able to do anything about it, if our grasp on reasons that are truly practical is as flimsy as this, then it is not the sort of rational control we thought we had—and not the sort of control that seems required to underwrite moral responsibility. This suggests that we ought to look elsewhere for a solution—indeed, to the sort of solution which careful attention to import can provide. For by rejecting the notion of direction of fit and so reconceiving desire as simultaneously both responsive to import (as a justifying reason) and motivating us to act in light of that import (as a motivating reason), we thereby reject the inevitability of the motivational gap and make room for the possibility of rational control even in the face of weakness or listlessness. I shall briefly return to this suggestion in §3.

2. Emotions and Import

I have suggested that import is fundamentally important to human agency. Yet how can we make sense of import along the lines just described as something our desires and practical judg-

---

[3] For a clear expression of the sort of view I have just articulated, see, e.g., Michael Smith, *The Moral Problem* (Oxford University Press, 1994).

ments both respond to and constitute? The basic idea is this. For something to have import to you—for you to *care* about it—is (roughly) for it to be *worthy* of attention and action not merely in the sense that attending to it and acting on its behalf is a good thing, but more robustly in that such attention and action is rationally required: to fail to attend or act when these are called for by your circumstances is a rational failure, a failure to do what you rationally ought. At a first approximation, the relevant modes of attention and action are emotional and desiderative, such that individual emotions and desires respond to import and yet import itself is constituted by rational patterns of emotions and desires. To see this requires thinking more carefully about the emotions.

Emotions have traditionally been understood to have several different kinds of objects. Intuitively the most obvious is the emotion's *target*: that at which our emotional evaluation is directed. A second object of emotions is its *formal object*: the kind of implicit evaluation of the target characteristic of each emotion type. Thus, fear involves construing its target as dangerous, whereas anger involves evaluating its target as offensive. For example, I might be afraid that my paper will be rejected by a journal; here, the target of my fear is the paper's rejection, which I implicitly evaluate to be a danger (the formal object). At this point we might ask: how is this rejection dangerous? The answer must be given in terms of a background concern of mine—the import, say, of my philosophical success—for it is only because the target threatens (or intelligibly seems to threaten) this background concern that it is appropriate to evaluate it as dangerous. Such a background object that both has import to me and is related to the target in such a way as to make intelligible the target's having the evaluative property defined by the formal object is what I call the emotion's *focus*; as we shall see, this often overlooked object of emotions is fundamental to understanding import.

Together, these objects of emotions make intelligible the conditions of their warrant. Emotions are warranted just in case both:

1. the focus really does have import to the subject, and

2. the target is (or intelligibly seems to be) appropriately related to the focus so as to make intelligible its evaluation in terms of the formal object.

In the normal case, then, emotions are a kind of responsiveness to the import of one's situation, albeit a responsiveness that might get things wrong, as when I feel fear of getting my paper rejected when I don't care about philosophical success or when my publication record is solid enough that a single rejection would not reasonably impact that success. In this sense, we might say, emotions are essentially *intentional feelings of import*.

A further fact about the emotions is relevant here: emotions are not isolated mental states but instead are rationally interconnected to each other. Thus, being afraid that my paper will be rejected commits me to feeling other emotions, depending on what happens: relief or joy when my paper is accepted, disappointment or frustration or even anger when it is rejected, hope at a conditional acceptance, and so on. Which other emotions these will be is defined largely by their focus: in general, to feel one emotion is to be committed to feeling other emotions with the same focus in the relevant actual and counterfactual situations precisely because each emotion is a feeling of the import of that focus. In this way, such emotional commitments define a pattern of emotions with a common focus, a pattern which constitutes the subject's commitment to the import of this common focus. Moreover, to feel one emotion and yet fail to have the other emotions constitutive of the pattern in general undermines one's commitment to the import of its focus. This means that the relevant patterns here are *rational* insofar as belonging to the pattern is a necessary condition of the warrant of particular emotions. Indeed, given the nature of such emotional commitments to import, to exhibit a pattern of emotions with a common focus and yet to fail to have a further emotion that fits into that pattern when otherwise appropriate is itself a rational failure. Consequently, such patterns must in general be *projectible*: a condition of the intelligibility of one's having the capacity for emotions at all.[4]

Given this, I claim, *what it is for something to have import just is for it to be the focus of a projectible, rational pattern of emotions*. Recall that for something to have import is for it to be worthy of attention and action. From what I have already said we can see how the common focus of a projectible, rational pattern of emotions is thereby constituted as worthy of attention. For to

---

[4]This last claim presupposes the broadly Davidsonian approach to the mind I acknowledged at the beginning: insofar as rationality is the constitutive ideal of the mental, one's mental states must be by and large rational to be intelligible as such. Consequently, we cannot countenance an agent's having a capacity for some type of mental state if most of that agent's exercises of that capacity are irrational.

respond emotionally in accordance with the pattern is to attend to your circumstances as being of a certain kind: a kind not intelligible except in terms of the import of their focus. Given the rationality of the pattern, such responses are rationally demanded and so such circumstances are worthy of attention. Moreover, for such responses to be responses *to import*, they must normally motivate us to act on behalf of that import when otherwise appropriate. For although we can make sense in particular cases of emotions failing to motivate us, as when I feel sad without having any impulse to mourn, such a response will be defective insofar as for something to have import is for it to be worthy of action, so that a failure to be motivated accordingly is a failure properly to respond to import. Consequently, never or rarely to be motivated accordingly when otherwise appropriate is to fail to have the capacity for this kind of responsiveness to import—the capacity for emotions—at all. In short, the sort of commitment to import that emotions essentially are is normally motivating.

Emotions can also motivate us indirectly through their rational connections with desires and our broader understanding of the circumstances. Thus, I have claimed that fear normally motivates us to avoid the dangers to which they respond; precisely what we are motivated to do, however, depends on what we believe about how it is best to promote (or sustain) the focus of our emotions, the import of which makes intelligible the relevant evaluation of the target. So my fear that my paper might be rejected ought to motivate me to have the desire to send the paper around to colleagues for comments. Such a desire in turn motivates the relevant action in light of its background evaluation: the worthiness of avoiding rejection and, ultimately, of philosophical success. To feel the emotion and yet fail to have the relevant desires (and, other things being equal, be motivated to act by them) is a rational failure. All of this suggests that we ought to understand desires themselves to have a formal object (worthiness of pursuit), a target (that which is found in desire to be worth pursuing), and a focus (in light of the import of which the target is intelligible as worth pursuing). In short, desires are the same sort of commitment to import as the emotions are and consequently are equally a part of the relevant patterns of such commitments constituting import.

It might be suggested that I have gotten things backwards. It is not that emotions motivate us to have particular desires; rather, it is these desires that explain or even partly constitute our emotions. Indeed, such an understanding of the place of desires is widespread among philosophical accounts of emotion. Nonetheless, such an objection, although perhaps initially plausible, cannot be sustained in the context of the problem of import. For the challenge is to provide an account of desire that makes sense of it as evaluative—as responsive to import—in a way that could serve this role of explaining emotions. This, of course, requires a general solution to the problem of import, which I have argued requires an appeal to the emotions.[5]

In short, to be an agent is to be a subject of import, and being a subject of import requires having the capacities for not just desires but a wide range of emotions, all of which must be rationally structured in such a way as to constitute that import. Finally, it is normally only in terms of such import that we can understand how we are motivated to act.

3. Rational Control and Freedom of the Heart

I have sketched an understanding of emotions (and desires) as commitments to import. On the one hand, such commitments are like cognitions with mind-to-world direction of fit insofar as they enable us to understand emotions as intentional feelings of import, which they can get right or wrong. On the other hand, patterns of such commitments, when rationally structured in the right way, themselves constitute the very import to which particular emotions respond; in this respect, emotions are like conations with world-to-mind direction of fit, "projecting" import onto the world. This means that although import is an object of emotions in terms of which we can evaluate them for warrant, it is not a fully independent object; standard accounts of direction of fit therefore do not apply.

It is precisely this fact that import is not a fully independent object of emotions and desires that enables me to solve the problem of how we can have and exercise rational control over our actions in the face of phenomena like listlessness and weakness of will. I suggested above (§1) that what makes this problem seem so difficult is the thought that there is an inevitable motivational gap

---

[5] The arguments I have presented here are more suggestive than compelling. For more details, see Bennett W. Helm, *Emotional Reason: Deliberation, Motivation, and the Nature of Value* (Cambridge: Cambridge University Press, 2001), especially Chapters 2–3.

between evaluation and motivation, between that which justifies action and that which motivates it, for when what usually bridges this gap is ineffective, as in cases of weakness, the gap itself seems to make it impossible to exercise our capacity for practical reason to regain it. However, given my account of import in which our emotional evaluations are not independent of our being motivated, there is no such gap to be bridged, thereby preserving the potential for rational control. This needs further explanation.

I have claimed that import, as that to which we are rationally responsive in our emotional evaluations, is a property of objects that justifies not only our emotions themselves but also our actions on behalf of these objects. The import of the object, therefore, serves as a justifying reason for such action, and our emotions are in part an awareness of such reasons. Nonetheless, emotions are intelligible as such an awareness of import only insofar as this awareness is one aspect of a more general emotional commitment to import that, when rationally structured in the appropriate way, constitutes the very import to which individual emotions respond. And such commitments are intelligible as commitments *to import* only insofar as the appropriate rational structure includes one's normally being motivated on behalf of that import. Hence, unless the justifying reason that import provides normally motivates us to act accordingly, there would be no import and so no justifying reason in the first place. That is, it is because import is not a fully independent object of emotional commitment that justifying reasons normally just *are* motivating reasons: there is no inevitable motivational gap.

Moreover, as I have argued elsewhere,[6] evaluative judgments should also be understood to be commitments to import, where such commitments are in part commitments to have other responses to import—emotions and desires as well as other evaluative judgments—when these are otherwise appropriate. That is, evaluative judgments themselves are a part of the same rationally structured pattern of emotions and desires that constitute import such that the systematic failure to have these other responses therefore undermines the idea that the object really has import to you and so brings into question the genuineness of one's judgmental commitment.[7] This implies, first, that there is a con-

---

[6] Helm, *Emotional Reason*, op. cit., especially Chapter 5.

[7] Of course, bringing one's evaluative judgment into question does not mean repudiating it. As I will touch on briefly below, by making evaluative judgments we can impose a change in our patterns of emotions and desires and

ceptual connection between evaluative judgment on the one hand and emotion and desire on the other, such that a condition of the possibility of a subject's having the capacity for evaluative judgment is that such judgments normally motivate one to act indirectly through emotions and desires. Moreover, just as for other commitments to import, our judgmental commitments normally motivate action directly, for (again) it is a condition of the possibility of our having the capacity for such commitments to import that these commitments motivate us accordingly. Such direct and indirect connections between evaluative judgment and motivation therefore provide an account of the *will* as a capacity to exercise self-conscious control over what we do, an account that is possible only because import is not a fully independent object of evaluation. Once again, our justifying reasons normally just are our motivating reasons.

It should be clear that in saying that our justifying reasons *normally* are our motivating reasons, I am thereby leaving room for the possibility of weakness and listlessness, for these are abnormal cases in which our justifying and motivating reasons come apart. At this point we must confront the problem of rational control head-on: in cases of weakness or listlessness, how can we exercise our rational capacities so as to regain the control we have lost? In general, what we do to regain control is precisely what we need to do to exercise that control in the first place: we must make the relevant evaluations self-consciously in judgment and so focus our attention on the relevant features of the environment so as—normally—to allow import to impress itself on us in feeling and so to motivate us indirectly. In such a case, the exercise of control takes place entirely within the capacity for practical reason, with no extra-rational mediation required between evaluative judgment and motivation. Of course, in abnormal cases such an attempt to exercise control may fail, yet such failures are parasitic on the normal case in which there is no gap between evaluation and motivation, so that the possibility of such cases do not in general undermine our status as autonomous agents.

This account of rational control presupposes that something already has import to us. However, one important type of case in

---

so in what has import to us; indeed, this can be an important part of our deliberations about what *should* have import to us. These issues, of course, are quite tricky, and I cannot discuss them here. For details, see Helm, *Emotional Reason*, op. cit., especially Chapters 6–7.

which we need to exercise control is that in which we do not already care about something we think we ought, for in such cases, lacking the import, we lack the justifying reasons. How, then, can we exercise control not merely over what we do but also over what has import to us and thereby over our actions? To control what has import, we must control our habits of emotional and desiderative response so as to institute the relevant rational patterns constituting that import. We can do this by exercising our wills to control our behavior directly, getting ourselves to behave as if we have these emotions and desires in the appropriate circumstances. That is, we must develop, through repeated exercise of the will, both the habit of attending to circumstances in which, as one judges, emotional or desiderative response is warranted and the habit of responding to such circumstances in ways characteristic of the relevant emotions and desires. When these two habits are in place and the one following immediately upon the other, we have responses to situations of a type that can be characterized only in terms of its apparent import, responses that are rationally appropriate to the presence of such import; such responses are genuine emotions, and when they form the appropriate patterns they constitute that import as not merely apparent. Hence in exercising our wills in this way, we can exercise what I have called *freedom of the heart*—the freedom to control what we care about, what has import to us; such freedom of the heart is distinct from both freedom of action and freedom of will.[8]

4. Looking Back and Looking Ahead

What I have proposed, then, is a radical overhaul of our understanding of intentional mental states, including especially their connection to motivation and reason. To be an agent is to be a subject of import, where such import is not a fully independent object of our emotions, desires, and evaluative judgments. Consequently, there is normally no distinction between justifying and motivating reasons, and so exercising the will is a matter of making

---

[8] Contra Harry G. Frankfurt, 'Freedom of the Will and the Concept of a Person', *Journal of Philosophy*, 68:1 (1971), 5–20, who claims that freedom of action and of the will are "all the freedom it is possible to desire or to conceive" (17). Of course, this discussion of freedom of the heart is much too quick; I have worked out the details in Bennett W. Helm, 'Freedom of the Heart', *Pacific Philosophical Quarterly*, 77:2 (1996), 71–87 and in Helm, *Emotional Reason*, op. cit., especially Chapter 6.

evaluative judgments and thereby committing oneself to import.

We might draw from this the moral I voiced at the outset: philosophers interested in human agency, including questions of free will, the nature of intention, the nature of practical reason, and even the agency of social groups, have not paid careful enough attention to issues that arise within philosophy of mind. For attempts to understand these phenomena of human agency tend simply to presuppose the truth of standard accounts in philosophy of mind of what various types of mental states are and how they motivate action, accounts that are, as I hope to have shown, inadequate to the task. The reverse, I believe, is also true: philosophers of mind, primarily focused on working out various puzzles of intentionality and consciousness, have not paid careful enough attention to the ways in which an understanding of various psychological states bear on broad questions of human agency. The result is that we need to provide more systematic attention to big-picture questions concerning the nature of persons and the way such an overall understanding ought to shape particular debates in more narrowly defined areas.

In arguing that we should not sharply distinguish justifying and motivating reasons, I have here focused on the idea that attending to the justifying reasons we have itself can motivate us to act: there is no inevitable motivational gap. Yet, the connection between justification and motivation cuts both ways: we cannot understand what justifying reasons we have apart from the ways those reasons motivate us. This does not mean that where we are not motivated we do not have justifying reasons, for there can clearly be cases in which someone has justifying reasons—whether "internal" or "external"[9]—to act in some way and yet is simply blind to those reasons and so is never motivated to act accordingly. It does mean, however, that our capacity for practical reason should not be understood to be located simply in our capacity to make judgments but instead extends to include our emotions and desires. Attempts to understand human agency ignore this at their peril.

---

[9] Cf. Bernard Williams, 'Internal and External Reasons', in: *Moral Luck: Philosophical Papers* 1973–1980 (Cambridge: Cambridge University Press, 1981), 101–13.

9
Ted Honderich

Grote Professor Emeritus of the Philosophy of Mind and Logic
University College London, UK

Determinism and Freedom: Which Theories Are Dead and Which Alive?

1. Unpredictability

Theorizing about determinism and its relation to freedom and responsibility was something that a new graduate student could be drawn to by Professor Sir Stuart Hampshire, Grote Professor at University College London. He had written a free-thinking book on it, *Thought and Action*. I worked awfully hard on the book, and finally supposed it to be ineffective in its main idea against determinism, which was that our attempted predictions of our coming actions turn into decisions.[1]

England's Logical Positivist, A. J. Ayer, the previous holder of the Grote chair, was still in the neighborhood, and also compelled attention. His contribution to the subject was one paper.[2] It was pretty clear, but, like so very much else written about the matter, it did not seem really to take it far forward, indeed not beyond David Hume in the 18th Century. So here too there was room for an idea or two from a graduate student.

No doubt my Canadian boyhood, in particular my mother Rae Laura Armstrong in her religious progress, and my father in his progressive pamphlets, had contributed to an inclination on my part to large human questions. The meaning of life would turn up in our family discussions. Also, my mother did not leave her youngest child unaware of his moral responsibility for things. Nor did a tough brother later.[3]

---

[1] Hampshire, 1959; Honderich 1988 or 1990, 342-7 in both cases; 1993, 74-75 or 2002a, 86-87.
[2] Ayer, 1954.
[3] Honderich, 2001.

That boyhood past does not make it less accidental that my labor as a graduate student was on the subject it was. If the stately Stuart had had another interest, maybe space and time, I might well have joined him. This brings to mind the fact that a life subject to determinism, and a life truly taken as subject to determinism, will be quite as unpredictable as an undetermined life in the main way.

The main way in which life is a matter of accidents or seeming chance is in its unpredictability to us, its human unpredictability, its apparent fortuity as both lived and looked back over. This unpredictability, despite the fact that determinism entails complete predictability in principle or in theory, is preserved in the determined life. You don't know what's going to happen, or see that it had to happen when you look back, any more than in the undetermined life, since you lack the particular knowledge needed for predictions and explanations.

Can it be that the fundamentality and extent of the lived and remembered unpredictability consistent with determinism has been insufficiently felt or remembered or stated by philosophers, and hence that determinism has been made less believable? Have we not really seen that determinism leaves untouched the natural way of thinking about life? Can it be, too, that this insufficiency contributes to audacious rejections of determinism as unnatural, say Helen Steward's conviction of "fresh starts," even when determinism is officially and rightly taken as entailing only predictability in principle?[4]

2. Three Sides to Determinism

There is a larger subject. At least since the dispute in the 17th Century between Hobbes and Bishop Bramhall, philosophers of determinism and freedom have divided into Compatibilists and Incompatibilists. Things have changed somewhat, but philosophers still tend to divide up that way today. Compatibilists and Incompatibilists are concerned with the question of *the consequences of determinism* – more particularly, the consequences of human determinism, a causal account of our human existence, rather than a universal determinism. What follows from this human determinism? How does it affect our lives if it is true? Can we have freedom and moral responsibility along with this determinism?

---

[4]Steward, forthcoming.

What about the justification of punishment by the state? Philosophers of determinism and freedom, as distinct from philosophers of science, have indeed stuck to the question of the consequences of human determinism. They have not been much concerned with the question of *the truth of this or any wider determinism*. This is explained, presumably, by an idea that is natural enough that philosophy is not in itself a factual inquiry but something somehow different from science. Philosophers of determinism and freedom have also taken little care with respect to another question that is less avoidable for them than the question of truth and prior to it. It is the question of *the conceptual adequacy of determinism* – whether and how a clear, consistent and complete theory of human determinism can be put together.

Philosophers in the 1960s, notably J. L. Austin and Peter Strawson,[5] were skeptical about our having a conceptually adequate theory. If they were not explicit about the grounds of their skepticism, they surely were moved by the fact that human determinism must come together with the philosophy of mind, and in particular the nature of consciousness and the mind-body problem. Certainly there can be no adequate theory of determinism that does not assume something about these dark and troubled waters. Austin and Strawson may also have been daunted by the large philosophical problem of causation, the problem of what it is for an event to be an effect. It too has divided great and other philosophers.

It is possible to construct a theory of human determinism that contains a traditional and reasonable assumption of the nature of consciousness, having to do with a kind of subjectivity, and locates our consciousness inside heads, and contains an account of the relation of consciousness and the brain, a kind of union. Also an account of a particular causal sequence issuing in the unions of conscious and simultaneous neural events, and an account of actions and their particular causation.[6]

The theory depends on an explicit account of the general nature of causal and other necessary connections. It clarifies the connection between a causal circumstance and its effect, the different connection between other law-governed correlates, the distinction

---

[5] Austin 1956; P. F. Strawson 1962.

[6] Honderich 1988 & 1990a, 71-258 in both cases; 1993, 22-54; 2002a, 22-64. The theory set out very fully in the long earlier books is summarized in the later two editions of a short one.

between a cause and the other conditions in a causal circumstance, and the nature of causal sequences.[7] Certainly it does not confuse an effect with any lesser thing, say an event of a certain probability, even of a probability of 1. Such an event might be certain to you because God let you know it would happen or because you could see into the future but it could still be an unnecessitated event.

Who could maintain that all philosophers attracted to determinism should first work out philosophies of consciousness and causation, and then consider such alternatives as those of John Searle and Benjamin Libet?[8] I don't. It is indeed true, however, that our freedom and human determinism is the subject of events in or of *our consciousness*. Maybe you are not straying into supererogation if you pay it attention. Is there more reason now than in the time of Austin and Strawson to attend to the general subject? Can my fellow workers be as confident as their predecessors in leaving it out?

Should they take care, at least, not to be predisposed in their reflections by an unexamined leaning to either of the main commitments in the philosophy of mind – devout physicalism and the traditional dualism associated with Descartes that is a kind of spiritualism? Do some of us fall into free speculation about causation as a result of no serious thinking about it? Free speculation about freedom as a result of no engagement with the philosophy of mind? There are now theories of consciousness that do not confine it to the cranium – externalisms rather than internalisms. Will they have some relevance to the matter of the consequences of determinism? Where do they leave conscious decisions and choices?

Putting aside the question of an adequate theory of determinism until later, consider for a minute the question of the truth of determinism. It is natural to take it that the factuality of science as against philosophy is good reason to excuse philosophers from entering into the question. My own inclination, however, is to excuse them less readily here than with conceptual adequacy and particularly the philosophy of consciousness.

This critical inclination has to do with what is probably an uncontroversial idea of philosophy. What it is, according to this idea, is a concentration on the logic of ordinary intelligence. That is a concentration on clarity, usually by way of analysis, and on

---

[7] Honderich 1988 and 1990a, 13-70; 1993, 6-18; 2002a, 18-21.
[8] Honderich, 2005b, 2005c.

consistency and validity, and on completeness – a concentration usually on large and general subjects. Philosophy does not own this logic, and it would be absurd to take it as no part of science or history or whatever. But philosophy is less distracted from it by other things. It is less distracted from this indubitable side of all inquiry, this particular contribution to truth.

This idea of philosophy as concentration on ordinary logic in no way limits its subject-matters – indeed it does not limit them to the large and general subjects. And, to come to the point, obviously it does not exclude philosophy from questions of fact. This idea of philosophy does not exclude it from consideration of the subject of the truth of determinism. It does not exclude philosophy from the judgment that interpretations of Quantum Theory that are taken to refute determinism are indeed failures with respect to the three requirements of logic.

So much has long been admitted about the interpretations, although in wonder and a kind of self-satisfaction rather than embarrassment, by physicists expounding the interpretations. If it were not for the ascendancy of science and a residual ascendancy of physics in science – the first of those being another subject for philosophy as logic, if a small one – it would indeed be said that interpretations of Quantum Theory are a mess, and thus of doubtful use in evidence for or against determinism. It does not need adding that they tend to be disputable philosophy themselves. Neuroscience is surely of greater evidential force.[9] So, on certain questions, is the reflective extra-scientific experience of the world on which all science rests at bottom.

3. Compatibilism and Incompatibilism

Leaving the questions of conceptual adequacy and truth, return now to the question of the consequences of determinism, the question that has most concerned philosophers.

It is indubitable that Compatibilists and Incompatibilists agree in one proposition. It is that we have a single, settled and fundamental conception of freedom and engage in linked ascriptions of responsibility, which conception and ascriptions are fixed in our language and inform and direct our lives. The freedom is real or true or clear or sensible freedom. So with the ascriptions of responsibility – holding people responsible and crediting them with

---

[9] Honderich 1988, 1990a, 261-336 in both cases; 1993, 55-67 or 2002a, 65-80.

responsibility. Compatibilists and Incompatibilists, however, disagree about what this freedom and responsibility is. They offer proofs and persuasions of their idea of it. These proofs and persuasions have been the stuff of the philosophy of human determinism and its relation to freedom and responsibility.

Compatibilists, in a sentence that sums up a certain amount of variety, take our single freedom to be *voluntariness* – to consist in choices and actions owed to a certain kind of causes, causes in certain senses internal to the agent. These are, say, intentions of one's own or unreluctant desires. I am not free when in jail, or facing a man with a gun, or subject to a psychological compulsion only in a different sense internal to my personality.

Incompatibilists, in a sentence, take our freedom to be *origination* – to consist in an initiation of choices and actions that somehow is not subject to standard causation but remains somehow within the control of the person in question. More particularly, the choices and actions are uncaused but such as to make possible holding people responsible and crediting them with responsibility in a particular way – taking such attitudes to them as are exemplified by the retribution or desert theory of the justification of punishment by the state, backward-looking thinking as distinct from the forward-looking prevention theory of punishment. This origination, I take it, is what has traditionally been named free will, despite the existence of a wider use of the term.

It is a professional failing of philosophers, you can think, to take things to be obvious. Moritz Schlick the Compatibilist did so in as declamatory a fashion as F.H. Bradley[10] the Incompatibilist. Others have been as confident. I confess to such a failing, if that is what it is, with respect to this prolonged and now boring dispute, now carried forward mainly by American philosophers, maybe called to the platform by the religion of their society.

4. Dead Theories?

Compatibilism and Incompatibilism surely are dead ducks, old dead ducks. Is that judgment a triumph of desire over truth? Could be, but I can't believe it. To my mind it can be and has been proved that we have a conception of freedom as voluntariness, a conception both settled and fundamental to our lives. However, it can be and has been proved that we also have a conception of

---

[10] Schlick 1956; Bradley 1927.

freedom as origination, quite as settled and fundamental.[11]

It seems to me reasonable, despite being based in a certain confidence in the history of philosophy, to take the history itself of the philosophy of determinism and freedom since the 17th Century to throw into serious doubt the assumption that we have a single, settled and fundamental conception of freedom and one linked practice of ascribing responsibility. It is surely impossible or very difficult indeed to suppose that the history of philosophy could have had in it the endless regiments of Compatibilists and Incompatibilists, each advocating an understanding of freedom and responsibility, and each about as able to defend itself, without that understanding existing at least to a great extent in the meaning-intentions and the language and the life of the rest of humanity. Decent philosophers aren't actually dreamers.

Something better, surely one proof of the existence of our conception of freedom as voluntariness, consists in the pervasive existence of our claims to *rights*, legal or moral or human or occupational or whatever. To claim a right, in brief, is to assert or demand a freedom to get or to keep something, maybe food. It is transparent that the freedom in question is voluntariness. The defense, demand and struggle for rights is endeavor against facts of compulsion, constraint, incapability and the like – against external causes rather than *any* causes of action and inaction. It is no less than absurd to suppose that the starving are demanding from their societies or the world that something be added to their own natures as persons, demanding that they be given a power of origination by presidents or prime ministers. As for the importance of rights in our lives, and hence voluntariness, it would be difficult to overstate it.

One proof of the existence of our conception of freedom as origination is the patent existence of a certain way of holding others and ourselves responsible and also crediting others and ourselves with responsibility. Is it missed by Compatibilist philosophers, just as the different responsibility involving voluntariness is missed by Incompatibilist philosophers, because what it is to ascribe responsibility is left vague? In short, to ascribe responsibility to another or oneself for a choice or action is to have an attitude – an evaluative thought of the person and the choice or action, feelingful and bound up with desire.[12]

---

[11] Honderich, 1988, 379-487, or 1990b, 11-119; 1993, 80-94, or 2002a, 91-121.
[12] Honderich, 1988, 380, 382-383, 448-450, 478-480, or 1990b, 12, 14, 80-82,

Reflect on our implicit and explicit justifications of punishment in terms of desert, including the retributive theories as to punishment by the state. It is impossible to suppose, to speak generally, that our attitude here is our taking choices and actions to have been only necessitated effects, whatever else is said. We typically resist the idea when it is offered in explanation or defense of an injurious action against ourselves. We have a conception of human existence, of choices and actions, that is different in kind.

What this comes to is that all of us, or close enough to all of us, not only condemn an action on account of its low or small or vicious initiation in an agent's own caused and necessitated intention, but on account of the conviction or at least the tendency to believe that as things were, and not merely if things had been different, he or she could have done otherwise. If this is a fact of a culture, perhaps not a law of human nature, what did you expect? Our subject is our lives as they are, partly formed by a culture.

That all or as good as all of us have at the very least a tendency to the two ideas of freedom and the two kinds of ascription of responsibility containing them is also established by considering something other than moral responsibility – on which traditional Compatibilists and Incompatibilists have concentrated far too much. They have not seen or have disregarded or underestimated other consequences of determinism – for attitudes other than those of holding people responsible and crediting them with responsibility.

P. F. Strawson led the way to consideration of determinism and what can best be called the personal attitudes.[13] Some, on which he concentrated, are exemplified by gratitude and resentment. There are certainly more. They include our hopes, and in particular what can be called life-hopes. They also include confidence in belief – epistemic confidence. Who can doubt that each of us has or has the possibility of the kind of life-hope whose content is future actions taken as voluntary? Who can doubt that each of us has the kind of life-hope whose content is future actions taken as originated? If we hope not to be compelled, we as certainly hope as much to rise over our pasts.[14]

It is my own view, therefore, that the supposed proofs of Compatibilism and the supposed proofs of Incompatibilism must fail.

110-112; 1993, 81-82, or 2002a, 92-93.
[13] Strawson 1962.
[14] Honderich, 1988, 379-400, 496-501, 510-13; 1993, 80-87, or 2002a, 91-97.

That they do so can surely also be seen directly by looking at them. What they come to are proofs, some of them strong and indeed decisive, of the existence of the idea of freedom as voluntariness or of the existence of the idea of freedom as origination – none of which proofs, however successful, shows that the favored conception is the only one.[15]

It is my own view that the tradition of Compatibilism is owed to no proof at all but owed instead partly to a disinclination to a shortage of content in the idea of origination – an unexplained idea of control in a non-causal initiation of choices and actions that warrants certain attitudes and reactions to them, at bottom certain desires. Compatibilism is also partly owed to clear-headedness as to moral judgment and moral reasons, that necessarily they are consequentialist, and a conviction that the consequences involved in retributive punishment are quite insufficient to make for a justification of it.[16]

As for Incompatibilism, it has become increasingly evident, and is now more or less admitted by prominent advocates, such as Robert Kane, that it is partly owed to a certain resistance to naturalism – a resistance to taking us all to be within the natural world rather than somehow above it. Incompatibilism, in short, has been demanded for *standing*.[17] It is, to my mind, although not all Incompatibilists are to be accused of this, also tied up with a determination to maintain forms of life, societies and indeed a world. Those of us who benefit from them, naturally enough, take enemies of them, down to simple burglars, to be worthy of responses other than those in place with persons whose actions are conceived as just effects.

None of this motivation comes near to establishing that we, or we in our cultures, have only a single, settled and fundamental conception of freedom. The very short story is that determinism is neither compatible nor incompatible with freedom. To say either is to say what is false on account of referential ambiguity that amounts to reference-failure. It is no more true that determinism is either compatible or incompatible with freedom than it's either raining or not raining in Muswell Hill if the latter term picks out two places. What is provable and proved, in place of Compatibil-

---

[15] Dennett 1984 and 2003, Frankfurt 1969, Ginet 1990, Lehrer 1966, Magill 1997, Pereboom 2001, van Inwagen 1983, Honderich 2006a, 151-155.

[16] Honderich, 2003b, 2006a.

[17] Kane 1996, Ekstrom 2000.

ism and Incompatibilism and their factitious dispute, is what can have the name of Attitudinism – that we have two conceptions of freedom entering into two families of attitudes.[18]

5. A Real Problem of Determinism and Freedom – And Another One

Thus it has seemed to me in the past that the true problem of the consequences of determinism has been only the essentially practical or attitudinal one of accommodating our attitudes to the truth of determinism. It is the problem of giving up attitudes whose content includes the conception of actions as originated, and seeing the value of the attitudes whose content has to do only with voluntariness. We need to escape the response of Dismay, which focuses only on the end of origination-attitudes, and the response of Intransigence, which only declaims voluntariness-attitudes. We need to try to come to an attitude of Affirmation, seeing what we actually have in our lives and worth of it despite a loss.[19]

This is a real rather than a fictitious problem, if not a philosophical one in a narrow sense, not a conceptual one. It is in a way unsolved, not a dead problem. It may remain a live one despite various efforts until we really come to believe determinism, if that ever happens. Maybe it is only that, belief which may never happen, that would put a real end to the problem.

The first of two last remarks on both Compatibilism and Incompatibilism is that they are right about something.

They are right in taking responsibility and freedom to be inseparable. Any ascription of responsibility contains a conception of freedom – that is what such an attitude is. Any conception of freedom enters into ascriptions of responsibility. If you ascribe responsibility, your having an idea of freedom goes with this, and vice versa. So you cannot have only responsibility tied to voluntariness together with only freedom as origination. And you cannot have responsibility being a matter of origination tied to freedom as only voluntariness. Remembering what the attitude of ascribing responsibility is defeats the possibilities. If you try, you are in fact espousing the existence of two sorts of freedom and two sorts of responsibility. 'Semi-compatibilism' and related views necessarily

---

[18] Honderich, 2004c.
[19] Honderich, 1988. 488-540, reprinted in 1990b, 120-172; 1993, 107-118, or 2002a, 122-132.

collapse into just Attitudinism.[20]

The other remark, which can be no more than that, is that it is possible to conjecture and indeed argue, as the good philosophers Anthony Kenny and E. J. Lowe have or do, that voluntariness entails or is somehow bound up with origination. It is also possible to remain unconvinced. Certainly people struggling for their rights, to food or against torture, do not value food or hate torture for a reason having to do with origination.[21] It cannot be that what they do, or the point of what they do, depends on origination or a belief in it.

6. Ideas as To Independence

But if Attitudinism and the practical problem and responses to it still seem to me to resolve the problem of the consequences of determinism, and if these ideas are gaining ground,[22] this no longer seems to be the end of the story.[23]

The seeming need to go beyond the main problem has to do importantly or mainly with the demand for human standing mentioned earlier – what can be thought to be the motive, maybe the motor, of Incompatibilism. You can suppose that this need is not simply a matter of desire but also a matter of conviction, indeed of plain truth. You can think of your past life as determined but also have feelings about it that have some similarity to feelings traditionally based on origination. This is to join the great Kant in his motivation, if definitely not in his two-worlds response.[24]

Speaking for myself, it seems to me evident that my past actions issued from causal circumstances – circumstances open to a decent degree of description, certainly enough as to be evidence for determinism. I feel no temptation at all to suppose that some past actions of mine, say those most regretted by me, had initiations that were and are partly mysterious, initiations identified partly in terms of attitudes to them. Rather, I think that these actions had partial explanations I can see, and that there is overwhelming

---

[20] Fischer, 1986, 1994; Cf. Galen Strawson, 1986.
[21] Kenny, 1975, 1978; Lowe, forthcoming; Honderich, 2005a, 49-70, especially 52, 63-66.
[22] Vargas, 2005.
[23] Compare the different final chapters of Honderich, 1993 and 2002.
[24] Honderich, 2002a, 145-6.

inductive reason to believe that in each case they came together into a causal circumstance.

As against that, however, it is impossible in a way to let myself off the hook, or all the hooks. It is somehow impossible to diminish some unclear role of mine. It is at least hard to resist thoughts that seem to make sense – say that if my life has had a dependence owed to causation, it also had some other *independence*. Despite determinism, it has been *my* life in a large sense or senses. It seems to me somehow true, in part unfortunately true, that I have *been my own man*, as others have been their own man or woman. Some reality of our existence is overlooked by the proposition that determinism leaves us, however tolerably, with only a family of attitudes having to do with voluntariness.

Future work on determinism should direct itself partly towards the identification and articulation of an additional fact or facts. Let me mention what have seemed to be some possible lines of inquiry, the first of which now seems confused and hopeless.

(1) It has been natural enough to suppose that what the stuff about independence and the like comes to is a recognition of a moral responsibility different in kind from the moral responsibility consistent with determinism or hitherto perceived as such – at bottom the existence of good or bad intentions of one's own. That supposition, tending in the direction of the responsibility of origination, now seems to me clearly impossible. Evidently the believing determinist cannot suppose that ascribing responsibility to someone can have in it any understanding of a choice or action as originated. Nothing similar to that sort of ascription of responsibility, defined by its content about freedom as origination, is possible.

The only possible supposition of responsibility that is of use, perhaps, is a new recognition of the reality and size in our lives of the fact of the responsibility of voluntariness.[25] Is it not conceivable that we have failed to see this as a result of being distracted or tempted by the illusion of the responsibility of origination? Here as elsewhere with the problem of determinism and freedom, our lived existence has perhaps been insufficiently decisive in our philosophizing. But this supposition about voluntariness is not really separable from the response of Affirmation to determinism.

(2) Is there a better speculation as to new thinking about determinism? As you have heard, and no doubt known, it is a fact that

---

[25] Cf. Honderich, 2002a, 142-6.

retributive feelings or feelings having to do with desert, in fact desires for the distress of someone, have always been predicated on assumptions or beliefs as to the origination rather than the voluntariness of bad or worse actions. There is the same fact about origination with respect to our desires and policies having to do with reward – responses in feeling to fine or good or creditable actions. Another fact, anyway a fact of philosophy, is that desires having to do with prevention of more bad or worse actions. And encouragement of additional fine, good or creditable ones, have assumed only the voluntariness of the past actions. The outstanding expression of the fact is theories of the justification of punishment in terms of prevention, say the Utilitarian theories.

There is no connection of logic between origination and desert or voluntariness and prevention such that voluntariness cannot be a ground of feelings not having to do with prevention. We can certainly think of rewarding fine and voluntary actions without having the aim of changing the future. Indeed we do this already, without feeling the need for a blessing in moral philosophy. Something else is conceivable. It is that we reward the good and voluntary and not punish the bad and voluntary except for the purposes of prevention. No doubt, like many other seeming inconsistencies, something can be done to deal with this one. We need the right principle of right and wrong, and of course the support of facts.[26]

If there are these lines of thought having to do with independence despite determinism, there is another, not having to do with ascriptions of responsibility, anyway ascriptions of responsibility as we have known them. This speculation takes us back to the subject of ordinary or actual consciousness.

(3) What is it for you to be aware of the room or other place you are in? More generally, what is it for you or anything else to be perceptually conscious? There are also two other questions. What is to be reflectively conscious? What is it to be affectively conscious? The three questions, to be brief, have to do with seeing, thinking without seeing, and desiring. They have to do with parts, sides or elements of consciousness in general, however related those things are.

One externalist theory of perceptual consciousness, different from those of Hilary Putnam[27] and Tyler Burge,[28] is that what

---

[26] Cf. Honderich, 1988, 478-481, or 1990b, 110-113.
[27] Putnam, 1975 Burge.
[28] Burge, 1979.

it is for you to be conscious of the room you are in is for a room in a way to exist. Your being conscious is indeed a fact external to you. This state of affairs external to you is akin to the physical world but in clear and strong senses subjective. Your world of perceptual consciousness now – the world as it is for you, which is certainly out there – is different from that of anyone else, and different from the physical world. Further, it has a dependency on the physical world and also, to come to the proposition of most relevance to thinking about the consequences of determinism, a dependency on you, you neurally.

To speak too grandly in order to have something clear quickly, you are part of what sustains a unique world, part of a creation. You in your nature are one of two necessary grounds of a world, the other being the physical world or a lower level of it.[29]

So here is an independence consistent with determinism. Here is what can be called more than *standing*. You can suppose that it plays or can play a large part in the idea and feeling that determinism, Attitudinism and the three responses are not the whole story. The fact of your perceptual consciousness is not merely the thin stuff of spiritualism. Nor is it the neuralism of most devout physicalism. The fact of your perceptual consciousness is a reality prior to any other. It is a reality untouched by determinism. Is there a related fact with respect to reflective consciousness and what is more relevant, the affective consciousness that includes choices and the like?

(4) Another speculation that seems less promising now than earlier,[30] but maybe is worth further inquiry, has to do with causal explanation. It is familiar that with a causal circumstance and an effect, we pick out one of the contained conditions, say a human action or a personality rather than the presence of oxygen, call and regard this as cause of the effect rather than a mere condition, and thereby at least seem to accord it greater explanatory weight. We can think, too, of an explanatory *line* within and through a causal sequence – the line that consists of causes rather than conditions.

There is the problem about a cause in a causal circumstance is that the cause is only as necessary to the effect as any other condition. In that sense and related ones it is obviously equally explanatory with respect to the effect. There is the same situation

---

[29] Honderich, 2004a; Freeman, 2006; Honderich, 2002, 142-153; Honderich, 2007.
[30] Cf. Honderich, 2002a, 151-153.

with a causal line through a causal sequence as against some other succession of conditions, maybe the ongoing presence of oxygen. Is there some unique explanatory strength of a causal line of which the conditions comprise persons, person-stages, choices, actions, or the like? If the idea can seem promising, I myself have got nowhere with it.

(5) A final speculation here, which can be no more than mentioned, is that the truth of determinism does not threaten, for example, the freedom or autonomy celebrated by Kant, the capacity of an agent to act in accordance with objective morality rather than the dictates of desire. The speculation does not need to be tied to Kantian morality, of course. Contemporary philosophers trying to leave the dead theories of Compatibilism and Incompatibilism behind could usefully spend some time getting through the machinery of a large work of philosophical history that does not depend on the machinery. This is Mortimer J. Adler's *The Idea of Freedom: A Dialectical Examination of the Conceptions of Freedom*.[31] I have in mind its survey of what has been forgotten, theories of what is called the Acquired Freedom of Self-Perfection, which are distinguished from the theories of voluntariness and origination.

7. Punishment, Autonomy, Humanity

So much for five further lines of thinking. To return now for a minute to the main problem of the consequences of determinism, let me add a few remarks on punishment by the state and one further remark about morality.

If or since determinism is true, there is no possibility of justifying state punishment by talk of desert or retribution based in a proposition of origination. We have also at least flirted with the idea of something like good or bad desert based in voluntariness – and the further idea that we might reward good and voluntary actions but not punish bad and voluntary ones.

What is also possible, and familiar, is justification of punishment in terms of consequences of prevention of crime. In fact this is also the tolerating, endorsing or encouraging kinds of behavior in a society, those left legal. This idea of the justification of punishment reduces to the question of what is to be prevented and what is to be tolerated, endorsed, and encouraged. The question of

---

[31] Adler, 1958.

punishment dissolves into the central question of political, social and indeed moral philosophy – what kind of society is right?[32]

One way of thinking about both matters, and also the matter of freedom as Kantian or other autonomy, is in terms of what has the name of being the Principle of Humanity. It is the principle that the right thing as distinct from others – action, practice, institution, government, society or possible world – is the one that according to the best judgment and information is the rational one, in the sense of being effective and not self-defeating, with respect to the end of getting and keeping people out of bad lives.[33]

There is an argument for something, in philosophy and elsewhere, if it hangs together with some other true or good thing. It is reassuring to me to suppose that the independent clarity and decency of the Principle of Humanity needs and espouses only the large freedom of voluntariness that determinism leaves to us. That is a further kind of argument for that freedom and for determinism.

Acknowledgements

This paper was a talk given to various audiences, including the Bath Royal Literary and Scientific Institute, the British Neuroscience Association, the Humanities Conference 2006, the University of Bath, and the University of Durham, and I am particularly grateful for comments by Richard Frackowiak, Ingrid Honderich, E. J. Lowe and Nicholas Zangwill.

References

Adler, Mortimer J., 1958, *The Idea of Freedom: A Dialecical Examination of the Conceptions of Freedom*. Garden City: Doubleday.

Austin, J. L., 1956, "Ifs and Cans," *Proceedings of the British Academy*. Reprinted in *J. L. Austin, Philosophical Papers*, ed. J. O. Urmson and G. J. Warnock. Oxford: Oxford University Press.

Ayer, A. J., 1954, "Freedom and Necessity," in his *Philosophical Essays*. London: Macmillan.

---

[32] Honderich, 2006a, especially 195-206.
[33] Honderich, 2002a, 1-57; 2006b, 1-82; 2003c.

Bradley, F. H., 1927, *Ethical Studies*. Oxford: Oxford University Press.

Burge, Tyler, 1979, "Individualism and the Mental," *Midwest Studies in Philosophy*.

Campbell, Joseph Keim, Michael O'Rourke, David Shier, 2004, eds., *Freedom and Determinism*. Cambridge, Mass: MIT Press.

Dennett, Daniel, 1984, *Elbow Room: The Varieties of Free Will Worth Wanting*. Oxford: Oxford University Press.

———, 2003, *Freedom Evolves*. London: Penguin Press.

Ekstrom, Laura W., 2000, *Free Will: A Philosophical Study*. Boulder: Westview.

Fischer, John, 1986, *Moral Responsibility*. Ithaca: Cornell University Press.

———, 1994, *The Metaphysics of Free Will*. Oxford: Blackwell.

Frankfurt, Harry, 1969, "Alternate Possibilities and Moral Responsibility," *Journal of Philosophy*.

Freeman, Anthony, 2006, ed., *Radical Externalism: Honderich's Theory of Consciousness Discussed*. Exeter & Charlottesville: Imprint Academic.

Ginet, Carl, 1990, *On Action*. Cambridge: Cambridge University Press.

Hampshire, Stuart, 1959, *Thought and Action*. London: Chatto and Windus.

Honderich, Ted, 1988, *A Theory of Determinism: The Mind, Neuroscience, and Life-Hopes*. Oxford: Oxford University Press. Reprinted as Honderich 1990a and 1990b. Summarized in Honderich 1993, 2002.

———, 1990a, *Mind and Brain*, parts 1 & 2 of 1988. Oxford: Oxford University Press.

———, 1990b, *The Consequences of Determinism*, part 3 of 1988. Oxford: Oxford University Press.

———, 1993, *How Free Are You? The Determinism Problem*, 1st ed. Oxford: Oxford University Press. German, Italian, Spanish, Swedish, Japanese translations.

———, 2001, *Philosopher: A Kind of Life*. London: Routledge.

9. Ted Honderich

———, 2002a, *How Free Are You? The Determinism Problem*, 2nd ed. Oxford: Oxford University Press. French translation.

———, 2002b, *After the Terror*. Edinburgh: Edinburgh University Press. Expanded and Revised Edition 2003.

———, 2003a, *On Political Means and Social Ends*. Edinburgh: Edinburgh University Press.

———, 2003b, "Consequentialism, Moralities of Concern, and Selfishness," in Honderich 2003a.

———, 2003c, "The Principle of Humanity," in Honderich, 2003a.

———, 2004a, *On Consciousness*. Edinburgh: Edinburgh University Press.

———, 2004b, "Anti-Individualism v. the Union Theory," in Honderich 2004.

———, 2004c, "After Compatibilism and Incompatibilism," in Campbell, O'Rourke, Shier.

———, 2005a, *On Determinism and Freedom*, collected papers. Edinburgh: Edinburgh University Press.

———, 2005b, "Is the Mind Ahead of the Brain? Behind It?," in Honderich, 2005a.

———, 2005c, "Mind the Guff," in Honderich, 2005a.

———, 2006a, *Punishment: The Supposed Justifications Revisited*. 2nd edition of *Punishment: The Supposed Justifications*. London: Pluto Press.

———, 2006b, *Right and Wrong, and Palestine, 9-11, Iraq, 7-7....* New York: Seven Stories Press. Also published as *Humanity, Terrorism, Terrorist War: Palestine, 9/11, Iraq, 7/7....* London: Continuum.

———, 2007. "Honderich on McGinn on Honderich on Consciousness," at http://www.homepages.ucl.ac.uk/~uctytho/.

Kane, Robert, 1996, *The Significance of Free Will*. New York: Oxford University Press.

Kenny, Anthony, 1975, *Will, Freedom and Power*. Oxford: Blackwell.

———, 1978, *Freewill and Responsibility: Four Lectures*. London: Routledge.

Lehrer, Keith, 1966, *Freedom and Determinism*. New York: Random House.

Lowe, E. J., forthcoming, *Personal Agency: The Metaphysics of Mind and Action*. Oxford: Oxford University Press.

Magill, Kevin, 1997, *Freedom and Experience*. London: Macmillan. New York: St. Martin's.

Pereboom, Derk, 2001, *Living Without Free Will*. Cambridge: Cambridge University Press.

Putnam, Hilary, 1975, "The Meaning of 'Meaning'," in his *Mind, Language and Reality*, vol. 2. Cambridge: Cambridge University Press.

Schlick, Moritz, 1956, "When Is a Man Responsible?," in his *Problems of Ethics*, trans. David Rynin. New York: Dover.

Steward, Helen, forthcoming, "Fresh Starts," *Proceedings of the Aristotelian Society*.

Strawson, Galen, 1986, *Freedom and Belief*. Oxford: Oxford University Press.

Strawson, P. F., 1962, "Freedom and Resentment," *Proceedings of the British Academy*, reprinted in Strawson, 1968, *Studies in the Philosophy of Thought and Action*. Oxford: Oxford University Press.

Van Inwagen, 1975, "The Incompatibility of Free Will and Determinism," *Philosophical Studies*.

———, 1983, *An Essay on Free Will*. Oxford: Oxford University Press.

Vargas, Manuel R., 2005, "The Revisionist's Guide to Responsibility," *Philosophical Studies*.

10
Jennifer Hornsby

Professor of Philosophy
Birkbeck College, University of London, UK

---

1. Why were you initially drawn to theorizing about action and agency?

I wrote a thesis in philosophy of language as a Masters student, and intended then to write a Ph.D. thesis on verbs and times. This was in the late 1970s. In those days, one didn't have to prepare elaborate proposals in order to get funding as a research student in the U.K., and I didn't have a very clear idea of the project at the start. But I had some naïve ideas about the relation between surface structure and deep structure (then so-called), and was enthusiastic about systematic semantics. I wanted to test some hypotheses in linguistic theory by looking at causative constructions and verb aspect. It was through thinking about 'lexical decomposition' in connection with causative verbs that I was drawn into theorizing about action and agency.

The importance of causative verbs, so far as I came to be concerned, is that one of them occurs in the claim that every (human, "physical") action is someone's moving (a bit of) her body. I saw this claim as the nub of Donald Davidson's account of agency. It records Davidson's view of actions' individuation by putting in place the idea that bodily actions, when they are described in terms that reach beyond the agent's body, are described in terms of their *effects*. That idea belongs with a view which holds that there is simple psychophysical causation in case of agency. And given that view, one needs only a certain conception of causality to reach Davidson's theory of mind—anomalous monism. This was a theory that I found very attractive, combining as it does an anti-reductionism about the mental with an anti-dualist ontology. So my rather cursory exploration of verbs and times had led me somewhere slightly unexpected, but somewhere I was happy to find myself.

The claim that every action is someone's moving her body is sometimes given a putative alternative statement by Davidson and those who take his lead: 'Actions are bodily movements.' This would seem to make a different claim, however, inasmuch as someone's moving her body appears to be someone's *doing* something, and a movement of their body does not appear to be anyone's *doing* anything. On the face of it, then, agents' movings of their bodies are candidates for actions, but bodily movements are not. This is where causative verbs come in. For 'move' belongs to a class of English causatives (along with 'break', 'sink', 'melt' and plenty of others) which have both transitive and intransitive occurrences (occurrences both with, and without, grammatical objects.) 'Someone's moving her body' contains a trace of transitive 'move,' whereas 'bodily movement' contains a trace of the intransitive. This fits with the entailments there are between sentences: just as one can infer 'B moved' from 'A moved B,' so one can infer that there was a movement of X's arm from there having been an event of X's moving her arm. It then seems that Davidson was wrong to think that actions could be identified with bodily movements. Those who make the identification appear to rely upon the false assumption that the nominal 'bodily movement' contains an occurrence of transitive 'move.' They wrongly think that (for instance) an action which is X's moving her arm is the same as the movement of X's arm.

There was more to be said. For an account of causative verbs ought to reveal how actions and bodily movements are actually related. A plausible account says that if A moves B, then A causes B to move. (Similarly: if A breaks B, then A causes B to break; if A melts B, then A causes B to melt; and so on.) And if one supposes, as I used to, that the occurrences of 'cause' here, which follow the name of an agent, are to be understood *au fond* as expressing a relation between events, then one will take the relation between an action and a bodily movement (X's arm's movement, say) to be the relation of causation in which pairs of events stand one to another. That would mean that actions are described in terms of effects even when they are described in bodily terms. Indeed it would mean that any event picked out as an action (at least as a "physical" action) is picked out in terms of some effect that it has.

So I thought. I pursued this line of enquiry, because the conception of actions it led towards belonged in what appeared to be a neat overall account. As it seemed to me, volitionists about action, in their different varieties, had been led to objectionable conclusions through a failure to distinguish between bodily movements and their causes. One could diagnose the volitionists' errors by making the distinction; and the alternative view one reached preserved such insights as the volitionists had hoped to capture but now without postulating acts of will (or the like) as the immediate precursors of actions. The alternative view had the resources to register what seemed to be an important distinction between two notions of basic *act*. And it led to a causal account of action which was a sort of mirror image of the most plausible causal account of perception. All in all, a pleasing theory resulted if one followed through, on what I took to be its logical conclusion, the observation that we describe and identify actions through their effects. This was the principal contention of *Actions* (1980).

I see now that claim about 'move' which was crucial to much of this is far from compulsory, and indeed needs to be rejected. Perhaps I was drawn into theorizing about action and agency on the basis of false assumptions. It may be that my undergraduate training in philosophy (with its quest then for analyses) had made the idea of lexical decomposition inappropriately attractive (given the primitive character of most interesting concepts.) Certainly my liking for Davidson's philosophy of mind drew me into an unduly monolithic conception of causality, and into a conception of the phenomena of agency too much based on thinking of agency's instances as confined to punctuate occurrences. It is somewhat galling in retrospect to think that I began from verbs and verb aspect. For the lesson to be learnt from causative constructions, as it now seems to me, is that that which is expressed with a sentence in which an agent is the subject of a causative verb like 'move' cannot be expressed using just the 'cause' which stands for a relation between events. Again, when it comes to verb aspect, one ought to be struck by the importance of the progressive (imperfective aspect) to an understanding of agency. (One starts to see this when one considers that an agent's distinctive ongoing knowledge of what she does is given when she answers the question "What are you *doing*?") A more processual view of the phenomena of human agency is called for than is got when one attempts to treat actions as the first links in causal chains of events.

2. What do you consider to be your own most important contribution(s) to theorizing about action and agency, and why?

Having just admitted to error on my own part, it might seem that I shouldn't profess to any genuine contribution. But I think that in work in the last twenty years, I have managed to do something to show why the "standard story of agency" must be relinquished. And although I now reject even the variant of that story that I myself once told, in the course of defending it, I made some points that still seem to me to be of some importance. I'll attempt to extract something of residual worth from my earlier work, and then say a little about the more recent work.

I mentioned that I reached a view alternative to volitionists'. Key to doing so was an appreciation of the difference between the notion of *willing* as it occurs in volitionist accounts and an everyday notion of *trying*. It can be made plausible that one tries to do everything one intentionally does. And if that is right, then events of agents' trying to achieve things are as ubiquitous as the phenomenon of human agency, and thus as ubiquitous as volitionists typically alleged willings to be. But someone's trying to do something, so far from being a cause of the event of her doing it, *is* her doing it (at least when she is successful; and, usually, if she is unsuccessful, it is her doing something else.) Now the traditional volitionists took willings to be mental and movements to be physical, so that their account of action belonged in a dualist philosophy. But when the notion of *trying* is introduced, and the identity of someone's Φ-ing with their trying to Φ is accepted, we start to see that agency is not to be characterized by reference to a division between mental ("inner") vs. physical ("outer"). It is true that what I said about *trying to* can appear to lead straight to the claim that I now reject—that actions cause movements. Actually, however, this claim is not a consequence of the idea that informs what I've written about *trying to*. My idea has been that trying to Φ is best understood as doing what one can to Φ. This still seems to me to be at least roughly right. But it needs to be combined with a correct conception of what is involved in an agent's capacity to move their body. Specifically: an exercise of such a capacity is a matter of the agent's causing movement (which can be their trying to make a movement), but not a matter of one event's causing another.

One thing that I should like to have done in my earlier work is to undermine the assumption that actions are both events and things that people 'do' or 'perform.' I understand why people slip into making the assumption: it is easy to lose track of talk of events. One doesn't often hear said such things as that there was an event of Jane's signing her name. One is more likely to hear it said that something that Jane did was to sign her name. Well, *sign her name*—something Jane did—is rather obviously not an event. That it is not an event comes out clearly, perhaps, if one adds that Jane entered a contract by signing her name. For now we have something else that Jane did—enter a contract. But we don't have another event, given that Jane's signing her name *was* her entering a contract. I take exception, then, to Davidson's saying that when 'I flip the switch, turn on the light, illuminate the room and [thereby] alert a prowler ... , I do not do four things' (1963, p. 686). Of course I agree with Davidson that we have here four descriptions of an action. But further descriptions of an action correspond not to further events, but to further things the agent did.

The importance of this becomes evident when one sees where people are led by supposing that 'do' stands for a relation between a person and an event. A certain kind of causal account then gains appeal. For 'doing,' if it is supposed to relate an agent to an event, comes to seem to be a sort of *bringing about*. And then it comes to seem as if a person who acts causes an event that is her action. Despite my best efforts, the idea that agents cause their actions remains rather popular.

If agents don't cause their actions, then we have two questions. What do agents cause? How do agents relate to their actions? I think that these are easy questions, once confusions are all set aside. By elaborating on answers to them, we get to see what's wrong with the so-called standard story of action. So I have urged.

Almost whenever one is told that a person, A, has done something, one can say something about some causal role that A played: A made a difference to whether p, or A brought it about that q, or A prevented x from being in state S, or A caused the occurrence of an F event, or .... A's action then is A's making a difference, or their bringing about, or ... No doubt A's playing a causal role can be a case of event-event causation: it is such a case when A's causing something is a matter of A's action causing an event. But there is no reason to think either that all causation by agents is causation by events, or that all the things that agents cause are events. The things that agents cause are many and various. It is often assumed that an account of human agency will embed neatly into an account of a causal order whose workings are fully intelligible in the absence of agency. But the assumption that such an embedding is possible can be cast in doubt by looking at the causal language actually involved in reports of pieces of agency.

What can be said about the relation between a person and her actions if she does not do them or cause them? The answer is present in the question: her actions are *hers*. An action is a person's doing something (when she does something intentionally); and the person we cannot but single out when we single out an action is the person whose action it is. One might put it thus: The person figures essentially in the event that is her action. Putting it thus, one comes to be in a position better to understand what sort of story is told when an agent's acting in some way is explained by saying what *reasons* she had for so acting.

Those who tell the standard story of action say that when an agent's having a reason to act results in her acting, causality operates in a world of states and events. "Beliefs and desires cause actions," according to the standard story's advocates. They say this, thinking that when the causal character of reasons-explanation is allowed, it becomes necessary to reconstruct ordinary such explanations so that these can be seen to record that certain events have causes belonging in a category of psychological occurrences. Such reconstruction has sometimes seemed necessary in order to avoid saying—what has struck some as metaphysically repugnant—that agents themselves do causal work. But we don't have to avoid this, inasmuch as we know that agents bring events about and affect the states of things beyond their bodies. It is only those who hold a 'naturalist' conception of causality inimical to human agency who find it repugnant to allow that human beings play an irreducible causal role.

Even those who favor the account of agency which the reconstruction of reasons-explanations is supposed to achieve have not found the account fully satisfactory. They have faced the problem of finding further requirements on actions, beyond being caused by beliefs and desires, which ensure that there is genuine, or "full-blooded," or "deep" agency. My contribution, as I see it, has been to show that this is a self-imposed problem. One avoids it as soon as one allows that human beings belong in an account of human agency.

I have argued, on grounds of several sorts, against the possibility of a "naturalist" reconstruction of agency and reasons-explanations. In doing so, I have endorsed some of the insights of philosophers who have denied that reason explanation is causal. I suggest that such philosophers have rightly wanted to deny that the dependencies recognized when people do things for reasons are discernible among the causal chains that constitute the world's "naturalistic" workings. Where such philosophers go wrong, I say, is in supposing that such dependencies cannot therefore be causal. Reasons-explanation can be allowed to be a species of causal explanation, without being assimilated to any kind of causal explanation which has no use for the notion of a reason. In the present philosophical climate, I think it can be liberating to realize that there is no need to endorse a naturalistic conception of causality. And I hope that I have demonstrated that such a conception of causality must be as erroneous as it is needless.

3. What other sub-disciplines in philosophy and non- disciplines stand to benefit the most from philosophical work on the nature of action and agency, and how might such engagement be accomplished?

Inasmuch as a great variety of work falls under the head of 'action and agency,' the work will have repercussions for, and connections with, a variety of fields, including moral philosophy (especially by way of moral psychology), philosophy of law, and political philosophy. So far as my own sort of work on action and agency is concerned, its repercussions for metaphysics, philosophy of mind, and epistemology seem to me of most importance, because they explain why it matters to relinquish the standard story of action.

Metaphysics. There are general questions about a correct ontology and about the nature of causality, which must have answers compatible with a truthful philosophy of action. Agency can't be left out of metaphysics, then. And the dispute I have with the standard story of action is at bottom a dispute in metaphysics.

Philosophy of mind. The conception of causality for which I've criticized theorists of action comes all too easily to philosophers of mind who rightly think that an account of mind must avoid postulating non-natural items, such as Cartesian souls, in the spatiotemporal world. Many suppose that the key to such an account is to treat the mind's place in nature as a causal place. And then they conceive causality according to the conception which I argue is inimical to human agency. It isn't all plain sailing for them, however. No sooner have they accounted for psychophysical relations in the kind of causal terms that they endorse than they find themselves up against "the problem of mental causation." As it seems to me, they need to review their assumptions.

Epistemology. The belief/desire idea of reasons for acting (which belongs with the standard story) has led philosophers to forget about how knowledge is *used*. A proper epistemology must be concerned with the deliverances of knowledge as well as its acquisition. And a correct account of our knowledge of ourselves—or our own minds—will embrace the special knowledge that an agent has of what she is doing in the course of doing it intentionally.

The non-philosophical disciplines on which philosophical work on action most immediately bears are, in my opinion, economics and psychology. Practitioners of these disciplines are at least as prone as philosophers to make assumptions of a broadly metaphysical or epistemological sort (about, for instance, the relation between persons and their longer-term projects, or the relation between persons and their brains); and these assumptions affect their interpretation of their data. At the same time, scientists are less likely than philosophers to appreciate that they are making assumptions which can be put into question.

So far as accomplishing engagement with other fields of philosophy is concerned, I think we all have to avoid the narrowness of vision that the increasing degree of specialization in philosophy encourages. So far as accomplishing engagement with non-philosophical disciplines is concerned, the only recipe can be to create space in which philosophers are heard by others. There are examples in which "results" that are supposed to be founded on the evidence of science have received devastating critiques by philosophers. A philosopher would say that, of course. But it needn't be immodest or imperialist to say so. For empirical findings can bear on generalizations that philosophers make. And philosophers must sometimes stand corrected. Indeed new data can put into question descriptions of phenomena that philosophers would be apt to give.

4. What do you regard as the most neglected issues in contemporary work on action and agency that deserve more attention?

I think that the best philosophical work usually emerges from an individual philosopher's wanting to know the answer to some question. Individual philosophers' individual intellectual ambitions are of course shaped by what they read and hear, and how they are guided. So I'm not suggesting that work should be carried out in isolation. And I'm well aware that such philosophy of action as I've just gone in for, in the course of saying something about my own work, touches on only a very few issues. But I'm reluctant to pick out issues on which people should be working, thinking as I do that the agenda for research cannot be set from on high. That said, the last ten years have seen something of a beneficial transformation in how the fundamental questions in philosophy of action should be articulated, so that attending to some of what is actually going on can be a good way to find good work to do. (And of course I'd have my personal favorites for someone seeking inspiration.)

5. What are the most important open problems in philosophical theorizing about action and agency, and what are the prospects for progress?

Nearly all problems in philosophical theorizing about action and agency are open problems if that means that there is no consensus on their solutions. Fortunately, however, there can be progress without general agreement. And there is progress when there's good work on important problems. As I've already suggested, I'm apt to think of philosophical problems as important to the extent that people well equipped to think about them find them important.

The transformation in the subject of which I've spoken corresponds to a new willingness to learn from older traditions, rather than to simply press on with the problematic set by early analytical work in philosophy of action. I've said that it's a beneficial transformation. So progress, in my own view, will depend upon twenty-first century work building from the transformation as I see it, and thus drawing on more than what was new in the literature in the last three or four decades of the twentieth century. I don't think I know what the prospects are. But I think that there's room for optimism.

Works Cited

Davidson, D. (1963) "Actions, Reasons, and Causes," *Journal of Philosophy* 60, 685-700.

Hornsby, J. (1980) *Actions*. London: Routledg & Kegan Paul.

11
Joshua Knobe

Assistant Professor of Philosophy
University of North Carolina, Chapel Hill, USA

---

1. Why were you initially drawn to theorizing about action and agency?

Back when I was a college freshman, I started working as a research assistant to a young graduate student named Bertram Malle. I hadn't actually known very much about Malle's work when I first signed up for the position, but as luck would have it, he was a brilliant researcher with an innovative new approach.

Malle was interested in understanding people's ordinary intuitions about intentional action – the way in which people's ascriptions of belief, desire, awareness and so forth ultimately feed into the process by which people determine whether or not a behavior was performed intentionally. Of course, this sort of question had already been pursued in countless philosophy papers, but Malle wanted to use a different approach. He wanted to study the problem *experimentally*. We ran a number of experiments together and then co-authored a paper, which was published in a social psychology journal (Malle & Knobe 2007).

Yet although I found this type of research interesting and engaging, my real passion lay elsewhere. I was obsessively reading Nietzsche, along with some heavy doses of Kierkegaard, Hume, Marx, Wittgenstein and Aristotle. What I really wanted to do was to continue working on the very same sorts of questions I saw addressed in these thinkers.

And so, after graduation, it seemed like the natural thing to do would be to get some sort of day job and then devote myself to writing philosophy. I made my way from one position to another – working with homeless people in Texas, teaching English in Mexico, translating documents in Germany – but all the while, I was writing out philosophical papers. Most of these papers were fairly awful, but I do think that I was wrestling with some important issues. I was especially interested in the idea that people's ordinary understanding of each other was suffused with moral notions but that it might be possible to create a new, quite different form of understanding which had no moral character and was simply an attempt to make sense of why people do the things they do.

By this point, I was leading a kind of intellectual double life. On one hand, I was continuing my work with Malle, ultimately coauthoring six papers in social psychology. On the other, I was writing out philosophical meditations on the role of morality in ordinary thought. I would struggle with these philosophical papers for months, and then – when I was finally satisfied – I would put them in my desk drawer. It never really occurred to me to try showing this work to anyone.

But then something strange happened. The philosopher Alfred Mele wrote a reply to the paper Malle and I had published back when I was an undergraduate (Mele 2001). Mele went over each aspect of our paper in detail, arguing that certain parts were mistaken, others were on the right track, and still others required further data before the relevant claims could be properly evaluated. But there was one aspect of his discussion that I found especially striking. Oddly enough, Mele tied these empirical questions about the concept of intentional action back to the very same questions I had been exploring in my more philosophical work.

In essence, Mele pointed out that our analysis of intentional action referred only to purely psychological states (belief, desire, etc.) and did not accord *moral* features any role in the concept of intentional action itself. This, he said, was exactly as it should be. On his view, the concept of intentional action was a purely psychological one, and any influence of people's moral judgments on their intuitions about whether a behavior was performed intentionally would have to be some kind of error.

To be perfectly honest, I had never actually made a conscious decision not to include moral features in the analysis. (The reason I had analyzed the concept of intentional action in terms of purely psychological features was just that it had never occurred to me to consider any other approach.) Mele was therefore moving the discussion in an important new direction. Where there had once been only an unarticulated assumption, there was now an explicit thesis that could be subjected to empirical tests.

But as soon as I saw my earlier assumption written out as an explicit thesis and declared to be right, I was overcome with the sense that it just had to be wrong. And so, I returned to experimentation – this time taking the empirical work seriously as a contribution to philosophy. My aim was to disprove the view I had argued for earlier, to show that the concept of intentional action could not be properly understood until one grasped the role of *moral* considerations. I began to cherish the hope that, this time, I might be able to publish the results in a philosophy journal.

2. What do you consider to be your own most important contribution(s) to theorizing about action and agency, and why?

Much of my work has been concerned with the relationship between two different ways of thinking about action. On one hand, there are questions about action that are explicitly *moral* – questions about right and wrong, praise and blame, and so forth. Then, on the other, there are questions that do not at first appear to be moral questions but seem instead to have a purely descriptive character – questions about intention and intentional action, about the agent's reasons for acting, about act individuation. A question now arises about the relationship between these two kinds of questions.

One obvious view would be that the relationship between people's thoughts about these two kinds of questions is, in an important sense, *unidirectional*. On this view, people first figure out what the agent intended, what her reasons were, what she caused. Then they use the answers to these purely descriptive questions to figure out how to address moral questions, such as whether or not the agent is to blame. But the relationship does not also go the other way. It does not happen, e.g., that people first figure out that the agent is blameworthy and then use their judgment about the agent's blameworthiness to determine precisely what she might have caused.

Plausible though it may seem, this view does not appear to be correct. Instead, it seems that the relationship here is *bidirectional*. People certainly do use information about intentions, reasons and causes to figure out whether an agent is to blame – but, surprisingly enough, it seems that they also use moral judgments to get at questions about intentions, reasons and causes.

My first experiments in this area were on people's use of the concept of intentional action (e.g., Knobe 2003). To assess the role of moral considerations, I constructed pairs of vignettes, such that the two elements of each pair were almost exactly the same except that one involved an agent doing something morally bad while the other involved an agent doing something morally good. Here, for example, is the 'morally bad' element of one of these pairs:

> The vice-president of a company went to the chairman of the board and said, 'We are thinking of starting a new program. It will help us increase profits, but it will also harm the environment.'
>
> The chairman of the board answered, 'I don't care at all about harming the environment. I just want to make as much profit as I can. Let's start the new program.'
>
> They started the new program. Sure enough, the environment was harmed.

After reading this vignette, try asking yourself: 'Did the chairman *intentionally* harm the environment?'

To form the 'morally good' version of the vignette, we can leave almost everything the same but simply replace the word 'harm' with 'help.' The vignette then becomes:

> The vice-president of a company went to the chairman of the board and said, 'We are thinking of starting a new program. It will help us increase profits, and it will also help the environment.'
>
> The chairman of the board answered, 'I don't care at all about helping the environment. I just want to make as much profit as I can. Let's start the new program.'
>
> They started the new program. Sure enough, the environment was helped.

After reading this second vignette, try asking yourself the corresponding question: 'Did the chairman *intentionally* help the environment?'

Comparing responses in these two cases, one comes upon a surprising result. The majority of subjects who receive the first vignette say that the chairman harmed the environment *intentionally*, while the majority who receive the second vignette say that the chairman helped the environment *unintentionally*. Yet it seems that the two vignettes are entirely parallel in the mental states ascribed to the agent and in the relationship between those mental states and the resulting behavior. The principal different appears to be a moral one – the agent brings about a bad effect in the first case, a good effect in the second.

Subsequent studies have shown that this effect is not limited to the concept of intentional action in particular but also arises for a wide variety of other concepts. Take the concept *deciding*. Faced with the vignettes about harming or helping the environment people are quite willing to say:

> The chairman decided to harm the environment.

but not to say

> The chairman decided to help the environment.

And one gets similar effects for the concept of doing something for a *reason*. People are willing to say:

> The chairman harmed the environment in order to increase profits.

but not to say

> The chairman helped the environment in order to increase profits.

Subsequent work has shown that one can get this same effect for the concepts *desire, in favor, opposed*, even *advocating* (Pettit & Knobe 2008).

In recent years, I have been examining the impact of moral considerations on concepts that go beyond the psychological. A particularly interesting case here is the concept of *causation*. Consider in this connection the following vignette:

> The receptionist in the philosophy department keeps her desk stocked with pens. The administrative assistants are allowed to take the pens, but faculty members are supposed to buy their own.
>
> The administrative assistants typically do take the pens. Unfortunately, so do the faculty members. The receptionist has repeatedly emailed them reminders that only administrative assistants are allowed to take the pens.

> On Monday morning, one of the administrative assistants encounters Professor Smith walking past the receptionist's desk. Both take pens. Later that day, the receptionist needs to take an important message... but she has a problem. There are no pens left on her desk.

And now ask yourself whether you agree or disagree with the sentences:

> The professor caused the problem.
>
> The administrative assistant caused the problem.

When Ben Fraser and I gave these sentences to experimental subjects, most agreed with the first, but disagreed with the second (Knobe & Fraser 2008). Yet, from a purely scientific standpoint, it seemed that the professor and the administrative assistant stand in precisely the same relation to the event that results. The key difference is just that the professor is doing something wrong while the administrative assistant is doing exactly what she is supposed to do. Somehow people's moral judgments appear to be shaping even their understanding of the causal relations among events.

In my view, these effects reveal something fundamental about the human capacity to understand action. It seems that this capacity is not designed to deliver the same sort of understanding we seek when we are engaged, e.g., in a scientific investigation. Instead, our most basic concepts for understanding action appear to be suffused through and through with moral considerations.

3. What other sub-disciplines in philosophy and non- disciplines stand to benefit the most from philosophical work on the nature of action and agency, and how might such engagement be accomplished?

In my view, we have much to gain from a greater dialogue between work in philosophy of action and work in the history of philosophy. Of course, research in the history of philosophy might profit from an examination of recent ideas in action theory, but there is probably even more potential for influence in the opposite direction.

The great philosophers of the past developed quite sophisticated theories about how people's minds actually worked. They asked about whether the mind was composed of separate parts and how these parts might interact. They discussed the ways in which reason and emotion might shape our moral understanding. Above all, they were concerned with questions about the moral implications of facts about human nature.

For reasons I don't quite understand, the twentieth century witnessed a peculiar decline in interest in these traditional issues. Scholars continued to work on questions about precisely what the great philosophers meant in their discussions of these questions, but there was surprisingly little interest in actually pursuing original research on the topics themselves. This has always struck me as a shame.

To take just one prominent example, Spinoza provides a complex and, I think, highly promising account of the relationship between emotion and scientific understanding. One implication of this account is that if we truly come to understand the ways in which a person's actions are determined by prior events, we can continue to feel love for that person but will no longer feel anger at her transgressions. The key question that arises now is, *Is that actually true?* Does anger diminish when one comes to have an understanding of the causal chain that led up to an action? Is it true, as Spinoza elsewhere suggests, that we would no longer blame people for their actions if we knew precisely why those actions were performed? These questions lie right at the heart of the debate concerning freedom of the will, and I think it would be foolish to let our scruples about disciplinary boundaries get in the way of a wholehearted attempt to go after them.

In talking with other philosophers, I find that they quite often express an interest in more 'traditional' questions one sees addressed in work of Spinoza, Hume, Nietzsche and others. Still, it seems that this interest is sometimes mixed with a certain feeling of trepidation. There is a sense that one cannot address the traditional questions unless one can somehow connect the discussion back to the sorts of issues one more typically finds in contemporary journal articles. In my view, this is all a big mistake. The traditional questions truly are profound and important, and if these questions do not connect up sufficiently closely to whatever appears in the latest journal articles, well then, so much the worse for the view that one must always be relating one's work back to debates in the contemporary literature.

4. What do you regard as the most neglected issues in contemporary work on action and agency that deserve more attention?

There has been a great deal of interesting work exploring the precise patterns of people's intuitions – numerous papers revealing surprising new facts about intuitions regarding intentional action, causation, reason explanation, and so many other properties and relations – but it often seems to me that there has been a striking neglect of questions about the philosophical *significance* of the various patterns that have been uncovered. In other words, there has been a neglect of questions about why it even matters whether people have this intuition or that one.

The usual answer here is that, e.g., a careful study of intuitions about the proper use of the adjective 'intentional' will help us to answer questions about which behaviors truly are intentional. I am not quite sure, though, whether this sort of claim can really answer the question. To see the worry here, imagine that a researcher is giving a talk and begins discussing a distinction which she refers to as the distinction between 'intentional' and 'unintentional.' And now suppose that a philosopher stands up and says: 'Well, technically, the distinction you are discussing there is not actually the distinction between intentional and unintentional behavior. Our analysis shows that the intentional/unintentional distinction is actually a somewhat different distinction from the one you have in mind.' At least to a first glance, it might be difficult to see how this could be anything more than some kind of nit-picky point. Something further has to be said before we could understand why it was supposed to be philosophically important.

But perhaps these issues are only distracting us from the things that are most deeply significant here. Amidst all the talk about how exactly one can use intuitions to get at various properties and relations within the world, there has been a striking lack of attention to another, far more straightforward way in which intuitions can be philosophically significant. Our intuitions do not merely give us information about properties and relations within the world; they also give us information about *ourselves*. Thus it seems that the fact that moral considerations play such an important role in so many concepts might be telling us something deeply important about the sorts of creatures we are.

What we face now is an enormous untapped opportunity. We already have before us an incredibly rich and nuanced understanding of the patterns in people's intuitions. The thing to do now is to *philosophize* about those patterns, to ask about their meaning, their significance, what they might have to tell us about human life.

5. What are the most important open problems in philosophical theorizing about action and agency, and what are the prospects for progress?

When people consider the idea of a deterministic universe, they often find themselves pulled in a number of different directions. Something draws them to the view that people in such a universe could not possibly be morally responsible for their behavior, but it seems that there is also something that draws them toward the opposite view – the view that, even in such a universe, people could still be morally responsible. Faced with this conflict between opposing intuitions, where exactly should we put our trust? The question is a difficult one, but it seems that one helpful way to make progress here would be to think about why exactly we have come to have the intuitions we do.

One of the most exciting developments in this domain in recent years has been the emergence of systematic empirical studies that really help us to get a handle on the origins of people's philosophical views. These studies paint a complex portrait of people's ordinary intuitions about freedom of the will. When the question is posed in a way designed to trigger emotional responses, people tend to say that an agent can be morally responsible even if her actions are entirely determined. However, when the question is posed in a way designed to trigger abstract theoretical reasoning, people tend to reach precisely the opposite conclusion – that people in a deterministic universe cannot possibly be responsible for anything. This pattern of results suggests a particular hypothesis about the origins of our conflicting intuitions. Perhaps our emotions are pulling us toward compatibilism, while our capacity for more abstract theoretical reasoning is somehow pulling us toward incompatibilism.

This incompatibilist strand in people's thinking appears to be remarkably robust. One recent study examined the intuitions of people in Hong Kong, India, Colombia and the United States. When the question was framed in a way designed to promote abstract theoretical cognition, subjects in all four of these cultures said that no one in a deterministic universe could be morally responsible (Sarkissian et al. 2008). Many of these subjects had presumably never thought about the free will problem before the moment the experiment began, and yet when the problem is put before them, people in these very different cultures somehow all converge on the same answer.

What on earth could be going on here? The answer is not yet known, but just in the past year or so, there has been a surge of interesting work that explores the processes by which people ordinarily arrive at these intuitions. Misenheimer (2008) showed that people's intuitions about moral responsibility vary depending on whether they are explicitly told that something 'caused' the agent to perform the action; Roskies and Nichols (forthcoming) showed that intuitions vary depending on whether the event is described as taking place in the actual world or in the counterfactual world; Sias (2008) showed that intuitions vary depending on whether people are explicitly told that the agent 'decided' to perform the action; Nahmias, Coates, and Kvaran (2007) showed that intuitions vary depending on whether subjects are told that the behavior is determined by psychological facts and neurological facts. Each of these studies gives us a tantalizing clue about the nature of people's intuitions here, but I do not think that any of these studies, taken in isolation, can tell us everything we need to know about the nature of the underlying phenomenon. What is needed now is an integrative theory that can account for the full range of data and explain why it is that people have the intuitions they do.

References

Knobe, J. & Fraser, B. (2008). Causal judgment and moral judgment: Two experiments. In Sinnott-Armstrong, Walter, *Moral Psychology Volume 2: The Cognitive Science of Morality: Intuition and Diversity.* Cambridge, Mass.: MIT Press, 441- 448.

Knobe, J. (2003). Intentional action and side effects in ordinary language. *Analysis.* 63, 190-193.

Malle, B. F. & Knobe, J. (1997). The Folk Concept of Intentionality. *Journal of Experimental Social Psychology,* 33, 101-121.

Mele, A. (2001). Acting Intentionally: Probing Folk Notions. In B. F., Malle, L. J. Moses, & D. Baldwin (Eds), *Intentions and intentionality: Foundations of social cognition.* Cambridge, MA: M. I. T. Press.

Misenheimer, L. (2008). Predictability, causation, and free will. Unpublished manuscript. University of California, Berkeley.

Nahmias, E., Coates, D. J. and Kvaran, T. (2007). "Free will, moral responsibility, and mechanism: Experiments on folk intuitions." *Midwest Studies in Philosophy* 31(1): 214-242.

Nichols, S. and Knobe, J. (2007). "Moral responsibility and determinism: The cognitive science of folk intuitions." *Nous* 41(4): 663-685.

Pettit, D. & Knobe, J. (2008). The Pervasive Impact of Moral Judgment. Unpublished manuscript. UNC – Chapel Hill.

Roskies, A. & Nichols, S. (forthcoming). Bringing Moral Responsibility Down to Earth. *Journal of Philosophy*.

Sarkissian, H., De Brigard, F., Chatterjee, A., Knobe, J., Nichols, S., Sirker, S. (2008). Is Belief in Free Will a Cultural Universal? Unpublished manuscript. Baruch College – City University of New York.

Sias, J. (2008). Decisions, decisions: On folk intuitions about determinism and decision-making. Unpublished manuscript. University of North Carolina, Chapel Hill.

12
Storrs McCall

Professor of Philosophy
McGill University, Canada

---

1. Why were you initially drawn to theorizing about action and agency?

There's a long causal chain here. At the end of my B.Phil. at Oxford, Jonathan Bennett lent me the proofs of Arthur Prior's *Formal Logic* (1955). I fell under Prior's spell, devouring his work on modal and tense logic and being captivated by the idea of branching time and the diagrams that showed this. A natural interpretation of branching is that an agent has a choice of actions at the branch point; another interpretation is that branching is caused by indeterministic set-ups with different outcomes having different probabilities of occurring.

Could the entire temporal history of the world be represented as a branching set of four-dimensional manifolds in which a single "actual" branch gets progressively selected from a branching set of "possible futures", and the unselected branches vanish? I worked out this idea in my book *A Model of the Universe* (1994). The physical world takes the shape of a tree, with a single 4D spatio-temporal trunk representing the past, multiple sets of branches representing the future, and the first branch point being the present. Time flow consists in progressive branch loss, as the first branch point works its way randomly up the tree, and the probability of any future event E is given by the numerical proportion of branches on which the event E occurs.

This may or may not be an acceptable model, depending on whether one is a determinist, and it does provide the objective built-in probabilities that quantum mechanics seems to demand, but how does it relate to human deliberation, decision-making, and action? It's taken me a long time to work this out. I'm a slow thinker, but lately I feel I've been making some progress.

What I've come up with is the idea of a *controlled indeterministic process*, and in section two I'll explain why I think this idea can unlock some of the puzzles about action and agency that have been worrying us over a considerable length of time.

2. What do you consider your most important contributions to theorizing about action and agency, and why?

Let me set the scene. The branched model I describe in section one is designed to serve as an interpretation of quantum mechanics, which (setting aside Bohmian interpretations) is indeterministic and provides only probabilities for outcomes of quantum experiments and other chance events, not certainties. Of course this could change, a new deterministic physics could replace QM for a century or two, and then a new probabilistic science could replace *that*. In any case, no worries, as they say in Australia. The branched model can represent a deterministic physical theory as well as a probabilistic one. (In a deterministic world, every branch bears the same set of outcomes.) At present, however, the branched model appears capable of satisfying our intuitions that in acting, humans have the power to choose what they *actually* do from a range of possible things they *could* do. In the philosophical tug-of-war between freedom and determinism, the branched model seems to come down on the side of freedom.

But does it really? In allowing for the openness and availability of possible futures in accordance with probabilistic as opposed to deterministic physics, how does the branched model provide for the availability of future human options? For possible actions which human beings can decide whether to perform or not to perform? We are still a long way from this.

When we act freely, a typical sequence includes (i) a period of deliberation in which we consider and weigh alternative courses of action, together with the reasons for and against them, (ii) a decision consisting of a choice of one of these alternatives, (iii) the formation of an intention, and finally (iv) a movement of the body that initiates the chosen action. Of these, (i), (ii) and (iii) are "mental" events, and (iv) is a "physical" event. Free, intentional action would seem to require some kind of mental causation, in which reasons, decisions and intentions can cause physical behavior. Somehow or other, we have to articulate a philosophy of mind and consciousness which permits ideas to cause bodily movements.

The traditional mind/body theories, Cartesian dualism, interactionism, materialism, the identity theory, etc. are not really up to this task. Action theory requires the possibility of mental causation, of a causal link between mind and body, but no satisfactory account of such a link has yet been given. Psychologists ridicule the idea: see for example Wegner (2002). A new point of departure is called for, and perhaps can be found in the "biological" theory of consciousness developed recently by John Searle in (1992), (2004), (2007).

Searle starts by considering a list of properties of the "mental" as opposed to the "physical" first given in Feigl (1958). Feigl's list, as amended by Searle ((2004), p. 81) is as follows:

Mental	**Physical**
Subjective	Objective
Qualitative	Quantitative
Intentional	Non-Intentional
Not spatially located	Spatially located
Not extended in space	Spatially extended
Not explainable by physical processes	Causally explainable by microphysics
Incapable of acting causally on the physical	Acts causally and as a system is causally closed

These categories specify two mutually exclusive distinct substances, mind and matter; a "First-person ontology" and a "Third-person ontology". Searle's radical suggestion is that we overcome Cartesian dualism by merging the list of "mental" with the list of "physical" characteristics in the following way. We can fit subjective, qualitative, intentional phenomena into the physical world by identifying them with, and defining them as, higher-level properties of the central nervous system. The brain consists of billions of neurons and other brain cells, in the same way that a table, for example, consists of billions of molecules. Just as the "solidity" of the table is not a property of any of its molecules taken separately, but is a higher-level collective property of many of them taken together, so Searle's suggestion is that "consciousness" is not a property of any of the brain's neurons taken separately, but is a higher-level collective property of many of them functioning together. If this is so, then a subjective first-person mental phenomenon, such as a belief or desire or intention, can indeed have a spatial location inside my head, can be spatially extended, can be causally explicable by physics and neurophysiology, and can act causally on the motor neurons of the brain to bring about a movement of my body. Searle's merger of Feigl's two mutually exclusive lists of "mental" and "physical" phenomena is based on the observation that the first three items of the "mental" list are not incompatible with the last four items of the "physical" list, but can be joined together as elements of a new "biological" concept of consciousness.

Searle insists that the new theory of consciousness, the new mind/body theory, is neither Cartesian dualism nor traditional materialism (2004, p. 126). It is not Cartesian because consciousness is a property or activity not of a "mind", but of a set of physical objects (neurons) located in physical space. It is not materialism as traditionally understood either, since the property of consciousness that characterizes the material brain is different from all other physical properties. Dan Dennett says "I declare my starting-point to be the objective, materialistic, third-person world of the physical sciences" (1987, p. 5). But in Searle's theory the first-person ontology of mental events is not reducible to the third-person ontology of physical events. His new theory is not an *ontological* reduction, although it involves a *causal* reduction. Consciousness is a higher-level property of the brain, and the causal efficacy of mental events is based on causal relations at the neural level. In similar fashion, the higher-level property of solidity in ice differs from the higher-level property of liquidity in water, both being properties of H_2O molecules. Both are grounded in, and realized by, the causal properties of the underlying molecular base. Here is Searle's explanation of how intentions cause actions:

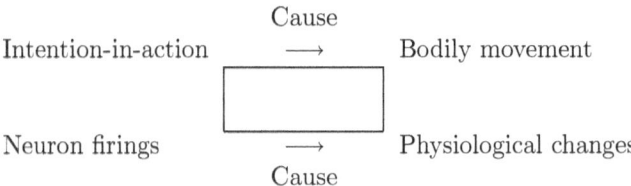

On the left, neuron firings cause and realize intentions, and on the right, physiological changes in the body cause and realize bodily movements. The first-person description of all this, which is perfectly accurate and perfectly correct, is that intentions cause actions. According to Searle, the engine that drives the causal process is located in the neurons.

There exists, in what is known as solid-state or condensed matter physics, a parallel to the higher-level causation of actions by mental events. Why does iron have a higher melting-point than lead? Although there is at present no way of deducing the melting points of either of these substances from elementary particle physics, the higher-level properties of the solids supervene upon the lower-level properties of the particles. But this is not to say that the causal laws of the two levels are the same. In an article in *Science* (1972) entitled "More is different", Philip Anderson lists a hierarchy of scientific disciplines with particle physics at the bottom and the social sciences at the top (see also Anderson (2001)). Anderson makes the point that at each level entirely new laws, concepts, and generalizations are necessary. Psychology is not applied biology, nor is biology applied chemistry, nor is chemistry applied physics. But chemistry supervenes upon physics in the sense that two chemical states cannot differ without an underlying difference in physical states, and chemical state A cannot cause chemical state B without underlying physical state X causing underlying physical state Y. Sometimes, as in the case of superconductivity, the higher-level states are causally related without there being any known parallel lower-level causal relations. Lowering the temperature of certain conductors below a critical level permits an electrical current to flow in them with zero resistance, a phenomenon that for some normal-temperature superconductors has no known explanation at the level of particle physics. In Searle's theory of consciousness, intention M cannot cause action N without neural state P causing neural state Q. But as in the case of superconductivity new laws, concepts and generalizations are needed at different levels, with the consequence that despite what Searle says mental causation may not be reducible to neurological causation. I return to the question of mental causation at the end of the paper.

Before moving on to controlled indeterministic processes, my contribution to the theory of action, I want to identify one more important feature of Searle's theory of consciousness. I'll give it a name: the "essential subjectivity" of consciousness, recognized by Descartes in stating the impossibility of my ever being deceived about my own existence. The way Searle puts it is worth emphasizing: in the first person ontology of consciousness, the distinction between appearance and reality disappears. If I *seem* to be thinking, or feeling hot or thirsty, then I *am* thinking, or feeling hot or thirsty. As Searle puts it, "you can't do an eliminative reduction of consciousness because it really exists; and its real existence is not subject to the usual epistemic doubts because those doubts rest on a distinction between appearance and reality and you can't make that distinction for the very existence of your own conscious thoughts." (2004, p. 123). Philosophers sometimes refer to the "incorrigibility" of first-person experiences. This is OK, but we must be careful. A *false* first-person report is certainly corrigible, normally by the person who reported it, but sometimes by lie detectors and mothers of small children. Only *true* first-person reports are incorrigible.

Now on to controlled indeterministic processes, or "CI-processes" for short (see McCall, forthcoming). Examples of CI-processes are (i) human actions or activities such as running, swimming, skiing, playing squash, playing the piano, sinking putts, writing a novel. There are also (ii) CI-processes that lead to actions, most importantly the mental process of deliberating and deciding. In what sense are CI-processes indeterministic, and in what sense are they controlled? Indeterminism is most easily seen in the case of deliberation. As noted earlier, decision-making consists of (i) listing one's available courses of action, (ii) evaluating them, (iii) choosing one of them, (iv) performing the chosen action by moving one's body. This process is indeterministic in that given a fixed starting-point, there are always at least two different possible terminations, i.e. different bodily movements (or omissions of bodily movements) that could result from it. (I discuss the question of underlying physical determinism below.)

The indeterminism of CI-processes that are actions follows from the indeterminism of decision-making. When I walk down a crowded sidewalk other people come at me from different angles, and I have constantly to make small changes in speed and direction to avoid collisions. This may require hundreds of mini-decisions per minute. But we are all remarkably successful at this, and only rarely do two people bump into each other. (Contrast Brownian movement, which is indeterministic but uncontrolled.) Another prime example of a CI-process is skiing, in which again many tiny adjustments per second have to be made, in order to accommodate small irregularities in the slope. There is in addition a huge difference between skiing in control and skiing out of control, with the difference sometimes hanging on a hair. Playing bridge is another example of a CI-process, where the indeterminism lies in what the opponent may do and how to react to it. Bridge is a good example of decision-making under uncertainty.

Now control. In each instance of a CI-process it is a human (or sometimes a group of humans) who do the controlling, not for example a thermostat in a house or a governor on a diesel engine. How do humans control their behavior? There is *unconscious* control, exemplified by the control the body has over its heart-rate or digestive process, but more interestingly there is *conscious* control. "Better to be silent and thought a fool, than open your mouth and prove it." So many of us deliberately remain silent; or do not, as the case may be. This is conscious, voluntary control, and is based on the ability of first-person subjective thinking to cause third-person objective behavior.

As I remarked earlier, psychologists and social scientists tend to ridicule the notion of mental causation and the conscious will. But in accord with what I earlier called the "essential subjectivity" of consciousness, in the first-person ontology there is no difference between appearance and reality, between what seems to be and what is. Consequently if I seem to be feeling hungry, then I *am* feeling hungry. If I am conscious of being irritated by my bridge partner, then I *am* irritated. And if I decide after due deliberation to sacrifice my rook and say "check", then I do just that. This last is an example of mental causation:- the first-person conscious decision causes the third-person objective move on the chessboard. A philosopher or a psychologist could disagree with this by attacking the essential subjectivity of consciousness and trying to drive a wedge between "intentionally moving my rook" and "seeming to intentionally move my rook". But someone who launched such an attack would *ipso facto* be exercising mental causation. One cannot show there is no such thing as mental causation by (a) intending to attack it and then (b) attacking it, where (a) causes (b). This is an *ad hominem* argument, but none the worse for all that.

Returning to the concept of control, John Martin Fischer distinguishes between "guidance" and "regulative" control (Fischer (1994), Fischer and Ravizza (1998)). I exercise *regulative control* over a car's turning to the right, for example, if (i) when I turn the steering wheel to the right it goes right, (ii) when I turn the wheel to the left, it goes left, and (iii) I have the power to turn the wheel either way I choose. But imagine now that the steering mechanism is defective; it works properly when I steer the car to the right, but if I were to try to steer in any other direction, the car would still go right. Alternatively, the car may be an instruction vehicle with dual controls, so that if I had neglected to steer right, or had tried to go in any other direction, the instructor would have intervened and caused the car to go to the right. In such circumstances Fischer says I exercise not regulative control but *guidance control* (Fischer (1994), pp. 132-3 and footnote 3). Why does he consider the notion of guidance control to be important in action theory? Because he wishes to devise a species of control that is consistent with overall determinism. Suppose an agent X is deliberating what to do in a deterministic context, and suppose, in the actual sequences of events that precede X's actions, whenever she has an appropriate reason for doing something, she does it. In these circumstances, Fischer says that X's action is "responsive to reasons". But X's actions are not always motivated by appropriate reasons. Sometimes, like the car that goes right without being steered right, she does something without having an appropriate reason. Fischer would say that X has only guidance control, not regulative control, over what she does. His thesis of guidance control and "reasons-responsiveness" in action theory seems a reasonable position for a determinist to take.

However, it is regulative control, not guidance control, that humans exercise over controlled indeterministic processes. We regulate them using (i) first-person causation, in combination with (ii) the "principle of indeterminism", that every CI-process has at least two different possible outcomes, and (iii) the "principle of control", that an agent controls her weighted evaluation of reasons during deliberation and then performs an action if and only if she decides to do it (including the rapid mini-decisions one makes to avoid colliding with people on the sidewalk). Unlike guidance control, which is consistent with determinism, regulative control requires the availability to the controller of at least two different possible alternative actions, which produce the different outcomes of the CI-process that the controller is controlling. E.g. when driving a car, it's physically possible for me to turn the wheel to the right, and it's physically possible for me to turn it to the left. In each case the car behaves differently. This kind of control is impossible in a deterministic world.

Turning now to the subject of responsibility, we may ask under what conditions an agent is responsible for performing an action? In a seminal paper (1969) Harry Frankfurt states his "Principle of alternate possibilities" (PAP) to the effect that a person is morally responsible for what he has done only if he could have done otherwise. Frankfurt provides an example that shows, or apparently shows, that PAP is false. His counter-example, and variations on it devised by other philosophers, are known as "Frankfurt-style examples". An excellent collection of papers on the subject is Widerker and McKenna (2003): see especially Mele and Robb's

(2003) paper in that volume.

Like Carl Ginet (1996) I don't find Frankfurt-style examples convincing, but rather than defend PAP I choose to build upon the notion of CI-processes to propose a new criterion of responsibility. PAP states only a *necessary* condition, whereas I believe a *necessary and sufficient* condition can be based on the idea of control, as in the following "Principle of Responsibility and Control" (PRC):

> PRC. A person is responsible for having done A at time t if and only if, throughout some time interval immediately before t, the doing of A, including whether or not to do A, was in her control.

The principal differences between PRC and PAP (apart from the latter's being only a necessary condition) are, first, that PRC refers to control rather than alternative possibilities, and second that PRC does not state conditions for moral responsibility, but for responsibility in general. But moral considerations are additional to those that pertain to responsibility as such. E.g. I go to shoot my donkey, but at the last moment you jog my arm, so that by accident I shoot your donkey instead (Austin (1961)). Whatever the morality of shooting defenseless animals may be, my action was uncontrolled so I'm not responsible. Alternatively, I go to shoot my donkey, but because of the similarity of the animals I shoot yours by mistake. Here I *am* responsible, though because of the absence of *mens rea* I may not be held morally responsible. I conjecture that while there may be Frankfurt-style counter-examples to PAP, there are no counter-examples to PRC. I may be wrong here of course, but let me throw it out as a challenge: find a counter-example if you can.

A final question needs to be discussed: how can indeterminism and control be combined? How are human beings able to act in such a way that what they do is under their control, but at the same time is in principle unpredictable from the point of view of objective science? This question is so vital to what has already been said, that I skip directly to question 5 in order to deal with it.

5. What are the most important open problems in philosophical theorizing about action and agency, and what are the prospects for progress?

The most important open problem is how it is possible for human actions to be simultaneously controlled and free: 'free' in the sense that at the moment person X performs action A there were other actions X could have performed but didn't (including refraining from A'ing). The major difficulty here, faced by all libertarians who reject determinism, is that rejecting determinism would appear to imply accepting the occurrence of indeterministic events in the process of deliberating and deciding. But indeterministic events are *chance* events, controlled by nobody. How is it possible for a controlled deliberative process to contain uncontrolled chance events? (See for example Kane (2005), p. 65, and Mele (2006), p. 50 ff.) Generations of libertarians have wrestled with this problem.

Indeterminism can enter into the process of deliberating and deciding in four different ways. (i) When one is trying to make up one's mind what to do, a random thought may enter one's mind, or a chance perception may serve as an input to the deliberative process. To borrow an example of Robert Kane's, when trying to decide whether to vacation in Hawaii or Colorado, Mike's attention may be caught by a chance glimpse of a poster showing the sun setting on the Grand Canyon. This chance event need not affect Mike's overall control over his deliberative process, because it is his *reaction* to E rather E's occurrence that is important. E may or may not be a significant factor in his deliberation: whether it is, is up to him. Importance is a subjective quality, not an objective one.

Secondly, (ii) the weight or importance of the different reasons for and against a possible course of action that an agent is considering is indeterministic, in the sense that the deliberator is free to attach whatever weight she wants to these reasons. Causal theories of action have certainly been constructed in which actions are deterministically caused by desires and beliefs, the strength of the latter being treated as outside the agent's control. But that the weight of the reasons to do A is outside the agent's control is simply not true. Weighing reasons is not like weighing sugar. Reasons do not come with an objective pre-determined degree of heaviness. Instead, before we can weigh one against another we have to *weight* them (see McCall and Lowe (2005), p. 686). And this weighting is under the control of the deliberator. Nothing prevents one from preferring the destruction of the whole world to the scratching of one's finger. Weighting is a conscious, subjective act. Consequently, although the strength of the reasons for and against any given course of action is *undetermined*, it is also *controlled*.

Thirdly, (iii) indeterminism can enter into the decisional process at the very last stage, once the different possible options have been evaluated and one of them has been judged the best thing to do, all things considered. Searle (2001), pp. 14 and 62 ff, calls attention to what he describes as the "gap" between decision and action. By a "gap" he means a causal gap, a gap where one stage of a process contains no causally sufficient conditions for the occurrence of the next stage. We have already dealt with the gap between "having a reason to choose option A" and "choosing A". This gap exists, but is bridged at the subjective level by the controlled weighting and weighing of reasons. The next gap is between judging that something is the best thing to do, and doing it. On this, Plato takes the position in the *Meno* that we always do what we think best, while Aristotle allows for the possibility of knowing what is best but not doing it. Could it be that we evaluate options A-D and conclude that C is best, but end up doing B instead? Yes. We all know that going to the dentist is the best thing to do, but sometimes we just don't go. This needn't imply that not going is a random, chance, or uncontrolled event. The fact that our going to a movie instead of to the dentist was causally undetermined by events 15 minutes before the appointment does not mean that going to the movie was an uncontrolled act. On the contrary, it doubtless was a controlled, undetermined, akratic action, unsupported by the weight of reasons.

Finally, (iv) indeterminism enters into the entire process of deliberating and deciding in a systemic and fundamental way, at the neurological level. If the functioning of the brain were 100% deterministic, then its initial neural state at the beginning of deliberation would causally necessitate one and only one neural end-state. That end-state would consist of the firing of motor neurons initiating a bodily movement, the only movement causally consistent with the initial state and the intervening neural inputs. Under these conditions, human beings would be marvelous deterministic mechanisms, and freedom and regulative control would be illusions. When the situation is described in these terms, the answer is obvious. For regulative control to be possible, the brain must function as a complex *indeterministic* mechanism.

Let me suggest a naturalistic hypothesis to account for the existence of brains as indeterministic mechanisms. If the brain functioned deterministically, decision-making with more than one available outcome would be impossible. But a decision-making process with only one outcome is a useless tool, an evolutionary dead-end. It contributes nothing to the struggle for survival. Competing against a creature with many possible options, any of which it could employ to surprise its opponent, the creature with the inflexible one-track brain would not survive for long. So let us imagine that the possession of a multi-option brain would be highly advantageous. The function of this indeterministic brain would be to keep future options open, no more and no less.

If the brain were a complex indeterministic mechanism, on what would its indeterminism be based? The obvious (perhaps the only) answer is quantum mechanics. A deliberating brain, for example, might have three future possible actions A, B and C. Let the motor neuronal states that lead to these be n(A), n(B) and n(C) respectively. Then random variations in the phase of neural impulse cycles, brought on by quantum fluctuations in the speed of neuronal synaptic transmissions, might cause each of n(A), n(B) and n(C) to change from being physically available to being physically unavailable, and back again, several times a second. A brain that functioned in this way would be, in effect, a macroscopic amplifier of microscopic quantum indeterminism. So far so good, but how would the indeterministic brain *choose* which of the options A, B, C to implement via a motor neuronal discharge?

Keeping options open by exploiting random quantum fluctuations seems possible for a network composed of billions of neurons. But choosing and intending are subjective, conscious, first-person activities. The only way I can see of translating the options-open capacity of the indeterministic brain into intentional action is to recognize the possibility of mental causation. As was seen earlier, in Searle's biological theory of consciousness higher-level subjective states of the brain are caused by lower-level states of sets of neurons. But, as remarked earlier, the laws, concepts and causal properties of the higher-level states may be entirely different from those at the lower level, as for example holds in the case of normal-temperature superconductivity. For there to be such a thing as controlled intentional action, an instance of mental causation, there may be causal connections at the level of consciousness that are not mirrored by causal connections at the lower level of neural activity.

When (I) a higher-level conscious state of the brain causes a bodily movement, as when a feeling of thirst causes us to drink, there will be (II) a corresponding causal connection between a lower-level neural state of the brain and a motor neuronal discharge. But this is not to say that causal connection (I) is reducible to causal connection (II). Each type of causal connection may hold at its own level, and mental causation may be no more reducible to lower-level neural causation than superconductivity is reducible to elementary-particle physics. Despite what Searle says about "causal reducibility,"[1] this is the conclusion I believe we are led to by the new and exciting biological theory of consciousness.

References

Anderson, Philip (1972) "More is different", *Science* 177 pp. 393-396.

(2001) "More is different – One more time", in N.P. Ong and R.N. Bhatt, ed., *More is Different* (pp. 1-8). Princeton: Princeton University Press.

Austin, J.L. (1961) "A plea for excuses", in his *Philosophical Papers*. Oxford: Clarendon Press.

Dennett, Daniel (1987) *The Intentional Stance*. Cambridge, MA: MIT Press.

Feigl, H, (1958) "The 'Mental' and the 'Physical' ", *Minnesota Studies in the Philosophy of Science*, vol.2.

Fischer, John Martin (1994) *The Metaphysics of Free Will*. Oxford: Blackwell.

and Ravizza, M. (1998) *Responsibility and Control*. Cambridge: Cambridge University Press.

---

[1] Searle says (2004, p. 208) "In every case the higher-level causes, at the level of the entire system, are not something in addition to the causes at the microlevel of the components of the system. Rather, the causes at the level of the entire system are entirely accounted for, entirely reducible to, the causation of the microelements." In the light of Anderson's contention that new causal laws come into effect at each level of his scientific hierarchy, I would question whether what Searle says here is either necessary for his new theory of consciousness or true. When I act following a difficult decision, the first-person cause of my action may be "new", and may act *across* to the bodily movement. Not all causes need be "upward working" in the system, nor need they be reducible to causes at the microlevel.

Frankfurt, Harry (1969) "Alternate possibilities and moral responsibility", *Journal of Philosophy* 68, pp. 829-39.

Ginet, Carl (1996) "In defense of the principle of alternative possibilities: Why I don't find Frankfurt's argument convincing", *Philosophical Perspectives* 10, pp. 403-17.

Kane, Robert (2005) *A Contemporary Introduction to Free Will*. Oxford: Oxford University Press.

McCall, Storrs (1994) *A Model of the Universe*. Oxford: Clarendon Press.

McCall, Storrs (forthcoming) "Controlled indeterministic processes in action theory", to appear in D. Vanderveken (ed.) *Attitudes and Actions in Discourse*, papers in honour of R. Klibansky.

McCall, Storrs and Lowe, E.J. (2005) "Indeterminist free will", *Philosophy and Phenomenological Research* 70, pp. 681-89.

Mele, Alfred R. and Robb, David (2003) "Bbs, magnets and seesaws: The metaphysics of Frankfurt-style cases", in Widerker and McKenna.

Mele, Alfred R. (2006) *Free Will and Luck*. Oxford: Oxford University Press.

Prior, A.N. (1955) *Formal Logic*. Oxford: Oxford University Press.

Searle, John (1992) *The Rediscovery of the Mind*. Cambridge, MA: MIT Press.

    (2001) *Rationality in Action*. Cambridge, MA: MIT Press.

    (2004) *Mind: A Brief Introduction*. Oxford: Oxford University Press.

    (2007) "Putting consciousness back in the brain: Reply to Bennett and Hacker", in Bennett, Dennett, Hacker and Searle, *Neuroscience and Philosophy*. New York: Columbia University Press.

Wegner, Daniel M. (2002) *The Illusion of Conscious Will*. Cambridge, MA: MIT Press.

Widerker, David and McKenna, Michael (2003) *Moral Responsibility and Alternative Possibilities*. Aldershot: Ashgate.

13
Hugh J. McCann

Professor of Philosophy

Texas A&M University, USA

---

1. Why were you initially drawn to theorizing about action and agency?

Like many action theorists, I am sure, what first drew me to the subject was the free will problem, which I can remember discussing with my elders as early as the age of fifteen. I grew up in a religious household, and in my thinking at that time the problem appeared in the guise of theological fatalism: If God was omniscient, it seemed, the entire future had somehow to be fixed in advance of any human decision. And if that was so then our decisions and actions could not be free, could not truly be "up to us." How, then, could we be responsible for them? It emerged pretty quickly that my elders were as stumped as I was, and their fallback position—that these were mysteries, not to be fathomed by feeble creaturely minds—was anything but reassuring to me.

Things got better in college, where I learned about Boethius's God, who exists entirely outside of time. Such a God, I was assured, could observe the entire course of history in one, timeless glance, and so could know all things regardless of when they occurred, or how they came about. So God could know our decisions and actions without their being fixed by any temporally prior condition. For a long time this answer satisfied me, at least on the theological front.[1] But of course I was in no way out of the woods, for in the meantime I had encountered causal determinism, which taken as a universal thesis about the world implied exactly what

---

[1] It should not have. The God of classical theism is supposed to be impassible—that is, incapable of being acted upon—and therefore not dependent on anything external to himself for his knowledge. It is not possible that such a God could learn of our doings by passive observation.

theological determinism does: that our decisions and actions are settled long before their occurrence, far in advance of any opportunity we have to control them. And this time there would be no handy Boethian way out.

There might, of course, be other means of escape. One lesson of twentieth century physics is that the world is not, at the microlevel, deterministic. The implications of this have not been lost on philosophers, some of whom have argued that subatomic events in the brain might manifest themselves at the level of neuron firings, so that the physiological and behavioral events that occur in exercises of agency would be undetermined causally, making libertarian freedom possible.[2] This is a valuable point for philosophers who, like myself, view libertarian freedom as necessary for moral responsibility—but it is still speculative relative to present empirical knowledge and investigative capability. And even if true, this kind of indeterminacy would not be sufficient to secure responsible freedom since, as determinists are fond of pointing out, there would then be the question how agents are able to control behavioral events whose origin, empirically speaking, appears strictly random, and hence accidental.

2. What do you consider to be your own most important contributions to theorizing about action and agency, and why?

Here is a question that makes one wonder. Is it possible to have made contributions that are "most important" without having made any that are important? And even if it is, can one be trusted to represent them fairly? I have doubts on both scores. But most of my work on action has focused on its etiology—specifically, on the formation and execution of intention—and if I have made a contribution it is on these two topics. In full-blown cases of action we first make up our mind to do something and then, perhaps after an interval of time, proceed to do it. The focus of my early work was on the doing part as it occurs in bodily movement, which of course lies at the foundation of virtually all overt behavior. Bodily movement, when it counts as action, arises out of voluntary physical exertion (muscle flexing, if you want to get kinesiological

---

[2] For a nice summary of this discussion see David Hodgson, "Quantum Physics, Consciousness, and Free Will," in *The Oxford Handbook of Free Will*, ed. R. Kane (New York: Oxford University Press, 2002), pp. 85-110.

about it) which, on my account, is grounded in volition—a mental activity that is intrinsically actional.[3] Volition is not a staccato event that precedes overt motion. It is the means by which the agent exerts control over what he does, and it is carried on by the agent throughout the exertional activity that the intended movement requires.

There are, I think, two things about volition that are of paramount importance. The first is simply that it is there. The motion of an arm or finger is never an action. It is the *bringing about* of the motion that counts as action, and this cannot occur except through the interior involvement of which we are all aware when we reflect on what we do in acting. This is a simple enough point, but it was fervently ignored for about a generation during the postwar period, when the influence of logical behaviorism made it difficult to speak without apology of almost any kind of mental doing.[4] The revival of the notion of willing—or "trying," as some called it—made it possible to lay to rest certain problems about the etiology of action, especially that of "causal deviance" in the progression from merely intending to doing.[5] The second important feature of volition, one that I think is still too little appreciated, is its essential actional character: its spontaneity, and its intrinsic intentionality or purposiveness. Volition does not befall us. It is impossible to will the exertion appropriate for raising one's arm by accident or inadvertence, or without meaning to engage in precisely that volitional activity. If one thinks of volition as trying, then the point becomes this: that we cannot accidentally try to do anything. The same goes for all other exercises of active willing—for example deciding, and the act of selectively directing one's attention to one or another conscious content. That willing is both spontaneous and intrinsically intentional is crucially important for the study of agency because, at least from the agent's practical perspective, it lays to rest the determinist's claim that an action not subject to nomic causation must, as a "random" event, be out of the agent's control and hence accidental or fortuitous.[6]

---

[3] See my *The Works of Agency* (Ithaca, New York: Cornell University Press, 1995), chs. 4 and 5.

[4] The *locus classicus* for criticism of volitional theories in that era is Gilbert Ryle, *The Concept of Mind* (London: Hutchinson, 1949), ch. 3.

[5] Other defenses of volition include Brian O'Shaughnessy, "Trying (as the Mental 'Pineal Gland')," (*Journal of Philosophy* 70 (1973): 365-86; and Carl Ginet, *On Action* (New York: Cambridge University Press, 1990), ch. 2.

[6] For an argument of this kind see Alfred R. Mele, *Free Will and Luck*

From the point of view of the agent no such thing is even possible, phenomenologically or logically, because decision and volition are anything but random. Both are intrinsically actional. We cannot decide or will anything without meaning to decide exactly what we do decide, and to will exactly as we will.[7]

From the practical perspective, then, there is no coherence to the idea that decision or volition might be fortuitous, or that an agent might be "lucky" to have decided or acted well rather than foolishly or wrongly. The conceptual content of notions like *deciding* and *willing*, which is founded upon the experience we have of engaging in such activities, simply precludes any such judgment. And I think there can be little doubt that this experience is largely responsible for the widespread belief that when we act what we do is "up to us" in some fairly radical, and implicitly antideterministic, sense. There are, however, perspectives other than that of the agent, a point to which I shall return below.

3. What other sub-disciplines in philosophy and non- disciplines stand to benefit most from philosophical work on the nature of action and agency, and how might such engagement be accomplished?

Let me address this question first as it pertains to non-philosophical disciplines. Philosophical treatments of action and agency have obvious bearing on psychological studies human behavior, for certain areas of sociology, and for jurisprudentialists concerned with the subject of punishment and responsibility. Of these, the most active arena of mutual interest and interchange these days is psychology. Most philosophers interested in the way agency gets exercised have become familiar with the work of Benjamin Libet on neural readiness potential and intentional movement, and a useful discussion has resulted.[8] On another front, several action theorists, myself included, have been involved with experimentation having to do with the so-called "Simple View" of the relation between intention and action, according to which a necessary condition of performing an action intentionally is that one intend to perform

---

(New York: Oxford University Press, 2006), pp. 6-9.

[7] *The Works of Agency* ch. 7.

[8] Summarized in Libet, "Do We Have Free Will?" *The Oxford Handbook of Free Will*, pp. 551-64. For critical discussion see Mele, "Free Will: Action Theory Meets Neuroscience," in *Intentionality, Deliberation and Autonomy* ed. C. Lumer and S. Nannini (Burlington, VT: Ashgate, 2007), pp. 257-72.

it.⁹ Experimental results in these areas can be interpreted in more that one way, and dramatic conclusions are not easy to establish. I think, however, that the empirical subtlety of experimenters combined with conceptual sophistication of philosophers can only be beneficial to both sides, so that cooperation of this kind is bound to continue.

As for other subdisciplines of philosophy that might benefit most from discussions in action theory, there are many. Most prominent in my own work has been the philosophy of religion, for which the study of agency has a number of implications. There is, in particular, an age-old problem about the relationship between divine sovereignty and human freedom—that is, about how the providential control that the God of traditional belief is supposed to exercise over the universe can be squared with the idea that creatures have any genuine control over their destiny.¹⁰ Related to this question are theological disputes concerning salvation and the operation of grace, over which in centuries past more than a little blood was shed. A proper understanding of the way agency is exercised and of how responsible freedom may best be understood is indispensable for addressing issues such as these—especially since, with a few notable exceptions, neither theologians nor philosophers of religion have found compatibilist accounts of freedom attractive.

Theories of action and agency have implications for other areas of philosophy as well. Perhaps the most important is the philosophy of mind, in particular for the topic practitioners in that field refer to as "mental causation." It is generally allowed that in action explanations an agent's reasons have explanatory force *qua reasons*. Thus, if I turn on the radio out of desire to hear the Met's latest performance of *Don Giovanni*, the mental *content* of my desire—the thought we might express as, "Would that I hear this performance of *Don Giovanni*"—has explanatory force. The importance of this is twofold. First, if it is the content of my desire that explains here, then the explanation would presumably not be causal, at least in the sense of nomic causation. This is because the content is not an event but an abstraction, something proposition-like, and nomic causes have to be events. Yet

---

⁹See my "Intentional Action and Intending: Recent Empirical Studies," *Philosophical Psychology* 18 (2005): 737-748.

¹⁰I address this topic in "The Author of Sin?" *Faith and Philosophy* 22 (2005): 144-159.

the content does explain what I did, at least to some extent. If we acknowledge this then we must be prepared to except the legitimacy of forms of explanation that are not causal. Second, this kind of explanation, because it proceeds in terms of mental content, is inherently dualistic in its implications. That is, it is hard to see how this kind of explanatory force can be retained in a reduction of the mental to the purely physical or physiological. Thus even if, as many assume, mental events and states are either identical with physiological states of the brain or "supervene" upon them, it seems still to be the case that, whatever physiology we might finally invoke to explain voluntary behavior, its full explanation will have to proceed at least partly in terms of some mental dimension that comes with the physiology.[11]

A third subdiscipline of philosophy to which theories of agency have relevance is value theory. Intentions are formed and executed for reasons, which frame some end that the agent deems worth attaining, and which by way of practical reasoning issue in intention and action. Sometimes the end is only a matter of desire; other times it is thought or felt to be obligatory. When it comes to obligation, the difference between "thought" and "felt" is of vital importance, because it has to do with whether moral principles enter into practical thinking merely as matters of judgment or belief, or as intrinsically motivating—that is, as matters of felt obligation. There is a big difference between the two, a difference that is important for dealing with such questions as why a person should be moral at all, and how weakness of will is possible. The contrast between moral belief and moral motivation reaches, in fact, to the foundations of ethics, since it leads directly to the question whether moral injunctions are best framed as judgments of truth or falsity, or as imperatives. In some of my work I have argued that truly practical reasoning—that is, reasoning in which premises that are inherently conative issue in intention formation—is itself an exercise of agency.[12] If that is so then the study of the foundations of agency should have a good deal to contribute to value theory.

4. What do you regard as the most neglected issues in

---

[11] An excellent introduction to this issue can be gotten from J. Heil and A. Mele, eds., *Mental Causation* (Oxford: Clarendon Press, 1993).

[12] See, for example, "The Will and the Good." In Lumer and Nannini, *Deliberation, Intentionality, and Autonomy*. pp. 119-133.

contemporary work on action and agency that deserve more attention?

It is not obvious to me that action theorists themselves have ignored many fundamental issues. What I do think is that, apart from the topic of free will, the entire field is presently somewhat neglected. With regard to some questions that may be for the best. For instance, one sees little written these days on the individuation of action, but in fact that was always a topic that stood pretty much on its own—a special problem in the study of time and change, which is really a part of metaphysics rather than action theory. One's views on act individuation are not likely to influence what one will say about how decisions are made, how intentions get executed, how values enter into practical thinking, and what constitutes legitimate freedom. As I have tried to indicate above, however, these latter questions and the views we take on them have important bearing on a number of central areas of philosophy, and progress in those areas can only be enhanced if philosophers have a firm grasp of action theory.

It is of course a normal thing for attention to shift from one subject area to another as philosophy evolves, and the flurry of activity devoted to the study of action in the fifties and sixties of the past century was not likely to persist. Perhaps it diminished in part because of what turned out to be unrealistic expectations. It was not uncommon to hear it argued in those days that, although there could be no recourse to mental activity to help explain how voluntary action came about, it was nevertheless the case that the motion of an arm or finger, when viewed as an action, was not susceptible of causal explanation, but was rather to be explained in terms of the agent's reasons.[13] This was bound to fail, inasmuch as it is possible for an agent to have reasons but not act upon them. Inevitably, therefore, the objection would arise that in order to explain why a limb or digit moved for one of the agent's reasons rather than another, causation by the reason would have to be invoked.[14] When mental action has been ruled out of the discussion, this may well be the only plausible view that remains. Its effect, however, is to make voluntary agency seem just one more mechanistic process—not to be distinguished, in this re-

---

[13] For an extended defense of this position see A. I. Melden, *Free Action* (London: Routledge & Kegan Paul, 1961).

[14] Donald Davidson, "Actions, Reasons and Causes," *Journal of Philosophy* 60 (1963): 685-700, p. 691.

spect, from any other psychological phenomenon, and hence not deserving of special attention or intensive study. In my opinion, however, mid-twentieth century action theorists were in fact correct in insisting that reason explanations, as ordinarily used and understood, are not causal. Their mistake was not in making this claim, but in thinking that the situation it described could be understood while at the same time denying that anything relevant was going on within the agent. If this is correct then there is indeed something quite unique about agency. It will inevitably become an object of renewed attention, even if it does not appear an attractive or promising topic to many at the moment.

5. What are the most important open problems in philosophical theorizing about action and agency, and what are the prospects for progress?

The most important problem is that of free will. I stated above that it is not possible from the practical perspective of the agent for an exercise of will to be fortuitous or accidental. The reason for this is simply that the phenomenology of agency is the phenomenology of libertarian freedom. From our own standpoint in acting, agency can only be exercised spontaneously and intentionally. It can never, therefore, be a matter of luck that we act well or rightly. Just the opposite: it is the actor in a deterministic world who would be lucky to behave well—lucky, because he was born into a world whose causal structure was such, and its prior conditions so arranged, that he would act as he did rather than in some less fortunate way, as no doubt he would have in many other worlds. And of course no matter how he acted he could not be responsible for his deed, for it was in the cards that he would so behave ten thousand years before he was born.[15] There are, of course, accounts of free will that seek to make it compatible with determinism. In my view, however, these are no more than the creations of philosophers. My experience with students and other laypersons is that they have difficulty even fathoming

---

[15] The principle that an agent is responsible only if he could have done otherwise was rejected by Harry G. Frankfurt in "Alternate Possibilities and Moral Responsibility," *Journal of Philosophy* 66 (1969): 829-39. The example upon which Frankfurt's argument was based is, however, question-begging against libertarian accounts of freedom. To my mind, a satisfactory replacement has yet to be found. For discussion, see Kane, *The Oxford Handbook of Free Will*, chs. 12-14.

compatibilist accounts of freedom, and that when they finally do understand they are not at all prepared to agree that this is what *they* have always thought freedom was. Their view, which is born of their experience in acting, is that we are free in a far more radical sense than compatibilism allows. If they felt any other way, there would be no such thing as the free will problem.

As was stated earlier, however, there are perspectives other than that of the agent engaged in action. In particular, there is the standpoint of the third person observer, who may wish to be able to predict and control the behavior of others, and rightly finds libertarian accounts of agency an unpromising basis for so doing. Or, someone may simply be impressed with the progress of science, and believe that exercises of agency will eventually receive complete, naturalistic explanations. From this standpoint, agency that is indeterministic can only be seen as an embarrassment. It is not, or at least not finally, predictable, and is to that extent fortuitous as far as external control is concerned—notwithstanding the fact that, from his internal perspective, the agent feels completely in control. And even if from the agent's perspective there can be no such thing as luck in exercises of the will, the third person predictor or would-be controller will indeed be lucky to predict the outcome of undetermined deliberation, and he can at most influence the outcome, not control it. But that is as far as the luck argument goes. Someone might protest that there is a deeper, metaphysical sort of luck that pervades indeterministic world, manifested simply in the fact that the agent in a given case wills A rather than B. But there is at least as deep an element of luck that pertains to deterministic worlds, in that the causes are from the beginning such that A rather than B is bound to occur—and this sort of luck must trouble the agent's perspective as well as that of the observer.

Which perspective, then, is correct? Are exercises of agency causally determined or not? It is natural to think this is strictly an empirical question, but there is a case to be made that it is not entirely so. For suppose the neurophysiology of decision and action proves to be deterministic through and through, and that we find consistent and reliable correlations between neurological elements in the causal chain from stimulus to response on the one hand, and such mental states and events as desire, felt obligation, decision, intending, volition and all the rest on the other. Perhaps we would then be driven to conclude that libertarian freedom is an illusion, and would revert to some compatibilist treatment of moral responsibility as the best that can be made of what, for libertarians at least, would be an unhappy situation. But would we be compelled to do so? That depends on what we take the relation between the mental and the physical to be. If we believe that conscious thought simply rides piggyback on brain events—in virtue of an identity relation, or perhaps a weaker form of metaphysical supervenience—then I would say that the answer is certainly yes. But it is not obvious that the relation of mind to body is in itself an empirical matter. Can empirical evidence *alone* tell us that mental events and brain events are identical rather than distinct, or that when it comes to explaining decision and volition physiology always has the upper hand? I do not see how it could, at least as science has so far evolved. Perhaps, then, there could be found alternative accounts of the relation of mind to body that would allow libertarian accounts of freedom and responsibility to survive even in this seemingly dire situation. Kant, to cite perhaps the most notorious example, certainly thought something like this was possible.

In any case, we are not presently in a position to say whether voluntary agency is determined or not, even in its neurological correlates. There are, however, cases where voluntariness seems to be impaired, and the agent's responsibility at least diminished if not destroyed. And it is interesting to note that there is broad agreement between determinists and libertarians about such cases. Both sides are at pains to excuse precisely the same failures—e.g., actions undertaken under threat or duress, or those of the mentally deranged. Moreover, both sides of the debate tend to excuse such actions on roughly the same ground: that in the circumstances that obtained, the agent could not reasonably have been expected to appreciate and act upon the true nature and value of the alternatives available. What this suggests if that the issue of determinism is, in practical circumstances, more or less moot. We decide questions of responsibility based on the agent's frame of mind, rather than by examining questions of causation—on which, after all, we are not in a position to give a definitive answer. Perhaps, then, it would be possible without resolving the free will problem to frame an account of responsibility on which determinists and libertarians could agree, thus sidestepping in large part the metaphysical issue of freedom.

14
Michael McKenna

Professor of Philosophy
Florida State University, USA

Naturalism and Free Agency

1. Why were you initially drawn to theorizing about action and agency?[1]

My initial interest in theory of action arose from general questions about the relationship between human beings and the natural world. As it was once quaintly put, "What is man's place in the world?" Wilfred Sellars spoke of the manifest and the scientific images and the apparent tension between them (1966). According to the manifest image, creatures like us are capable of acting purposively, morally, freely, and responsibly. Furthermore, from the manifest image, it seems that humans are capable of creating beauty, of living meaningful lives, of self-reflection and abstract thought, of crafting just societies, and so on. But it is unclear how to make room for these diverse phenomena from the standpoint of the scientific image. According to this image, the laws of nature are pervasive, and human beings are just as much within their domain as are the heavenly bodies. This suggests a leveling of the presumed colossal differences between us and mere inanimate matter. According to the scientific image, especially in light of Darwin, humans are the upshot of an entirely natural history, one in which the features of our selves have arisen from purely physical conditions. We at the top of the food chain are simply on a continuum; the differences between us and amoebas come in degrees, not kinds. Cutting edge work in behavior and brain

---

[1] For helpful comments, I would like to thank Jesús Aguilar, Andrei Buckareff, Justin Capes, Randolph Clarke, Ishtiyaque Haji, and Storrs McCall. I would also like to thank Jesús Aguilar and Andrei Buckareff for kindly inviting me to contribute to this volume.

sciences only further solidifies the picture of the scientific image as one in which human beings are grounded in physical realities that, it seems, entirely settle the facts about us. If so, what are we to make of the idea that humans have free will, that it is up to us what sorts of lives to live, that there is a difference between a life lived meaningfully and one squandered, or that beauty can issue forth from the likes of John Coltrane or Michelangelo? Where are these properties to be found in the causal interstices of the Big Bang, our DNA, and the spinning of the earth's axis in the vastness of space? There is the thought—the skeptical worry—that these humanistic notions issuing from the manifest image are by and large myths built out of ignorance and to be wiped away with the enlightened understanding contemporary science offers.

Although crude, I think three rough categories help to characterize the different strategies philosophers have taken in response to the apparent tension between the scientific and manifest images. One might be called an *insulating strategy*. The insulating strategy seeks to protect at least some features of the manifest image from the domain of the scientific image. One can be a realist about the pertinent features, but these features cannot be explained within the framework of the natural sciences. The reality that they pick out is non-natural (some might say 'supernatural', though the connotations cast the insulating strategy in an uncharitable light). A second stance might be called a *supplanting strategy*. The supplanting strategy bows to the advances of science wherever those advances suggest that the manifest image is untruthful. In these cases, the supplanting strategy is unabashedly revisionist in its attitude towards our understanding of human nature. Whether it be free will or creativity or the reality of moral truth, if science suggests that there is no room for these phenomena in nature, then philosophy's task is to supplant our earlier manifest image with one that is true to the natural facts. And so the crucial move involves eliminativism. Finally, the third stance involves what might be called the *reconciling strategy*. The reconciling strategist seeks to preserve as much of the manifest image as possible by showing that, despite any appearances to the contrary, the scientific image does not undermine it; the standpoints are, at least with respect to some domains, reconcilable. The properties of human nature identified from the manifest image are not crowded out by the scientific image, and this is not because, as is suggested by the insulating strategy, the properties at issue are non-natural ones. Rather, the properties themselves are natural properties, as much a part of the natural order as any other.

The above categories are indeed rough, and few philosophers, if any, adopt wholesale the same stance toward the entire range of phenomena identified from the manifest image. One could, for instance, be a supplanter about free will and a reconciler about intentional agency or instead meaning in life (e.g., Pereboom, 2001). Regardless, one important alliance is between the supplanters and the reconcilers. Both can be characterized as *naturalists*. That is, both respect the standpoint of the scientific image and use as an ontological litmus test the prospect that the humanistic qualities in question could be grounded in what our best sciences tell us about the natural world.

I am a naturalist, at least with respect to matters bearing on the nature of persons,[2] and I seek to push the reconciling strategy as far as possible. I wish to show that the manifest image—at least large swaths of it, such as those bearing on theory of action—can be reconciled with the scientific image. The reality of human life might be entirely grounded in the natural world, but there is room in this world for moral goodness (and badness), right (and wrong), virtue (and vice), meaning in life, justice, free and morally responsible agency, and so on. Nothing about the scientific image of the human condition undermines this.

The particular reconciling strategy I have tried to defend is focused upon a specialized topic within the broader arena of theory of action: free will and moral responsibility. The typical characterization of "the problem of free will" concerns the seeming conflict between free will and determinism. Although much disputed, I understand *free will* to be whatever is sufficient to satisfy all of the control required for morally responsible agency. A *free action*, that is, an exercise of free agency, just is one that issues from the agential capacities constitutive of this control. As for *morally responsible agents*, I understand such agents as an important subset of persons, ones who are sufficiently developed so as to be fitting objects of our moral demands, accountable for their conduct and liable to the full spectrum of the moral emotions, which include resentment and moral indignation.

The traditional worry is that if determinism is true, then no one

---

[2] I do not mean to commit to a naturalism so unrestricted that I would deny ontological status to anything if it could not be grounded in natural facts. For instance, I am open to Platonism about, for example, mathematical objects, propositions, or universals. (Thanks to Andrei Buckareff for pressing me on this point.)

has free will, and thus, there are no morally responsible agents. *Determinism* is most simply understood as the thesis that only one future is possible due to something that settles or determines it, such as God's foreknowledge. I focus exclusively on the thesis of *causal determinism*, which can be understood as the metaphysical thesis that a true proposition expressing all the atemporal facts at a time (fixing the entire state of the universe at that time), in conjunction with a proposition expressing all of the laws of nature, entail every atemporal truth about every later time. If causal determinism is true at this world, then at some time in the remote past, perhaps just after the Big Bang, given the laws of nature, every truth at every later time is entailed. Therefore, if you raised your arm just now, or had pancakes for breakfast this morning, these facts were entailed by those facts obtaining at a much earlier time (in conjunction with the laws of nature). The problem *seems to be*—and this is the crux of the dispute—that if determinism is true, no one controls her actions in the way required for moral responsibility because no one can do otherwise. No one could, for instance, not raise her arm or have pancakes for breakfast if that is what she did, since these facts were, in a sense, "settled" long ago.

This way of specifying the free will problem does have drawbacks. Crucially, some have thought that the problem is irrelevant because our best sciences tell us that the universe is not deterministic. The fundamental laws of physics are probabilistic laws, and the laws at higher levels of nature are not exceptionless. So, at best determinism poses a hypothetical threat. We can worry about whether, if it is true, anyone is free or morally responsible. But because we know it is not true, fretting about the implications that would follow if it were is mere idle speculation. This response, a most common reaction from outsiders to the discipline of philosophy, while understandable, is nevertheless misguided, and for two reasons. First, we learn something about the nature of certain phenomenon by understanding how it would behave were it exposed to conditions different from those it is typically in. Even if determinism is not true, supposing we do have free will and we are morally responsible, would that sort of freedom and responsibility be resilient in such a way that we would still possess it if the universe were set up differently than it is and we were fully determined? If so, we can understand something about the nature of the kind of freedom and responsibility we actually have. But there is a second and to my mind a more compelling reason for taking the free will problem seriously, even if we have strong scientific reasons for thinking that causal determinism is false. Although the thesis of determinism is sufficient for naturalism, it is not necessary for it. Naturalism might very well be true even though it looks pretty clearly that determinism is false.[3] Nevertheless, if we can establish that free will and moral responsibility are compatible with determinism, we can thereby establish that free will and moral responsibility are compatible with at least one form of naturalism. And this is a way to help make the case for the more general reconciling thesis that naturalism itself (whether in a deterministic or indeterministic form) poses no threat to free will or moral responsibility. Indeed, this is how I understand my work.[4]

2. What do you consider your most important contributions to theorizing about action and agency, and why?

As a *compatibilist*, I argue for the reconciling thesis that free will

---

[3] For example, consider the thesis of mechanism, which is consistent with causal determinism, but does not imply it. Mechanism is the thesis that for every mental state or event, there exist some microphysical state the either is or that fully realizes that state. These physical states stand in causal relations with other physical states and can in principle be explained adopting only the apparatus of purely (micro) physical descriptions, that is, ones that make no reference to the intentional states of agents. Mechanism of this sort will generate the same free will problem that determinism does. (On this point, see Dennett, 1973.)

[4] In correspondence, Jesús Aguilar has raised an important question about the relation between moral responsibility and the agential control I identify with free will. Can we not understand this control independently of the nature of moral responsibility? I think we can. For consider the control I identify as satisfying all of the freedom required for moral responsibility. Suppose I am right to locate a control of this sort, one only possessed by sufficiently developed persons. But suppose I am wrong about the conditions for moral responsibility. Perhaps moral responsibility requires more than what I maintain it does. Then while I have identified a certain type of control (or freedom), what I identify might not do duty for a full account of the freedom implicated in moral responsibility. Or instead, suppose I am right to link free will to the control bearing on moral responsibility. Even so, it might be that persons have this sort of control, but yet that none of them are morally responsible. Maybe there is some other condition on moral responsibility other than a control condition that these persons lack. If so, we have free will of the sort I identify, but with no moral responsibility. How could this be possible? Consider a world of amoral beings, ones who have no use for morality at all. They still might satisfy all of the control or freedom that is required of beings who are morally responsible agents. (On this point, see Mele, 1995: 3-4.)

is compatible with determinism. Because it is, I also believe that morally responsible agency is compatible with determinism. My primary philosophical opponent is the *incompatibilist*, who argues for the contrary thesis.[5] Incompatibilists offer different sorts of reasons for their thesis, and this has had some bearing on my work. Probably the majority of incompatibilists rest their thesis primarily if not exclusively on the claim that if determinism is true, no one has free will because no one is free to do anything other than what she does. If the past and the laws entail every truth about what I do at any time in my life, then I cannot do otherwise than as I do. Why? Here is an argument: Assuming causal determinism (as defined above) is true, for me to do otherwise, I would have to act in such a way that some law of nature that is true would not be, or to act in such a way that the past would be different than it is. But I cannot do these things, so I cannot do otherwise. Put differently, if it is not up to me that the past and the laws are thus and so, and if it is not up to me that they jointly entail every future fact, then it is also not up to me what the facts are now. It is not up to me in the sense that if it is true now that I raise my hand, I cannot render that truth false by not raising my hand. This is a very sketchy presentation of the *Consequence Argument* (Ginet, 1966; Wiggins, 1973; and van Inwagen, 1975).

The traditional compatibilist argues that there is a flaw in the Consequence Argument (and other arguments like it) so that even if determinism is true, at least some persons are free to do oth-

---

[5]Note that some incompatibilists share with me a commitment to naturalism, but instead adopt the supplanting strategy of eliminating free will and moral responsibility in light of the thought that determinism (or more credibly, naturalism) is true. Historically, these incompatibilists were called *hard determinists* (e.g., Edwards, 1958), and they restricted their supplanting project to the assumption of determinism. But in more recent times the thesis has evolved and now goes under the label '*hard incompatibilism*', which contends that free will and moral responsibility are incompatible not only with determinism, but more broadly with indeterministic forms of naturalism (Pereboom, 2001). Other incompatibilists, who are called *libertarians*, hold that although determinism is incompatible with free will and moral responsibility, determinism is false, and at least some persons do have free will and are morally responsible. Of these libertarians, some are insulators (e.g., Chisholm, 1964; and O'Connor, 2000) who maintain that the sort of relation between agent and action that bears on free will cannot be explained from the standpoint of the natural sciences. But others are, like me, reconcilers. They maintain that although free will and moral responsibility are incompatible with determinism, they are not incompatible with the wider thesis of naturalism (see, most notably, Kane, 1996).

erwise. For instance, David Lewis (1981) challenged the premise that the laws of nature are fixed. According to Lewis, assuming determinism, if a person acted otherwise than she did act, some law of nature that is true would not be. For reasons I will not offer here, I do not think that Lewis's strategy or others like it are convincing. I believe that the Consequence Argument is the most compelling of all incompatibilist arguments. In fact, I think it is so compelling that some variation on it is sound. It has convinced me of this much: Determinism is incompatible with the ability to do otherwise (insofar as this ability has any bearing on questions of free will). But notice that the Consequence Argument only directly establishes that if determinism is true, no one is able to do otherwise. It *assumes* that if no one is able to do otherwise, no one has free will and no one is morally responsible. Here I part company with the traditional compatibilist. I think *this* assumption is false.

I follow John Martin Fischer (1994) in defending what he calls 'semi-compatibilism', which I take to be the thesis that determinism is compatible with moral responsibility and the freedom that moral responsibility requires even if it is incompatible with the freedom to do otherwise. The first step in establishing this semi-compatibilist strategy is to argue that moral responsibility and the freedom required for it (what might be called an 'actual-sequence freedom') do not require the freedom to do otherwise. Although there are different routes to this conclusion, like Fischer and others following his lead, I think the best is by way of Harry Frankfurt's argument (1969), which is built upon a counterexample to the Principle of Alternative Possibilities (PAP): A person is morally responsible for what she has done only if she could have done otherwise. Here is an approximation of the example Frankfurt uses to make his point: Jones plans to and indeed does shoot Smith at a certain time, t. Jones is under no duress or anything of the sort. He acts freely. But Black is covertly watching Jones in the hope that Jones will shoot Smith on his own by t. Should Jones show any sign that he will not shoot Smith by t (a sign of the sort Black is specially equipped to read), Black will manipulate the inner workings of Jones's neural anatomy, causing Jones to shoot Smith by t. As it happens, Black never does intervene since Jones showed no such sign and did shoot Smith on his own at the requisite time. Here, Jones is morally responsible for what he did even though he could not have done otherwise. Ergo, PAP is false.

One of my contributions to work on agency and action is by way of my compatibilist effort to respond to the Consequence Argument. I try to do so by showing that, even if sound, it does not have the implication it is taken to have—that determinism rules out free will and moral responsibility by ruling out the freedom to do otherwise. I deny this implication in semi-compatibilist fashion by defending Frankfurt's argument against PAP from numerous critics. In this project, I am not alone. Numerous others have defended Frankfurt from the objections raised to his argument.[6]

What differs in my approach can be understood in relation to two standard lines of attack that are leveled against Frankfurt. One has it that in a Frankfurt example, while it is true that the agent (Jones in the case above) could not avoid doing what he did, there is something that the agent did and could have avoided doing (like the particular act token of shooting Smith), and this is the basis for the agent's free action and moral responsibility (e.g., van Inwagen, 1983). Furthermore, according to the second line, it has been argued that the 'sign' that a counterfactual intervener such as Black would rely upon cannot be one that takes place prior to the agent's action (Kane, 1996; Ginet, 1996; and Widerker, 1995). For it could only be thought to be a certain sign of future free action if the agent was already determined to so act before the act took place. But of course incompatibilists would resist this. The upshot of these two ways of resisting Frankfurt is that those who sought to defend his thesis assumed that the right way to do so was, *first*, to show that we can construct examples in which there is no action the agent could have performed other than the one she did perform, and *second*, to create conditions that ensure the action (e.g., in the role played by Black) so that those conditions do not presuppose that the agent is already determined prior to her so acting (e.g., Mele and Robb, 1998, 2003). The trouble with this approach, to my mind, is that it is difficult to construct an example that does both at once. Nail down the first one and you violate the second. Get the second one right and the first is unsatisfied.

I argued that others defending Frankfurt wrongly assumed that a *robust alternative* course of action—one that would be adequate for showing that the agent had a meaningful sort of freedom to do otherwise in a Frankfurt example—is simply any action that is 'open' to the agent. This is why Frankfurt's defenders think they

---

[6] See the articles in the collection I edited with David Widerker (2003). This collection is devoted exclusively to the debate over Frankfurt's argument.

have to close down all action paths other than the one that involves the action the agent actually performs, like shooting Smith. My thought was this: Suppose that some action paths remain open, but that no theorist about free agency would ever think that this open alternative would enhance an agent's freedom (2003). Suppose, for instance, that Black closed off all of Jones's alternative courses of action other than one in which he begins to eat his fist. Would Frankfurt's critic really want to say that Jones's moral responsibility is partially grounded in the fact that he could have begun to eat his fist by t rather than shoot Smith? How would the availability of an insane course of action bear on whether Jones is morally responsible for shooting Smith if he does so on his own? Given that such alternatives are not robust, I set about to create an example in which an agent could do otherwise, but only in insane ways. The sane alternatives were all closed down. In such a case, it is not causally determined that the agent perform only one action, since there are some action paths left open (the insane ones). And so Frankfurt's critic cannot object that the example assumes determinism. Yet the alternatives left open seem irrelevant to the agent's freedom and responsibility. This, I believe, is a sound way to defend Frankfurt's thesis: the freedom bearing on moral responsibility does not require the freedom to do otherwise.

Suppose I am correct about this. I have not fully replied to the incompatibilist. This brings into relief another aspect of my work. Recall, as I remarked above, the incompatibilist has different sorts of reasons for her incompatibilism, and only some of them fix on the thought that determinism conflicts with the freedom to do otherwise. Other reasons that incompatibilists enlist have to do with the sources of agency, and with the thought that if determinism is true, those sources originate in sufficient conditions external to the agent. The arguments bearing on these worries I have labeled *source incompatibilist* worries (2001). Source incompatibilists (e.g., Pereboom, 2001; and Stump, 1996) actually agree with Frankfurt's argument but argue that, nevertheless, determinism is incompatible with free will and moral responsibility. Because I also think that the freedom bearing on moral responsibility has to do with the sources of an agent's action and not whether she was free to do otherwise, I am a *source compatibilist*. As such, I bear the burden of answering those source incompatibilist arguments meant to show that if the sources of an agent's actions originate in sufficient conditions long before her birth, then she is not morally responsible for them.

Space does not permit a discussion of the three source incompatibilist arguments I have resisted. I'll just describe two briefly, as well as my general line of reply to each. One, the *Manipulation Argument*, has it that a deterministic history is no different than a history due to the manipulation of a demon, and no one would hold a person morally responsible if her actions were the result of such extreme manipulation. I have challenged this argument by holding that if the manipulation really is exactly like the way a deterministic history would produce actions, then the compatibilist should just say that agent is free and responsible. If not, then the agent need not be free and morally responsible (2004). Another argument, the *Transfer of Non-responsibility Argument* contends that one can 'transfer' non-responsibility for the laws of nature and past facts along entailment relations so that one is also not responsible for what is entailed by those facts. I have also resisted this argument (2008). I contend that claims about transferring non-responsibility are contentious when the examples meant to establish the transfer work through normally functioning agents. For instance, suppose it is determined that due to the state of the world just after the big bang, Janis is in a certain mental state prior to her deliberating, and that this state (along with the laws of nature) deterministically leads to her deliberating in such a way that she decides to and does steal Bobby McGhee's cigarettes. Is the fact that she is not responsible for being in the earlier state sufficient for us to conclude that she is also not responsible for the actions issuing from her own states of deliberation? I think this is just what is in dispute. In the context of the debate between compatibilists and incompatibilists, it is not reasonable for the incompatibilist to assume that if at a determined world an agent is not responsible for states leading to her processes of deliberation, she is also not responsible for her subsequent actions that issue from that process.

In summary, in response to the incompatibilists, I have adopted two different strategies. For those incompatibilist arguments meant to show that determinism is incompatible with the freedom to do otherwise, I have granted the point at issue, but then advanced the semi-compatibilist contention that the freedom to do otherwise is not required for the freedom that does bear on moral responsibility. As for those source incompatibilist arguments that hold that determinism pollutes the sources of free agency (irrespective of considerations about freedom to do otherwise), I have taken on what I take to be the three best arguments for this thesis. But notice that so far my project is merely a negative one. I have yet to give any positive account of what free agency is and to show how it is compatible with determinism.

This leads to a third aspect of my work. In my estimation, the best compatibilist account of free will is developed by John Martin Fischer and Mark Ravizza (1998), though I also find Ishtiyaque Haji's formulation extremely forceful as well (1998). Fischer and Ravizza, and also Haji, analyze the freedom required for moral responsibility, which Fischer and Ravizza call guidance control, in terms of responsiveness to reasons (in conjunction with further features that needn't be considered here). When a free agent acts and is morally responsible for what she does, she acts from agential characteristics that are sensitive to an appropriate range of rational considerations. This shows that when she does act, she is responding to reasons, and we can morally assess her—hold her responsible—on the basis of the moral value of the reasons she does act upon. All of this is compatible with determinism. Although I am an advocate of Fischer and Ravizza's work, several of the pieces I have published have been critical of the details of their analysis of reasons-responsiveness (2000, 2001a, 2005). But the differences between us should not cloud our similarities. I have only been at pains to show that there are further details that need to be corrected, and where possible I have offered ways to help advance their cause (e.g., 2005). Here again, space does not permit a proper presentation of the problems, but the general difficulty is due to the fact that even agents who are not free are responsive to some range of reasons. The drug addict who takes a drug due to (what seems to be) an irresistible desire still might be sensitive to some reasons not to take the drug. She might, for instance, not take it if she were given reason to believe that, were she to do so, she would explode, or cause the destruction of the world, or that her children would be eaten by wolves. Here she would be responsive to *some* reasons, but clearly if these were the *only* reasons to which she would be responsive, she would not be adequately or appropriately responsive to reasons in a way that would lead us to think that when she does take the drug, she does so freely rather than as the product of a defect of agency. The differences that I have had with Fischer and Ravizza all turn on how to specify properly just the right amount of responsiveness as needed to account for all that is required for the freedom relevant condition for moral responsibility.

A fourth aspect of my work has to do with the nature of moral responsibility itself rather than with the freedom condition required for it, or even the general question about its compatibility or incompatibility with determinism. The basic issue is simply, *What is moral responsibility?* What does the concept of moral responsibility come to? Some hold that moral responsibility does not essentially involve the moral emotions, the ones having to do with the moral sentiments bearing on holding morally responsible, such as resentment and indignation, and in the case of holding oneself responsible, guilt. I follow P.F. Strawson (1962), and many of his contemporaries (e.g. Watson, 1987), in arguing that moral responsibility is intimately connected with the moral emotions. It is my contention that this connection has to do with the expressive and communicative nature of moral responsibility and of holding morally responsible (1998, 2000b, 2004b). I maintain that our reactive moral emotions express our moral demands and are responses to the attitudes of good and ill will expressed in the conduct of those whom we hold morally responsible. Our moral emotions are, in a sense, the glue that holds together moral communities comprised of morally responsible agents.

3. What other sub-disciplines in philosophy and non- disciplines stand to benefit the most from philosophical work on action and agency, and how might such engagement be accomplished?

As for sub-disciplines in philosophy, those working in the closely related area of normative theory would benefit from tending more to questions about the nature of action, decision, choice, deliberation and will, which often seem to be conflated in differing ways. Special attention to compatibilist accounts of freedom would be useful in defeating the strikingly pervasive thought that free will and responsibility require "contra-causal" freedom (whatever that is). Areas as diverse as work in applied ethics related to questions of patient autonomy and competence in psychiatric care could benefit from more careful attention to work on the nature of morally responsible agency.

Clearly there are areas of the law that would profit from these inquiries, for instance, at the borderline between adolescence and adulthood when questions of criminal liability arise. There is more than likely a much better way to determine when a young person is appropriately regarded as a fully legally competent agent. Similar remarks probably apply regarding psychopathy and the law.

An area especially in need of attention is the exploding neurobiological sciences, wherein scientists are often announcing outrageous findings, such as that free will has been proven to be an illusion due to a 'discovery' as to how and where choice is located in the workings of the brain. Here, my colleague Alfred Mele has done the most to put the neuroscience in perspective, and he has a new book forthcoming on this topic.

As for how such engagement might be accomplished, there are many avenues, I suppose, and Mele is pursuing one by simply writing in a way that speaks directly to a discipline outside of philosophy. But another is to do the sort of work being done by the authors of this volume, creating a collection of accessible articles that will allow various sorts of inquirers to come to understand a philosophical subject such as action theory.

4. What do you regard as the most neglected issues in contemporary work on action and agency that deserve more attention?

Since I work mostly on the more narrow area of free will and moral responsibility, I'll focus upon this area. I have come to suspect that different theorists are operating with very different concepts of what moral responsibility is. It would be one thing if this were done consciously, but I fear that there is often a dialogue at cross-purposes with opposing sides not clear at all on what the other has in mind. A key question then concerns what moral responsibility actually is. Is it a matter of susceptibility to justifiable moral demands? Is it a susceptibility to being a target of the moral emotions should one fall short of (or exceed) moral expectations? Is it the more antiseptic notion of merely being expected to account for one's conduct?

A serious worry is that those with fairly stringent incompatibilist demands might hold those demands as in contrast with compatibilists due to the fact that what the incompatibilist has in mind by moral responsibility is far away from what the compatibilist is thinking about. In my estimation, one can place a magnifying glass on the issue by fixing upon the concept of desert. If a morally responsible agent is blameworthy, does this entail that she deserves a certain type of response, and if so, what type? Does she deserve to suffer? In what sense does she deserve this? Is the thought that it would be morally right to cause her harm, or is it the distinct thought that, if she were to be caused to suffer, that would be an intrinsic (*pro tanto*) good?[7] Here, I believe that a great deal of work has yet to be done, and in a sense, as regarding the differences between the various contestants to the debate, this is where the rubber meets the road. It is where theory is to inform action. Yet so little has been said.

If there is a hope that we can get clear on what our concept of moral responsibility is (as well as related notions like blame and praise, guilt, and so on), it might well be in the work of experimental philosophers who are doing the tough labor of trying to figure out just what the folk concept of moral responsibility is (e.g., Nahmias, Morris, Nadelhoffer, and Turner, 2006; and Nichols, 2006). Naturally, this would settle nothing, but only tell us what people's intuitions are and what concept we can extrapolate from those intuitions. But getting clear on those intuitions and concepts is a first step down the path to discerning what moral responsibility is and what concept we should have of it.

5. What are the most important open problems in philosophical theorizing about action and agency, and what are the prospects for progress?

Here again, I will restrict my answer to work on free will and moral responsibility. One open problem concerns the one mentioned just above, which has to do with just what the correct (veridical) concept of moral responsibility is. I'll not rehearse that again here. I'll mention two others. A second has to do with an alternative way to theorizing about free will that does not begin with action theoretic questions about the nature of intentional agency and the like, but begins with normative questions about the proper grounds for justifying our practices of holding agents morally responsible. Some, such as Jay Wallace (1994) and T.M. Scanlon (1998), adopt the normative approach and then come to conclusions very similar to those who approach the issue from an action theoretic standpoint (as I do). One question is whether the differences in approach suggest different extensions to moral responsibility. If they do, who gets it right? If not, is there some explanation for why we get a natural fit here?

---

[7] I am indebted to my colleague Randolph Clarke for helping me to get clear on these questions. I attended his seminar on moral responsibility in the fall semester of 2007 at Florida State University. In it, he drew into stark relief the vastly different notions of moral responsibility that opposing theorists have relied upon.

A third open problem concerns the relation between work in the behavioral and brain sciences and our understanding of the conditions of moral responsibility. It is one sort of empirical claim that some neuroscientific insight can settle wholesale whether any persons have free will. I am dubious that our brain sciences are that advanced, or that those espousing these theories have any clear sense of what free will is. But it is quite another to locate specific sorts of psychological conditions or processes that call into question the appearance of voluntary, rational control (as is suggested by the famed Millgram experiments). Here our sciences are now, it seems to me, well positioned to inform us about these matters, and to give us good reason to rethink our understanding of the scope and degree or responsibility. (Another example has to do with recent work that offers an explanation of limited impulse control for teenagers due to brain development.) As all good philosophers should, we need to remain open to scientific discoveries that might give us good reason to rethink long held categories about who is and who is not morally responsible, and to what degree, and in what arenas of agency. As a naturalist, it is my hope that philosophy can aid the scientists here while we philosophers learn from them.

Bibliography

Chisholm, Roderick. 1964. "Human Freedom and the Self." *The Lindley Lectures*. Copyright by the Department of Philosophy, University of Kansas. Reprinted in Watson, ed., 1982.

Dennett, Daniel 1973. "Mechanism and Responsibility." In Honderich (1973).

Edwards, Paul. 1958. "Hard and Soft Determinism." In Hook, ed. 1958, 117-25.

Fischer, John Martin.1994. *The Metaphysics of Free Will*. Oxford: Blackwell Publishers.

Fischer, John Martin, and Mark Ravizza. 1998. *Responsibility and Control: An Essay on Moral Responsibility*. Cambridge: Cambridge University Press.

Frankfurt, Harry. 1969. "Alternate Possibilities and Moral Responsibility." *Journal of Philosophy* 66: 829-39.

Ginet, Carl. 1996. "In Defense of the Principle of Alternative Possibilities: Why I Don't Find Frankfurt's Argument Convincing." *Philosophical Perspectives* 10: 403-17.

———. 1990. *On Action*. Cambridge: Cambridge University Press.

———. 1966. "Might We Have No Choice?" In Lehrer, 1966: 87-104.

Haji, Ishtiyaque. 1998. *Moral Appraisability*. New York: Oxford University Press.

Honderich, Ted, ed. 1973. *Essays on Freedom and Action*. London: Routledge & Kegan Paul.

Kane, Robert. 1996. *The Significance of Free Will*. Oxford: Oxford University Press.

Lehrer, Keith, ed. 1966. *Freedom and Determinism*. New York: Random House.

Lewis, David. 1981. "Are We Free to Break the Laws?" *Theoria* 47: 113-21.

McKenna, Michael. 2008 forthcoming. "Saying Goodbye to the Direct Argument the Right Way." *Philosophical Review*.

———. 2005. "Reasons Reactivity & Incompatibilist Intuitions." *Philosophical Explorations* vol. 8, No.2: 131-43.

———. 2004a. "Responsibility and Globally Manipulated Agents." *Philosophical Topics* 32: 169-92.

———. 2004b. "The Relationship Between Autonomous and Morally Responsible Agency." In J. S. Taylor, ed., *Personal Autonomy*. Cambridge: Cambridge University Press, pp. 205-34.

———. 2003. "Robustness, Control, and the Demand for Morally Significant Alternatives." In *Moral Responsibility and Alternative Possibilities*. Eds., Widerker and McKenna. 2003.

———. 2001a. "John Martin Fischer and Mark Ravizza, *Responsibility & Control*." *Journal of Philosophy*, XCVIII, No. 2: 93-100.

———. 2001b. "Source Incompatibilism, Ultimacy, and the Transfer of Non-responsibility." *American Philosophical Quarterly* 38: 37-51.

———. 2000a. "Assessing Reasons-Responsive Compatibilism: J.M. Fischer and M. Ravizza's *Responsibility and Control*." *International Journal of Philosophical Studies* Vol. 8, No.1: 89-114.

———. 2000b. "Toward a Speaker Meaning Theory of Moral Responsibility." In Ton van den Beld, ed., *Responsibility & Ontology*. Dordrecht: Kluwer Academic Publishers: 247-58.

———. 1998. "The Limits of Evil and the Role of Moral Address: A Defense of Strawsonian Compatibilism." *Journal of Ethics* Vol. 2, No. 2: 123-42.

Mele, Alfred. 1995. *Autonomous Agents*. New York: Oxford University Press.

Mele, Alfred, and David Robb. 2003. "Bbs, Magnets and Seesaws: The Metaphysics of Frankfurt-style Cases." In Widerker and McKenna eds. (2003) 127-38.

———. 1998. "Rescuing Frankfurt-Style Cases." *Philosophical Review* 107: 97-112.

O'Connor, Timothy. 2000. *Persons and Causes*. New York: Oxford University Press.

Nahmias, Eddy, Stephen Morris, Thomas Nadelhoffer, and Jason Turner. 2006. *Philosophy and Phenomenological Research*. 73: 28-53.

Nichols, Shaun. 2006. "Folk Intuitions on Free Will." *Journal of Cognition and Culture*. 6 (1&2): 57-86.

Pereboom, Derk. 2001. *Living Without Free Will*. Cambridge: Cambridge University Press.

Scanlon, T.M. 1998. *What We Owe to Each Other*. Cambridge, Mass.: Harvard University Press.

Sellars, Wilfred. 1966. "Fatalism and Determinism," In Lehrer, ed. 1966.

Strawson, P. F. 1962. "Freedom and Resentment." *Proceedings of the British Academy* 48: 187-211.

Stump, Eleonore. 1996. "Libertarian Freedom and the Principle of Alternative Possibilities." In Howard-Snyder and Jordan, 1996: 73-88.

van Inwagen, Peter. 1983. *An Essay on Free Will*. Oxford: Clarendon Press.

———. 1975. "The Incompatibility of Free Will and Determinism." *Philosophical Studies*. 27:185-99.

Wallace, R. Jay. 1994. *Responsibility and the Moral Sentiments.* Cambridge, MA.: Harvard University Press.

Watson, Gary. 1987. "Responsibility and the Limits of Evil: Variations on a Strawsonian Theme." In Schoeman, 1987: 256-86.

Widerker, David. 1995. "Libertarianism and Frankfurt's Attack on the Principle of Alternative Possibilities." *Philosophical Review* 104: 247-61.

Widerker, David, and Michael McKenna, eds. 2003. *Moral Responsibility and Alternative Possibilities.* Aldershot, UK: Ashgate Press.

Wiggins, David. 1973. "Towards a Reasonable Libertarianism." In Honderich 1973: 31-62.

15
Alfred R. Mele

Professor of Philosophy

Florida State University, USA

---

1. Why were you initially drawn to theorizing about action and agency?

That happened long ago; it's hard to know. The article that interested me most as an undergraduate, as I recall, was Donald Davidson's "How Is Weakness of the Will Possible?" I was also fascinated then by some of Aristotle's work – particularly the *Nicomachean Ethics*, and especially the theory developed there about how human actions – including those that manifest weakness of will (or *akrasia*, in Aristotle's Greek) – are to be explained. (I also took psychology courses as an undergraduate, but behaviorism was still very popular, and I found it uninspiring.) I suppose I had an antecedent interest in how human behavior is to be explained that was sharpened by some of what I read in undergraduate philosophy courses.

My dissertation was entitled *Aristotle's Theory of Human Motivation*. During my first few years as an assistant professor, I thought I would devote my career to ancient Greek philosophy. But I soon got caught up in the action theoretic issues that concerned Plato and Aristotle. At about the same time, owing to an invitation to serve as a commentator on a paper on self-deception by Robert Audi, I acquired an interest in self-deception. My first published articles outside of ancient philosophy were on self-deception and weakness of will. The subtitle of my first book (published in 1987) shows that those interests continued for a while: *Irrationality: An Essay on Akrasia, Self-Deception, and Self-Control*. And I still write articles on akratic action and self-deception.

Akratic action certainly is a topic in the philosophy of action. It isn't clear that self-deception is; but self-deception is connected in some interesting ways to akratic action (as several philosophers have observed), and lots of philosophers who are known for their good work in the philosophy of action have also written on self-deception: for example, Robert Audi, Donald Davidson, David Pears, and Amelie Rorty. In any case, by the time I completed my first book, I was definitely interested in developing a detailed theory about how intentional actions are to be explained; and because psychology had broken the chains of behaviorism, I was reading a lot of psychology then too – especially motivational psychology.

2. What do you consider to be your own most important contribution(s) to theorizing about action and agency, and why?

I suppose I consider my most important contribution in this area to be something approaching a general philosophy of action. I started with pretty specific questions: for example, questions about how to account for akratic actions, what is involved in exercising self-control, whether intentions play a role in producing actions that goes beyond any role that can be played by combinations of beliefs and desires, what it is for a desire to be irresistible, how decisions are related to intentions, what is it for a state essentially to constitute motivation to act, what can be added to an ideally self-controlled agent (self-control being understood as the contrary of *akrasia*) to yield an autonomous or free agent, and how compatibilists and libertarians about free will should reply to apparent problems that different kinds of luck pose for their theories. And I now have, among other things, something approaching a general theory about how actions are to be explained that includes accounts of such explanatory items as desires (including action-desires), intentions, and decisions. My philosophy of action also yields judgments about such things as what makes intentional actions intentional and what makes free actions free.

3. What other sub-disciplines in philosophy and non- disciplines stand to benefit the most from philosophical work on the nature of action and agency, and how might such engagement be accomplished?

My approach to the philosophy of action has always included an empirical component. For example, when I wrote *Irrationality*, I naturally wanted to tackle the conceptual possibility of akratic action; but I also wanted to understand how akratic actions are produced. In the latter connection, I drew on empirical work on impulsiveness and delay of gratification. In my opinion, the road here does not run just one way – from science to philosophy. Good work in the philosophy of action can shed light on data produced by scientific experiments and contribute to experimental design.

I will offer an example of this that is connected to some recent and current work of mine. The editors of a recent volume entitled *Does Consciousness Cause Behavior?* report that "the wide promulgation of two new lines of genuinely scientific (that is to say, experimental) evidence has seized the philosophical and scientific imagination and again brought the whole question [whether consciousness causes behavior] to the forefront of intellectual debate" (Pockett, *et al.* 2006, p. 1). They then identify neurobiologist Benjamin Libet and psychologist Daniel Wegner as the sources of these two new lines of evidence. Libet contends that the brain decides to initiate actions about a third of a second before the person becomes aware of the decision and that the remaining window of opportunity for free will to get involved is tiny – about 100 milliseconds. Wegner argues that conscious intentions are not causes of corresponding actions. Both Libet and Wegner focus on *proximal* decisions and intentions – roughly, decisions and intentions to do something *now*.

Scientific evidence is accessible to philosophers, and philosophical argumentation and analysis are accessible to scientists. Even so, some members of each group are dismissive of what the other group has to offer. After writing that "many of the world's leading neuroscientists have not only accepted our findings and interpretations, but have even enthusiastically praised these achievements and their experimental ingenuity" and naming twenty such people, Libet adds: "It is interesting that most of the negative criticism of our findings and their implications have come from philosophers and others with no significant experience in experimental neuroscience of the brain" (2002, p. 292). Later in the article, he writes of one of his critics, "As a philosopher Gomes exhibits characteristics often found in philosophers. He seems to think one can offer reinterpretations by making unsupported assumptions, offering speculative data that do not exist and constructing hypotheses that are not even testable" (p. 297). (Incidentally, Gilberto Gomes informed me that he works in a psychology department.) This is not a one-way street. More than a few philosophers, after hearing a talk of mine on Libet's or Wegner's work, have suggested, on a priori grounds, that they could not have been right anyway. I believe that this dismissiveness is a mistake – on each side.

I have written more than a few things on Libet's and Wegner's work, and I am currently writing a book – *Effective Intentions: The Power of Conscious Will* – that includes detailed critiques of the work of both scientists. I'll focus on Libet here. He contends that "If the 'act now' process is initiated unconsciously, then conscious free will is not doing it" (2001, p. 62).

Libet's claim that this process is initiated unconsciously is based largely on a well-known experiment of his. Subjects are regularly encouraged to flex their right wrists whenever they wish. In subjects who do not report any advance planning of their movements, electrical readings from the scalp (EEG readings) – averaged over at least 40 flexing actions for each subject – show a shift in readiness potentials (RPs) beginning about 550 ms before the time at which an electromyogram shows relevant muscular activity to begin. These are type II RPs. Subjects who are not regularly encouraged to aim for spontaneity or who report some advance planning produce RPs that begin about half a second earlier – type I RPs. The same is true of subjects instructed to flex at a prearranged time. (According to a common use of the expression "readiness potential," the RP is a measure of activity in the motor cortex that precedes voluntary muscle motion and, by definition, EEGs generated in situations in which there is no muscle burst do not count as RPs.)

Subjects are also instructed to recall where a revolving spot was on a special clock when they first became aware of something, x, that Libet variously describes as a decision, intention, urge, wanting, will, or wish to move. (The spot on this Libet clock moves about twenty-five times faster than the second hand on a normal clock.) On average, the onset of type II RPs preceded what the subjects reported to be the time of their initial awareness of x (time W) by 350 ms. Time W, then, preceded the beginning of muscle motion by about 200 ms. Libet's findings for type II RPs may be represented as follows:

Libet's findings for type II RPs
-550 ms   -200 ms   0 ms

RP onset   time W   muscle begins to move

(Libet finds independent evidence of what he regards as an error in subjects' recall of the times at which they first become aware of sensations. Correcting for it, time W is -150 ms.)

One inference that Libet makes on the basis of these findings is that the brain produces a proximal decision or intention to flex about a third of a second before the subject becomes aware of that decision or intention. Is this inference warranted? One alternative hypothesis is that what the brain produces around -550 ms is a *potential cause* of a subsequent proximal decision or intention to flex and that the decision or intention emerges significantly later. Libet's findings do not contradict this hypothesis.

How might one get evidence about whether the onset of the type II RPs at -550 ms is correlated with an unconscious proximal decision or intention to flex or instead a potential cause of a proximal decision or intention to flex? An apt question to ask in this connection is how long it takes a proximal intention to flex to generate muscle activity (a muscle burst). If, in fact, the brain produces proximal decisions or intentions in Libet's study about 550 ms before the muscle burst, then, in his subjects, it takes those decisions or intentions about 550 ms to produce a muscle burst. Is this a realistic figure?

Some reaction-time studies provide relevant evidence. In one relevant study (Haggard and Magno 1999), the mean time between the sounding of the go signal and the muscle burst was 231 ms. The subjects (who were watching a Libet clock) were instructed to respond as rapidly as possible to the go signal by pressing a button. If detection of the go signal produced a proximal intention to press the button, then the mean time between a subject's acquiring a proximal intention to press and the muscle burst was less than 231 ms. (Detecting a go signal takes time.) And notice how close this is to Libet's time W – his subjects' reported time of their initial awareness of something he variously describes as an intention, urge, wanting, decision, will, or wish to move (-200 ms). Even without putting a great deal of weight on the exact number, one can fairly observe that if proximal intentions to flex are acquired in Libet's studies, the finding just reported makes it look like a much better bet that they are acquired around time W than that they are acquired around -550 ms.

Someone might object that in reaction time studies of the kind described, muscle bursts and actions are not produced by proximal intentions but by something else. It may be claimed, for example, that the combination of subjects' conditional intentions to press whenever they detect the go signal together with their detection of it produces muscle bursts and pressings without the assistance of any proximal intentions to press. But if this claim is accepted, a parallel claim about Libet's studies should be taken very seriously. The parallel claim is that, in Libet's studies, the muscle bursts and actions are not produced by proximal intentions but by the combination of subjects' conditional intentions to flex whenever they detect a conscious proximal urge to flex together with their detection of such an urge. Someone who makes this claim may hypothesize that the onset of the type II RPs at -550 ms is correlated with a potential cause of a conscious proximal urge to flex. Libet's findings do not contradict this hypothesis.

Even if Libet is wrong in thinking that the brain produces proximal intentions or decisions to flex at about -550 ms, his claim about the 100 ms window of opportunity for free will is interesting. Libet's idea is that free will can only be exercised consciously and, therefore, can only be exercised after his subjects become conscious of proximal intentions, decisions, or urges to flex (and before it is too late to stop what is in place from generating a muscle burst). He contends that free will can be exercised only in vetoing the decision, intention, or urge of which the person has become conscious. One alternative hypothesis is that Libet's subjects exercise free will in consciously deciding to flex rather than after they become conscious of such a decision (or intention or urge). Given that Libet's findings do not justify the inference that proximal decisions to flex are made before the subjects are conscious of any such decision, they do not contradict the present hypothesis.

Libet's findings are sometimes said to support the thesis that conscious intentions and decisions do not play any role at all in producing corresponding actions. It is claimed that they are caused by the same brain events that cause actions and that they are not themselves in the causal chain that results in action. Sometimes the following assertion is offered in support of the preceding one: Subjects' conscious proximal intentions to flex cannot be among the causes of their flexing actions because those intentions are caused by unconscious brain events. This assertion is badly misguided, as attention to the following analogous assertion shows: Burnings of fuses cannot be among the causes of explosions of firecrackers because burnings of fuses are caused by lightings of fuses. Obviously, both the lighting of its fuse and the burning of its fuse are among the causes of a firecracker's exploding in normal scenarios. Other things being equal, if the fuse had not been lit – or if the lit fuse had stopped burning early – there would have been no explosion. There is no reason to believe that the more proximal causes of firecracker explosions cannot themselves have causes. Analogously, there is no reason to believe that items that are among the relatively proximal causes of flexing actions cannot themselves have causes and cannot be caused by unconscious brain events.

Might it be that conscious proximal intentions to flex are part of the causal chain leading to the flexing actions of Libet's subjects? Someone who wishes to answer this question should take a step backward and ask another: Is the brain activity registered by, for example, the first 300 ms of type II RPs – *type 300 activity*, for short – as tightly connected to subsequent flexing actions as lightings of firecracker fuses are to exploding firecrackers? In fact, no one knows. In the experiments that yield Libet's type II RPs, it is the muscle burst that triggers a computer to make a record of the preceding brain activity. In the absence of a muscle burst, there is no record of that activity. So, for all anyone knows, there were many occasions on which type 300 activity occurred in Libet's subjects and there were no associated flexing actions.

Libet mentions that some subjects encouraged to flex spontaneously report that they sometimes aborted or suppressed conscious proximal urges to flex. As he points out, because there was no muscle activation, there was no trigger to initiate the computer's recording of any RP that may have preceded the veto. So, for all anyone knows, type 300 activity was present before the urges were suppressed.

Notice that it is urges that these subjects are said to report and suppress. Might it be that type 300 activity is a potential cause of conscious urges to flex in Libet's subjects and that some subjects make no decision about when to flex – unconsciously or otherwise – until after the conscious urge emerges? And might it be that prior to the emergence of the conscious urge, subjects have no proximal intention to flex? That our urges often are generated by processes of which we are not conscious is not at all surprising. And if we sometimes make effective decisions about whether or not to act on a conscious urge, so much the better for free will. Moreover, Libet's data do not show that subjects have unconscious proximal intentions to flex before they have conscious proximal intentions to flex. The data do not contradict the hypothesis that what precedes these conscious intentions is a causal process that includes no unconscious proximal decisions or intentions to flex.

Two points made thus far merit emphasis. Libet's data do not warrant either of the following claims: (1) what happens earlier than, say, -200 ms in his subjects is causally sufficient for a muscle burst to occur at 0 ms; (2) his subjects have proximal intentions to flex before they think they do. Some related issues merit attention.

Even if claim 2 is not warranted by Libet's data, his idea that we have unconscious proximal intentions should not be lightly dismissed. Such intentions may be at work when, for example, experienced drivers flip their turn indicators to signal for turns they are about to make. In a study in which subjects are instructed to flex whenever they feel like it without also being instructed to report after flexing on when they first became aware of an intention, urge, or decision to flex, would they often be conscious of proximal intentions, urges, or decisions to flex? Might unconscious proximal intentions to flex – and, more specifically, proximal intentions of which they are never conscious – be at work in producing flexing actions in the imagined scenario?

Imagine that someone conducts the experiment just sketched and discovers (somehow) that the subjects were never or rarely conscious of proximal urges, intentions, or decisions to flex. Could it legitimately be inferred that, in Libet's own experiment, conscious urges, intentions, and decisions had no effect on the flexing actions? No. One possibility is that some of Libet's subjects treat their initial consciousness of an urge to flex as a go signal. If they do, the conscious urge seemingly has a place in the causal process that issues in the flexing. Another possibility is that some subjects treat the conscious urge as what may be called a "decide signal" – a signal calling for them consciously to decide right then whether to flex right away or to wait a while. If that is so, and if they consciously decide to flex and execute that decision, the conscious urge again seemingly has a place in the causal process, as does the conscious decision.

Perhaps it will be suggested that even if a subject treats a conscious urge to flex as a go or decide signal, that urge has no place in the causal process that issues in a flexing action because an unconscious brain event caused the conscious urge. But the inference here has the same form as the badly misguided assertion about conscious intention discussed earlier. An x can be among the causes of a y even if the x itself is caused. Possibly, it will be claimed that by the time the conscious urge emerges it is too late for the subject to refrain from acting on it (something that Libet denies) and that is why the conscious urge should not be seen as part of the process at issue, even if subjects think they are treating the urge as a go or decide signal. One way to get evidence about this is to conduct an experiment in which subjects are instructed to flex at a time, t, unless they hear a stop signal. By varying the interval between the stop signal and the mean time of the completion of a full flex when there is no stop signal, experimenters can try to ascertain when subjects reach the point of no return. (Time t can be a designated point on a Libet clock, and brain activity can be measured backward from t.) Perhaps it will be discovered that that point is reached significantly later than time W. (Of course, some researchers and theorists worry about how seriously subjects' reports of their first awareness of a proximal urge or intention to flex – time W – should be taken.)

Well, I've gone on longer about Libet's work than I originally intended. But I hope I have conveyed a sense of how knowledge of the philosophy of action can be useful both in interpreting scientific data and in experimental design. The philosophy of action has strong natural connections to many fields outside of philosophy – including neuroscience, various branches of psychology, law, economics, and even literary theory and theater. And, of course, the philosophy of action is tightly linked to a variety of issues in the philosophy of mind, ethics, and metaphysics.

4. What do you regard as the most neglected issues in contemporary work on action and agency that deserve more attention?

Here I must admit to being stumped. So much is being published now that it is difficult for any interesting topic to count as neglected.

5. What are the most important open problems in philosophical theorizing about action and agency, and what are the prospects for progress?

Almost any interesting topic in any area of philosophy is open in the sense that competing views about it are being advanced in the literature. It is difficult to predict what topics in the philosophy of action will receive the most attention in the next few years. But I don't mind guessing. The literature on free will is livelier now than ever, and I expect that to continue. Experimental philosophy, which is in its infancy, is getting a lot of attention; and it has a strong action theoretic component. Three hot topics there are folk concepts of intentional action, free will, and moral responsibility. (Data are gathered by asking lay folk to read vignettes and to make judgments about whether, for example, Ann intentionally did A.) I expect interest in action theoretic topics in this new field of philosophy to grow for at least a few years. Interest in topics at the intersection of the philosophy of action and science (especially neuroscience) is virtually certain to increase; and I do hope that young philosophers who take up these topics will have as firm a foundation in the philosophy of action as they do in the relevant sciences.

The prospects for progress are excellent in experimental philosophy, because it is such a young field. Interesting hypotheses will be generated by reflection on the data that have been gathered so far, new studies will be designed to gather pertinent data, and more will be learned about how lay folk use the relevant terms. In the area of action theory and science, progress will be promoted by scientific advances. Knowledge of what goes on in the brain when we act is growing by leaps and bounds; and it has a bearing on a host of issues in the philosophy of action, including how intentional actions are produced, why people sometimes resist temptation and sometimes succumb to it, and how we know what we're doing (when we do know this). Psychological research outside of neuroscience also is producing a lot of data of interest to philosophers of action. *Are We Free? Psychology and Free Will* (Baer, *et al.* 2008), edited by a trio of psychologists, merits special mention here.

What are the prospects for progress on free will? In my opinion, the main competing theories about the concept of free will (or free action) have been developed much more thoroughly than was the case even fifteen years ago, and we have a much clearer view of the main problems for each position and interesting proposed resolutions of some of those problems. Perhaps the dispute between compatibilists and incompatibilists will persist as long as philosophy does, but progress on an issue doesn't require universal agreement about it. My own tack – both in *Autonomous Agents* and in *Free Will and Luck* – has included developing two overlapping conceptions of free will: one for compatibilists and the other for incompatibilists. Given my incompatibilist conception, whether any human being ever acts freely is a challenging question. The answer depends on, among other things, whether human brains are suitably indeterministic. And who knows what future neuroscience may turn up? If my compatibilist conception of free will is correct, it is a good bet that there is a lot of free action. Naturally, I claim that my accounts of free action are superior to the others in the literature. I developed them partly in response to problems with other accounts, and I believe that I made progress in understanding free will. And when philosophers produce accounts that are superior to mine, they will have made further progress.

References

Aristotle. *Nicomachean Ethics*. Vol. 9 of W. Ross, ed. *The Works of Aristotle*. London: Oxford University Press, 1915.

Baer, John, J. C. Kaufman, and R. Baumeister, eds. 2008. *Are We Free? Psychology and Free Will*. New York: Oxford University Press.

Davidson, Donald. 1970. "How Is Weakness of the Will Possible?" In J. Feinberg, ed. *Moral Concepts*. Oxford: Clarendon Press.

Haggard, Patrick, and E. Magno. 1999. "Localising Awareness of Action with Transcranial Magnetic Stimulation." *Experimental Brain Research* 127: 102-07.

Libet, Benjamin. 2001. "Consciousness, Free Action and the Brain," *Journal of Consciousness Studies* 8: 59-65.

2002. "The Timing of Mental Events," *Consciousness and Cognition* 11: 291-99.

Mele, Alfred. 1987. *Irrationality*. New York: Oxford University Press.

1995. *Autonomous Agents*. New York: Oxford University Press.

2006. *Free Will and Luck*. New York: Oxford University Press.

2009. *Effective Intentions: The Power of Conscious Will*. New York: Oxford University Press.

Pockett, S., W. Banks, and S. Gallagher, eds. 2006. *Does Consciousness Cause Behavior? An Investigation of the Nature of Volition*. Cambridge, Mass.: MIT Press.

Further Reading

French, Peter, and H. Wettstein, eds. 2007. *Midwest Studies in Philosophy* 31, "Philosophy and the Empirical."

Libet, Benjamin. 2004. *Mind Time*. Cambridge, Mass.: Harvard University Press.

Mele, Alfred. 1992. *Springs of Action: Understanding Intentional Behavior*. New York: Oxford University Press.

───── 2001. *Self-Deception Unmasked*. Princeton, N.J.: Princeton University Press.

───── 2003. *Motivation and Agency*. New York: Oxford University Press.

Wegner, Daniel. 2002. *The Illusion of Conscious Will*. Cambridge, Mass.: MIT Press.

16

Timothy O'Connor

Professor of Philosophy
Indiana University, Bloomington, USA

The Significance of Persons
1. Why were you initially drawn to theorizing about action and agency?

My enduring interest in the nature of agency has two sources. The first is that it is central to the significance of persons. We understand ourselves as individuals bearing a distinctive kind of dignity, flowing in large part from our plight of having to engage in a project of limited self-creation. We understand one another in ethical terms, holding one another morally responsible for our actions and (to a lesser degree) our thoughts and more generally recognizing our achievements and failures, given what we had to work with. Finally, for many of us, agency is also central to our religious understanding of persons. As a philosopher who is also a traditional Christian, I am driven to understand Christian teaching that human beings live in a world that is 'fallen' through the misuse of the human power of choice and, what is more, that our fallen status affects forever more the very freedom of choice that got us into this mess! These doctrinal claims provide a rich problematic for philosophers drawn to difficult conceptual puzzles.

In philosophical training and inclination, I am first and foremost a metaphysician. The second source of my interest in the topic of agency is that, pursued properly, it leads to an exploration of many of the fundamental issues in metaphysics, especially causation, substance, property, and time.

2. What do you consider to be your own most important contribution(s) to theorizing about action and agency, and why?

My focus has been on the subset of human actions that appear to directly manifest our freedom or autonomy. Much of what we do is more or less 'automatic', involving the execution of familiar behaviors in familiar circumstances, with little or no forethought and without active, consciously-monitored control. If all of our actions were like that—or even if they occasionally also involved real deliberation whose outcome invariably yielded some one choice as the 'obvious' one, overwhelmingly preferable to any alternatives—then agency would have far less philosophical interest. As things stand, the whole range of phenomena that falls in the category of agency, from the most deliberately and autonomously initiated to the most inattentive and automatic, is of keen philosophical interest, but the interest largely derives, it seems to me, from its bearing on the puzzle of human freedom.

The puzzle of human freedom has both a purely conceptual side—what would it be, for any kind of agent, to have free will?—and a more empirical side—how can human persons wholly embedded within a world such as our own, a world of fundamentally impersonal causes, be free? Over the last half-century, there have been continued attempts to develop answers to these questions that are broadly reductionist, at least in an ontological sense of reduction: they attempt to understand human choices and actions as wholly consisting in physical processes of a more fundamental, subpersonal sort (even if the conceptual machinery required to give a theory of agency cannot be reduced to the conceptual machinery required to analyze physical processes generally). I take such reductionist approaches to have resulted in dead ends. When a phenomenon persistently resists reduction, you are faced with a choice between elimination (deeming the supposed phenomena to be illusory) or expansion in one way or another of the permissible conceptual and ontological primitives in your theoretical picture. I find elimination to be implausible (while not incredible), though a number of theorists endorse it either explicitly or tacitly, through the development of what look to be deflationary surrogates. My central contribution to action theory is to help to revive an older philosophical tradition that maintains a robustly nonreductionist account of autonomous agency. This tradition conceives our freedom to manifest itself through the exercise of a distinctively personal causal capacity, the capacity to directly generate one's own choices. (This view is commonly known as the theory of 'agent causation.')

The agent-causal approach to free action has been roundly dismissed in much of the twentieth century as obscure, mysterious, or downright incoherent. I have sought to respond to these charges by showing how non-reductive conceptual elucidation is possible, despite the primitiveness of the agent-causal relation itself (see my 1995 and more fully my 2000). This non-reductive analysis does vitally depend on certain metaphysical claims, such as the claim that causation more generally is a basic feature of the world. So it is not surprising that the agent-causalist picture has been especially disdained by those who shared in the long-standing antipathy to metaphysics that runs from the 18th-century Scottish philosopher David Hume through the logical positivists and their immediate heirs in the 20th Century. But I have had the happy fortune to come of age in the midst of a revival of metaphysics, and so long-dead views of many sorts are now back on the table, and I hope to see the theory of agent causation increasingly become one of them.

Thus, I approach action theory as a branch of metaphysics, and you can't see adequately the strengths and weaknesses of competing views until you set them in a larger metaphysical framework. Let me give a simple example of what I have in mind. Some philosophers (myself included) believe that freedom of action and moral responsibility are incompatible with causal determinism, the thesis (roughly) that the true laws of nature plus a complete description of the state of the world at any one time entails what happens at any other time, in every detail. If you like, deterministic laws take a snapshot of the universe at one time as 'input' and yield a determinate answer for what happens at every other time. Philosophers who see this picture of the way the world unfolds as incompatible with freedom reason as follows: it's not up to any human person right now either to determine the way the world was in the past or what constitute the laws of nature. But, given determinism, every action the person will perform henceforth is a logical consequence of those two things. And it seems true in general that whatever logically follows from things that are in no sense up to me are themselves things that are not up to me. Hence, if determinism is true, what I do in the future is not now up to me. (See my 2000 for a fuller discussion of this sort of argument, which was first articulated in formal terms by Peter van Inwagen.) Now, *some* philosophers who reject this line of thought do so because they think it rests on bad, antiquated metaphysics. They seem rather hastily to embrace the thought that determinism poses no challenge to freedom and responsibility once we follow Hume in discarding the 'mysterious' idea that either causation or the laws of nature involve or describe a 'necessary connection' between cause and effect, a kind of metaphysical glue that spreads from the past into the future, literally constraining what is to come. If instead causation and the laws are derivative features of the world, a mere reflection of the fundamental pattern into which events happen to fall through time, then the past and the laws don't literally control what the future will bring, including our own actions. *Go light on the metaphysics*, in other words, and the problem dissolves. But let us consider a consequence of the allegedly more palatable metaphysics on offer by the neo-Humeans. Whether the events involving my typing these words constitute an action partly depends, nearly all will agree, on whether there are appropriate causal connections at play. If the future were to unfold in accordance with very different fundamental patterns than those that held sway hitherto (or with no interesting patterns at all)—and it is precisely the neo-Humean's point that nothing that has occurred up to now ensures that they won't—then the series of events that might at the time have looked like an action will turn out not to have been any kind of an action at all. What conclusion should we draw from this strange, even grotesque state of affairs, on which whether you or I have ever performed so much as a single action is still an open matter, and will remain open long after our deaths? I suggest this: if all this is so, then however the radically contingent, 'loose and separate' events of the future fall out, whether validating certain events as actions or not, then for any one of them, it surely wasn't *up to me* just then—something I made to be the case at that very time— that I did what I did (if indeed I did anything at all). The very dependency of the facts of agency on the entire world history, in the neo-Humean scheme of things, itself supplies grave grounds for doubt about the possibility of freedom and responsibility in anything but a highly deflationary sense.

Now, the consequences drawn on either side of the exchange I have just sketched are much debated. My point was merely to illustrate that the broader metaphysics one adopts has prima facie consequences for how one should think about the nature of agency. This point is not as widely appreciated as it should be. In this respect, the state of play in much of recent action theory is similar to that of philosophy of mind in the same period, another area of metaphysical inquiry that has tended (wrongly, in my view) to see itself as independent of, rather than a special branch of, metaphysics. We're now seeing a degree of correction in the latter, and it's urgently needed in the philosophy of action.

3. What other sub-disciplines in philosophy and non- disciplines stand to benefit the most from philosophical work on the nature of action and agency, and how might such engagement be accomplished?

It is a curious and unfortunate fact that specialists in the philosophy of action and in the philosophy of mind are to a large extent non-overlapping. At any rate, it is certainly true that many of the most influential philosophers of mind have had little of depth to say regarding the theory of action. Much is written about the 'problem of mental causation,' but the problematic assumes nothing more than that beliefs and desires are among 'the causes' of other mental states and of physical behavior. Greater attention to the nature of human agency might lead more theorists of mind to see autonomous action as posing as significant a challenge to physicalism as consciousness and intentionality do.

Outside philosophy, the sciences of brain and behavior might likewise benefit from rigorous philosophical reflection on action. Such interaction is increasing—I am presently co-editing a volume of work bringing together scientists and philosophers under the title *Downward Causation and the Neurobiology of Free Will*. My impression is that psychologists and neuroscientists tend to think in very crude categories when characterizing commonsense thinking, and this leads many of them to see no prospects for integrating a robust conception of human control over their own actions with the detailed but very partial and localized findings that have steadily emerged from social psychology, neuroscience and clinical psychiatric studies. (A prime specimen of this crudity is Daniel Wegner's widely-discussed *The Illusion of Conscious Will*, which is otherwise a lively and informative survey of these scientific findings.) Theorists of action could hope, in turn, for insight from the sciences concerning the role of conscious awareness in agency and the detailed nature of one's awareness of one's own choices. (For me, a central moral of the famous studies by Benjamin Libet on the timing of conscious willing is the need for a better science of the phenomenal character of one's conscious awareness immediately prior to the forming of conscious choices.)[1]

Finally, certain views within philosophical ethics and the philosophy of religion begin from strong assumptions about the autonomous nature of human agency. Insofar as careful reflection on the sciences of human action suggests a revised conception, one that emphasizes the fragile and limited character of our control over our own actions, these other views need to be revised or discarded.

4. What do you regard as the most neglected issues in contemporary work on action and agency that deserve more attention?

The most neglected task in the theory of action until very recently has been that of allowing philosophical accounts of action to be shaped by the empirical sciences. Philosophers, especially those of us who are incompatibilists, are given to simple and idealized conceptions of human freedom. But the ever-accumulating empirical data and emerging partial theories present a messy picture that underscores the fragility of our freedom, and some elements of that picture cannot be readily mapped onto those idealized philosophical theories. The degree of automaticity in ordinary action, while already remarked upon, has been shown to be more pervasive than commonly supposed. Furthermore, it seems plain that human freedom of action, unlike the perfect freedom of God, is always limited, fragile, and variable over time and across agents. It is the sort of thing that can come in degrees, and so any realistic account will have to make room for these characteristics. A theory should indicate the freedom-relevance of factors such as the following:

- degree of awareness of y, for each influencing factor y (desire, intention, belief, or circumstance);

- the relative 'portion' of one's total motivational structure (the totality of influencing factors) of which one is aware;

- degree of likelihood that an unconscious influence y is a factor that one would reflectively endorse, were one to become aware of y's influence. (It is one thing to be partly moved

---

[1] For my own assessment of Libet and other studies sometimes taken to have negative implications for human freedom, see my 2005 and forthcoming.

to act by a presently unconscious desire or intention that is well-integrated into my character. It is another to be motivated by a factor—such as the level of ambient noise—whose relevance I would repudiate if asked.); finally

- the degree to which motivation y is a product of the agent's own past free choices.

This task of integration is just now being taken up by several theorists of action (especially Al Mele and Eddy Nahmias) and it has recently become a main focus of my own research.

A second neglected topic to which, by contrast, I've given no attention, is that of collective agency. Here I have in mind both the idea that in some contexts there are group-wide parameters that exert control over the behavior of its members to a degree that their individual agency seems compromised (some who like radical ideas will even contemplate here the thought that there is a 'group mind' that acts as a unity)[2] and the correlated issue of how the actions of several individuals manage to efficiently co-evolve within tightly-coordinated group contexts. (Is the nature of individual agency different, in interesting fundamental respects, within the context of groups and in the context of solo individual action?)

5. What are the most important open problems in philosophical theorizing about action and agency, and what are the prospects for progress?

It is still an open question whether teleological explanations of actions can in general be reduced to a special case of causal explanations, even setting aside the contentious issue of whether freedom of action requires a more 'metaphysically loaded' account than action *simpliciter*. I am not aware of any detailed causal account

---

[2] The idea that groups of individuals collectively possess intentional states and engage in goal-directed behavior, which states are possessed by and behavior is engaged in by none of the individuals themselves, has begun to receive attention in cognitive science. The most careful and sustained defense of this idea to date is the doctoral dissertation of Georg Theiner ("From Extended Minds to Group Minds: Rethinking the Boundaries of the Mental," Ph.D. thesis in Philosophy and Cognitive Science, Indiana University, 2008). Theiner's argumentative strategy extends the one advanced by Andy Clark and David Chalmers in defending the (individual) 'Extended Mind Hypothesis' ("The Extended Mind," *Analysis* 58 (1998), 10-23).

that provides a thorough and plausible account of the way reasons 'guide' or 'sustain' the performance of an intentional action (in a way that rules out clever philosophical counterexamples) that does not involve some degree of hand-waving.

For a specifically agent-causal approach to free choice and action of the sort I favor, the biggest problem is to develop a plausible account of how reasons guide and explain the agent's autonomous initiation of his own choices. One needs to show how we can be 'influenced' by our beliefs, desires, and longstanding intentions, as well as by environmental factors, without those influences directly producing the choices, thereby undercutting the agent's autonomy. I suspect that what is needed is an imaginative taxonomy of subtly distinct sorts of causal influence; I have made attempts along these lines (2000, 2005), but one thing I'm certain of is that I haven't provided the last word.

Short bibliography of work on agency by Timothy O'Connor:

1995. "Agent Causation," in T. O'Connor (ed.) *Agents, Causes, and Events*. New York: Oxford University Press.

2000. *Persons and Causes: The Metaphysics of Free Will*. New York: Oxford University Press.

2002. "Free Will," *Stanford Online Encyclopedia of Philosophy*. http://plato.stanford.edu/entries/freewill/. Revised in 2005.

2005. "Freedom With a Human Face," *Midwest Studies in Philosophy*, 29, 207-227.

2006. "Reasons Explanation And Agent Control: In Search Of An Integrated Account" (with John Ross Churchill), Philosophical Topics, 32, 241-254.

2009. "Agent-Causal Power," in Toby Handfield, ed., *Dispositions and Causes*, Oxford University Press.

Forthcoming-a. "Conscious Willing and the Emerging Sciences of Brain and Behavior," in T. O'Connor, George F. R. Ellis, and Nancey Murphy (eds.) *Downward Causation And The Neurobiology Of Free Will*. New York: Springer Publications.

Forthcoming-b. *Companion to the Philosophy of Action*, co-edited with Constantine Sandis, Wiley-Blackwell.

17
Derk Pereboom

Professor of Philosophy
Cornell University, USA

My interest in the topic of free will arose in response to the Calvinism with which I was raised. Calvinism *per se* takes no stand on whether theological determinism is true or false, or on whether compatibilism is true or false, although its main theologians tend toward theological determinism and compatibilism. Calvinism does take a specific stand on one issue that involves free will, its role in salvation. Whether one is saved depends on God's election, which is not conditional on any response of the human agent, let alone any freely willed response. The excluded position, advocated by Arminius from the late 16th century (and unfortunately deemed unacceptable by the Cavinism-defining Synod of Dordt of 1618-9), is that election is conditional on a freely willed response of the human agent. Many who grow up as Calvinists its view on salvation deeply disturbing, for the reason that it seems that many of us are caught in a horrific trap, in which one is consigned to a sinful nature independently of one's own agency, and for which one is destined to eternal suffering on the basis of an arbitrary divine decision. In my experience, many Calvinists ignore this central aspect of their theological position, or else compartmentalize it so that it does not affect their everyday thinking. But those who do not ignore or compartmentalize it often find it difficult or impossible to accept.

The most prominent way out is to accept Arminianism, and this sort of position currently dominates Protestant Christianity. In college and graduate school I sided with the Arminian view, advocating an agent-causal libertarian position in support. But another way out is to accept unconditional election together with universal salvation. Calvinist theologian Friedrich Schleiermacher accepted this view (1821-2/1831/1928), and Karl Barth (1936-69) developed it as well, and it is the position that I have found most attractive for the past twenty years (2005b). I think that this view expresses some of what is most valuable in Calvinism, the idea that the process of salvation is too significant to depend at all on the frailty of human volition, while it rejects what is seriously objectionable in some Calvinist views, that God decides to damn some people to hell for eternity in order to express his retributive justice. Since I can remember, I have found retributivism to be implausible, partly because it seems merely to be a cover for vengeful inclinations, and as a result I am skeptical of any view according to which God is motivated by retributivist considerations.

Calvinism's theological determinism and compatibilism undergird further troubling consequences for the drama of salvation, on the supposition that some are damned. Consider these remarks in a sermon on reprobation by a Calvinist with these convictions, Nathaniel Emmons, prominent New England Congregationalist theologian. The scriptural text for the sermon is from the passage in which God hardens Pharaoh's heart on various occasions prior to the exodus of Israel from Egypt (Exodus 8-14):

> It is often thought and said that nothing more was necessary on God's part, in order to fit Pharaoh for destruction, than barely to leave him to himself. But God knew that no external means and motives would be sufficient of themselves to form his moral character. He was determined, therefore, to operate on his heart itself, and cause him to put forth certain evil exercises in the view of certain external motives. When Moses called upon him to let the people go, God stood by him and moved him to refuse. When Moses interceded for him and procured him respite, God stood by him and moved him to exult in his obstinacy. When the people departed from his kingdom, God stood by him and moved him to pursue after them with increased malice and revenge. And what God did on such particular occasions, he did at all times. He continually hardened his heart, and governed all the exercises of his mind, from the day of his birth to the day of his death. This was absolutely necessary to prepare him for his final state. All other methods, without this, would have failed of fitting him for his destruction... Pharaoh was a reprobate. God determined him from eternity to make him finally miserable. This determination he eventually carried into effect. He brought

him into being, formed him a rational and accountable creature, tried him with mercies and judgments, hardened his heart under both, caused him to fill up the measure of his iniquity, and finally cut him off by an act of justice. (Emmons (1860), 327, 330/(1987), 391-2; 395)

Emmons has the firm intuition that while Pharaoh is causally determined by God to do wrong, he is yet free and thus morally responsible. The thought isn't simply that Pharaoh is blameworthy, but that he deserves eternal damnation because of his actions. This is a resolutely compatibilist position. My conviction has always been that the general sorts of anti-compatibilist reactions that Emmons's claims engender in response are correct. In fact, I do not have even the remotest intuition that Emmons's Pharaoh is blameworthy. Here again, one might advocate the libertarian version of incompatibilism, which I did for a time, or else one might side with Schleiermacher and claim that theological determinism is true, but that God does not intend a wretched final disposition for anyone. This is position that I have found more attractive.

Baruch Spinoza lived in the Netherlands in the mid-seventeenth century, where these concerns about free will and determinism, election and reprobation, were features of everyday culture. Spinoza maintained that due to certain general facts about the nature of the universe, which for him is the same thing as God, we human beings do not have the sort of free will required for moral responsibility. I agree. More exactly, he argues that it is because causal determinism is true that we lack this sort of free will; he is thus a hard determinist. By contrast, the position I defend is agnostic about causal determinism. I contend, with Spinoza, that we would not have the sort of free will required for moral responsibility if causal determinism were true, but also that indeterministic theories do not significantly improve the prospects for this sort of free will. As a result we need to take seriously the verdict that we lack the sort of free will required for moral responsibility. I call the resulting view "hard incompatibilism."

My contributions.

(1) Defending hard incompatibilism requires facing up to compatibilism. I believe that the strongest argument against the compatibilist begins with the intuition that if someone is causally determined to act by other agents, for example, by scientists who manipulate her brain, then she is not morally responsible for that

action. The argument continues by showing that there are no differences between cases like this and otherwise similar ordinary deterministic examples that can justify the claim that while an agent is not morally responsible when she is manipulated, she can nevertheless be responsible in the ordinary deterministic examples. This intuition remains strong even if when manipulated the agent satisfies the conditions on moral responsibility advocated by the prominent compatibilist theories. The following "four-case argument" first of all develops examples of actions that involve such manipulation, in which these compatibilist conditions on moral responsibility are satisfied (1995, 2001). These cases, taken separately, indicate that it is possible for an agent not to be morally responsible even if the compatibilist conditions are satisfied, and that as a result these conditions are inadequate. But the argument has more force, by virtue of setting out three such cases, each progressively more like a fourth, which the compatibilist might envision to be realistic, in which the action is causally determined in a natural way. The additional challenge for the compatibilist is to point out a difference between this fourth scenario and one or more of the manipulation cases that shows why the agent might be morally responsible in the ordinary scenario but not in the manipulation examples. I contend that the agent's non-responsibility generalizes from at least one of the manipulation examples to the ordinary case.

In my set-up, in each of the four cases Professor Plum decides to kill Ms. White for the sake of some personal advantage, and succeeds in doing so. I designed the cases so that his act of murder conforms to the prominent compatibilist conditions. Plum's action meets the Humean conditions, since for him selfish reasons typically weigh heavily – too heavily when considered from the moral point of view, while in addition the desire that motivates him to act is nevertheless not irresistible for him, and in this sense he is not constrained to act (Hume 1739/1978). It fits the condition proposed by Harry Frankfurt (1971): Plum's effective desire (i.e., his will) to murder White conforms appropriately to his second-order desires for which effective desires he will have. That is, he wills to murder her, and he wants to will to do so, and he wills this act of murder because he wants to will to do so. The action also satisfies the reasons-responsiveness condition advocated by John Fischer and Mark Ravizza (1998): Plum's desires are modified by, and some of them arise from, his rational consideration of the reasons he has, and if he knew that the bad consequences for himself that would result from killing White would be much more severe than they are actually likely to be, he would have refrained from killing her for that reason. Also, this action meets the condition advanced by Jay Wallace (1994): Plum possesses the general ability to grasp, apply, and regulate his actions by moral reasons. For instance, when egoistic reasons that count against acting morally are weak, he will typically regulate his behavior by moral reasons instead. This ability also provides him with the capacity to revise and develop his moral character over time. Now, supposing that causal determinism is true, is it plausible that Professor Plum is morally responsible for his action?

Each of the four cases I will now describe features different ways in which Plum's murder of White might be causally determined by factors beyond his control.

> **Case 1**: Professor Plum was created by neuroscientists, and they can manipulate him directly through the use of radio-like technology, but he is as much like an ordinary human being as is possible given these unusual features. The neuroscientists manipulate him to undertake the process of reasoning by which the desires at play in his act of murder are brought about and modified. They do this by pushing a series of buttons just before he begins to reason about his situation, thereby causing his reasoning process to be rationally egoistic. Plum does not think and act contrary to character since his reasoning process is typically rationally egoistic. His effective first-order desire to kill White conforms to his second-order desires. The process of deliberation from which his action results is reasons-responsive; in particular, this type of process would have resulted in his refraining from killing White in some situations in which the egoistic reasons were different. Still, he is not exclusively rationally egoistic, since he typically regulates his behavior by moral reasons when the egoistic reasons are relatively weak – weaker than they are in the current situation. He is also not constrained, in the sense that he does not act because of an irresistible desire – the neuroscientists do not provide him with a desire of this kind.

In Case 1, Plum's action satisfies all the compatibilist conditions we just examined. But intuitively, he is not morally responsible for the murder, because his action is causally determined by what the neuroscientists do, which is beyond his control. Consequently, it would seem that these compatibilist conditions are not sufficient for moral responsibility – even if all taken together.

Compatibilists might resist this conclusion by arguing that although in Case 1 the process resulting in the action satisfies all of the prominent compatibilist conditions, yet Plum's relevant states are directly produced by the manipulators moment by moment – he is locally manipulated – and this is the aspect of the story that undercuts his moral responsibility. In reply, could a time lag between the manipulators' activity and the production of the states in the agent plausibly make the difference as to whether an agent is morally responsible? If the neuroscientists did all of their manipulating during one time interval and, after an appropriate length of time, the states at issue were produced in him, would he only then be morally responsible? My sense is that such a time lag, all by itself, would make no difference to whether the agent is responsible.

Now consider a scenario more like the ordinary situation than Case 1:

> **Case 2**: Plum is like an ordinary human being, except that neuroscientists have programmed him at the beginning of his life to weigh reasons for action so that he is often but not exclusively rationally egoistic, with the consequence that in the circumstances in which he now finds himself, he is causally determined to engage in the reasons-responsive process of deliberation and to have the set of first and second-order desires that result in his killing White. Plum has the general ability to regulate his behavior by moral reasons, but in his circumstances the egoistic reasons weigh very heavily for him, and consequently he is causally determined to murder White. But at the same time he does not act because of an irresistible desire.

Again, although Plum meets each of the compatibilist conditions, intuitively he is not morally responsible. So Case 2 also shows that the prominent compatibilist conditions, either individually or in conjunction, are not sufficient for moral responsibility. Moreover, it would seem unprincipled to claim that here, by contrast with Case 1, Plum is morally responsible because the length of time between the programming and the action is now great enough.

Whether the programming occurs a few seconds or forty years before the action seems irrelevant to the question of his moral responsibility. Causal determination by factors beyond his control plausibly explains Plum's lack of moral responsibility in the first case, and I think we are forced to say that he is not morally responsible in the second case for the same reason.

Imagine next a scenario more similar yet to an ordinary situation:

> **Case 3**: Plum is an ordinary human being, except that he was causally determined by the rigorous training practices of his household and community so that he is often but not exclusively rationally egoistic (exactly as egoistic as in Cases 1 and 2). This training took place when he was too young to have the ability to prevent or alter the practices that determined his character. Consequently, Plum is causally determined to engage in the reasons-responsive process of deliberation and to have the first and second-order desires that result in his killing White. Here again he has the general ability to grasp, apply, and regulate his behavior by moral reasons, but in these circumstances the egoistic reasons are very powerful, and so the training practices of his upbringing, in conjunction with background circumstances, deterministically result in his act of murder. Nonetheless, he does not act on an irresistible desire.

If a compatibilist wants to argue that Plum is morally responsible in Case 3, he needs to come up with a feature of these circumstances that would explain why he is morally responsible here but not in Case 2. It seems there is no such feature. In all of these examples, Plum meets the prominent compatibilist conditions for morally responsible action, so a divergence in judgment about moral responsibility between these examples won't be supported by a difference in whether these conditions are satisfied. Causal determination by factors beyond Plum's control most plausibly explains the absence of moral responsibility in Case 2, and we are constrained to conclude that he is not morally responsible in Case 3 for the same reason.

Therefore it appears that Plum's exemption from responsibility in Cases 1 and 2 generalizes to the nearer-to-normal Case 3. Does it generalize to the ordinary deterministic case?

Case 4: Physicalist determinism is true – everything in the universe is in some sense physical, and every event is rendered inevitable by virtue of the past states of this physical universe in conjunction with causal processes governed by laws of nature. Plum is an ordinary human being, raised in normal circumstances, and he is typically but not exclusively rationally egoistic (just as egoistic as in Cases 1-3). His act of murdering White results from his engaging in the reasons-responsive process of deliberation, and he has the specified first and second-order desires. Although he possesses the general ability to grasp, apply, and regulate his behavior by moral reasons, in these circumstances the egoistic reasons weigh very heavily for him, and he is thus causally determined to kill White. However, it is not due to an irresistible desire that commits this act of murder.

Given that we are forced to deny moral responsibility in Case 3, could Plum be responsible in this ordinary case? It appears that there are no differences between Case 3 and Case 4 that might justify the claim that Plum is not responsible in Case 3 but is in Case 4. One distinguishing feature of Case 4 is that the causal determination of Plum's crime is not brought about by other agents. But the claim that this is a relevant difference is implausible. Imagine a further case that is exactly the same as, say, Case 1 or Case 2, except that the Plum's states are induced by a spontaneously generated machine – a machine with no intelligent designer. Here also Plum would lack morally responsibility.

I think that the best explanation for the intuition that Plum is not morally responsible in the first three cases is that his action is produced by a deterministic causal process that traces back to factors beyond his control. Since Plum's action is also causally determined in this way in Case 4, we should conclude that here again he is not morally responsible. So by this argument, his non-responsibility in Case 1 generalizes to his non-responsibility in Case 4. We need to conclude, I think, that if an action results from a deterministic causal process that traces back to factors beyond the agent's control, she will lack the control required to be morally responsible for it.

(2) While I accept incompatibilism, I reject a type of incompatibilism according to which the availability of alternative possibilities is crucial to explaining moral responsibility, and accept

instead a type that ascribes the more significant role to an action's causal history. I argue that an agent's moral responsibility for an action would be explained not by the existence of alternative possibilities available to her, but rather by the action's having a causal history of a sort that allows the agent to be the source of her action in a specific way. I thus opt for *source* as opposed to *leeway* incompatibilism (McKenna 1999). The standard argument for a source against a leeway position involves constructing appropriate Frankfurt-style examples. I have proposed a Frankfurt-style scenario (2000, 2001, 2003, 2005a) that avoids the objections that have been raised for examples of this sort, by for example, Robert Kane (1985), David Widerker (1995), and Carl Ginet (1997):

> *Tax Evasion*: Joe is considering claiming a tax deduction for the registration fee that he paid when he bought a house. He knows that claiming this deduction is illegal, but that he probably won't be caught, and that if he were, he could convincingly plead ignorance. Suppose he has a strong but not always overriding desire to advance his self-interest regardless of its cost to others and of even if it involves illegal activity. In addition, the only way that in this situation he could fail to choose to evade taxes is for moral reasons. He could not, for example, choose to evade taxes for no reason or simply on a whim. Moreover, it is causally necessary for his failing to choose to evade taxes in this situation that he attain a certain level of attentiveness to moral reasons. Joe can secure this level of attentiveness voluntarily. However, his attaining this level of attentiveness is not causally sufficient for his failing to choose to evade taxes. If he were to attain this level of attentiveness, he could, exercising his libertarian free will, either choose to evade taxes or refrain from so choosing (without the intervener's device in place). However, to ensure that he will choose to evade taxes, a neuroscientist has, unbeknownst to Joe, implanted a device in his brain, which, were it to sense the requisite level of attentiveness, would electronically stimulate the right neural centers so as to inevitably result in his making this choice. As it happens, Joe does not attain this level of attentiveness to moral reasons, and he chooses to evade taxes on his own, while the device remains idle.

In this situation, Joe could be morally responsible for choosing to evade taxes despite the fact that he could not have chosen otherwise than to evade.

The example does feature alternative possibilities that are available to the agent – his achieving higher levels of attentiveness to moral reasons. But these alternative possibilities are not robust. Note first that in ordinary circumstances, without the intervener's device in place, it is not the case that by achieving some higher level of attentiveness Joe would have avoided responsibility for choosing to evade taxes. For under these conditions achieving some higher level of attentiveness is compatible with his not refraining from making this decision, or even ever being seriously inclined so to refrain, and choosing to evade taxes instead. At this point one might object that given that the intervener's device is in place, by voluntarily achieving the specified higher level of attentiveness Joe would have voluntarily done something whereby he would have avoided the blameworthiness he actually incurs. For had he voluntarily achieved the requisite level of attentiveness, the intervention would have taken place, whereupon he would not have been blameworthy for deciding to evade taxes. In reply, Joe does not understand, and, moreover, he has no reason to believe, that voluntarily achieving the requisite level of attentiveness would preclude him from responsibility for choosing to evade taxes, and hence this alternative possibility is not robust. True, were he voluntarily to achieve this attentiveness, the intervention would take place, and he would then not have been responsible for this choice. Nevertheless, Joe does not understand, and has no reason to believe, that the intervention would then take place, and that as a consequence he would be precluded from responsibility for this choice. In fact, one might imagine that he believes that achieving this level of attentiveness is compatible with his freely deciding to evade taxes anyway, and that he has no reason to believe otherwise. Nevertheless, Joe is morally responsible for deciding to evade taxes.

(3) Defending hard incompatibilism also requires confronting libertarianism. There are two major types of libertarianism, the event-causal and the agent-causal versions. In event-causal libertarianism, actions are caused solely by events all actions are caused by solely by events, and some type of indeterminacy in the production of actions by appropriate events is the decisive requirement for moral responsibility (Kane 1996, Ekstrom 2000). I contend that event-causal libertarianism is undermined by a version of the

luck objection (Mele 2006; Pereboom 2001, 2004). Intuitively, for an agent to be morally responsible for a decision, she must exercise a certain type and degree of control in making that decision. In an event-causal libertarian picture, the relevant causal conditions prior to a decision – events that involve the agent – leave it open whether this decision will occur, and the agent has no further causal role in determining whether it in fact does. Thus whether the decision occurs or not is in this sense a matter of luck, and the agent lacks the control required for being morally responsible for it.

Libertarians agree that an action's resulting from a deterministic sequence of causes that traces back to factors beyond the agent's control would rule out her moral responsibility for it. One deeper point of the luck objection is that if this sort of causal determination rules out moral responsibility, then it is no remedy simply to provide slack in the causal net by making the causal history of actions indeterministic. Such a move would yield one prerequisite for moral responsibility – the absence of causal determinism for decision and action – but it would not supply another — sufficiently enhanced control. What needs to be added to the event-causal libertarian story is a further causal involvement of the agent in the making of the decision, a causal involvement that would enhance her control in making a decision over what is present in event-causal and deterministic contexts.

The agent-causal libertarian's solution is to specify a way in which the agent could have this enhanced control. The suggested remedy is to reintroduce the agent as a cause, this time not merely as involved in events, but rather fundamentally as a substance. The agent-causal libertarian claims that we possess a special causal power – a power for an agent, fundamentally as a substance, to cause a decision without being causally determined to do so (O'Connor 2000, Clarke 2003).

I think that the agent-causal position has not been shown to be incoherent (2001, 2004). But can agent-causal libertarianism be reconciled with what we would expect given our best physical theories? If the agent-causal position is true, then when an agent makes a free decision, she causes the decision without being causally determined to do so. On the path to action that results from this undetermined decision, changes in the physical world, for example in the agent's brain or some other part of her body, are produced. But if the physical world were generally governed by deterministic laws, it seems that here we would encounter divergences from these laws. For the changes in the physical world that result from the undetermined decision would themselves not be causally determined, and they would thus not be governed by the deterministic laws. One might object that it is possible that the physical changes that result from every free decision just happen to dovetail with what could in principle be predicted on the basis of the deterministic laws, so nothing actually happens that diverges from these laws. But this proposal would seem to involve coincidences too wild to be believed. For this reason, agent-causal libertarianism is not plausibly reconciled with the physical world's being governed by deterministic laws.

On the standard interpretation of quantum mechanics, however, the physical world is not in fact deterministic, but is rather governed by probabilistic statistical laws. However, wild coincidences would also arise on this suggestion. Consider the class of possible actions each of which has a physical component whose antecedent probability of occurring is approximately 0.32. It would not violate the statistical laws in the sense of being logically incompatible with them if, for a large number of instances, the physical components in this class were not actually realized close to 32% of the time. Rather, the force of the statistical law is that for a large number of instances it is correct to *expect* physical components in this class to be realized close to 32% of the time. Are free choices on the agent-causal libertarian model compatible with what the statistical law leads us to expect about them? If they were, then for a large enough number of instances the possible actions in our class would almost certainly be freely chosen close to 32% of the time. But if the occurrence of these physical components were settled by the choices of agent-causes, then their actually being chosen close to 32% of the time would amount to a wild coincidence. The proposal that agent-caused free choices do not diverge from what the statistical laws predict for the physical components of our actions would run so sharply counter to what we would expect as to make it incredible. (Pereboom 1995, 2001, 2005a)

At this point, the libertarian might propose that there actually do exist divergences from the probabilities that we would expect without the presence of agent-causes, and that these divergences are to be found at the interface between the agent-cause and that which it directly affects – an interface which is likely to be found in the brain. The problem for this proposal, however, is that we have no evidence that such divergences occur. This difficulty, all by itself, provides a strong reason to reject this approach.

Thus all versions of libertarianism face serious difficulties. Since compatibilism is vulnerable to an argument from manipulation cases, the position that remains is hard incompatibilism, which denies that we have the sort of free will required for moral responsibility. The concern for this view is not, I think, that there is significant empirical evidence that it is false, or that there is a good argument that it is somehow incoherent, and false for that reason. Rather, the questions it faces are practical: What would life be like if we believed it was true? Is this a sort of life that we can tolerate? In responding to these questions, I have been inspired by others who have done excellent work in answering them, including Spinoza (1677/1985), Galen Strawson (1986), Ted Honderich (1988); Bruce Waller (1990), and Saul Smilansky (2000).

(4) Accepting hard incompatibilism demands giving up our ordinary view of ourselves as blameworthy for immoral actions and praiseworthy for actions that are morally exemplary. At this point one might object that giving up our belief in moral responsibility would have very harmful consequences, perhaps so harmful that thinking and acting as if hard incompatibilism is true is not a feasible option. Thus even if the claim that we are morally responsible turns out to be false, there may yet be weighty practical reasons to believe that we are, or at least to treat people as if they were.

For instance, one might think that if we gave up the belief that people are blameworthy, we could no longer legitimately judge any actions as wrong or even bad, or as right or good. But this seems mistaken. Even if we came to believe that some perpetrator of genocide was not morally responsible because of some degenerative brain disease he had, we would still maintain that his actions were morally wrong, and that it was extremely bad that he acted as he did. So, in general, denying blameworthiness would not at the same time threaten judgments of wrongness or badness, and, likewise, denying praiseworthiness would not undermine assessments of rightness or goodness.

Does hard incompatibilism have resources adequate for contending with criminal behavior? Here it would appear to be at a disadvantage, and if so, practical considerations might yield strong reasons to treat criminals as if they were morally responsible. First of all, if hard incompatibilism is true, a retributivist justification for criminal punishment unavailable, for it asserts that the criminal deserves pain or deprivation just for committing the crime, while hard incompatibilism denies this claim. And retributivism is one of the most naturally compelling ways to justify criminal punishment.

Deterrence theories have it that punishing criminals is justified for the reason that it deters future crime. The two most-discussed deterrence theories, the utilitarian version and the one that grounds the right to punish on the right to self-defense, are not undermined by hard incompatibilism per se. Still, they are questionable on other grounds. There is, however, an intuitively legitimate theory of crime prevention that is neither undermined by hard incompatibilism, nor by other sort of considerations. This theory draws an analogy between the treatment of criminals and the treatment of carriers of dangerous diseases. Ferdinand Schoeman (1979) argues that if we have the right to quarantine carriers of serious communicable diseases to protect people, then for the same reason we also have the right to isolate the criminally dangerous. Notice that quarantining a person can be justified when she is not morally responsible for being dangerous to others. If a child is infected with a deadly contagious virus that was transmitted to her before she was born, quarantine can still be legitimate. Now imagine that a murderer poses a grave danger to a community. Even if he is not morally responsible for his crimes (say because no one is ever morally responsible), it would be as legitimate to isolate him as it would be to quarantine a non-responsible carrier of a dangerous communicable disease (Pereboom 2001).

Would an affirmation of hard incompatibilism undermine interpersonal relationships? Peter Strawson (1962) contends that the justification for judgments of blameworthiness and praiseworthiness has its foundation the reactive attitudes, reactions to how people voluntarily behave – such as moral resentment, guilt, gratitude, forgiveness, and love. Moreover, because moral responsibility has this kind of foundation, the truth or falsity of determinism is irrelevant to whether we are justified in regarding agents as morally responsible. This is precisely because these reactive attitudes are required for the kinds of interpersonal relationships that make our lives meaningful, and so even if we could give up the reactive attitudes we would never have sufficient practical reason to do so. Strawson believes that it is in fact psychologically impossible for us to give up the reactive attitudes altogether, but in a limited range of cases we can adopt what he calls the "objective attitude," a cold and calculating stance towards others. If determinism did imperil the reactive attitudes, and we were able to relinquish them, Strawson suggests that we would face the prospect of adopting this objective attitude toward everyone, as a result of which our interpersonal relationships would be undermined. Since we have extremely good practical reasons for maintaining these relationships, we would never have sufficient practical reason to adopt the objective attitude in most cases, and hence we would never have sufficient reason to give up our reactive attitudes, and thus to stop regarding people as morally responsible.

I agree that if we persistently maintained an objective attitude toward others, our relationships would be undermined. However, I deny that it would be appropriate to adopt this stance if we came to believe that hard incompatibilism were true. In my conception, some of the reactive attitudes would in fact be challenged by hard incompatibilism, for some of them, such as moral resentment and indignation, would have the false presupposition that the person who is the object of the attitude is morally responsible. But I argue that the reactive attitudes that we would want to retain either are not threatened by hard incompatibilism in this way, or else have analogues or aspects that would not have false presuppositions. The attitudes that would survive do not amount to the objective attitude, and they would be sufficient to sustain good human relationships.

Hard incompatibilism also promises substantial benefits for human life. Of all the attitudes associated with the assumption that we are morally responsible, anger seems most closely connected with it. The kind of anger at issue is the sort that is directed toward a person who is thought to have done wrong. But such moral anger is often destructive, and it is fueled by the belief that its object is morally responsible. Destructive moral anger in relationships is fostered by the assumption that the other is blameworthy. The anger that spawns ethnic conflicts is typically nurtured by the conviction that a group of people deserves blame for past wrongs. Hard incompatibilism advocates relinquishing such beliefs because they are false. As a result, moral anger might diminish, and its expressions subside. But would the benefits that would result if moral anger were modified in this way compensate for the losses that would result? Moral anger motivates opposition to immoral behavior. However, if for hard incompatibilist reasons the assumption that wrongdoers are blameworthy is given up, the belief that they have in fact behaved immorally would not be threatened. Even if those who commit genocide are not morally responsible, their actions are still seriously wrong, and a conviction that this is so would remain unthreatened. Accepting hard incompatibilism would allow us to retain the benefits moral anger can also yield, while also challenging its destructive effects (Pereboom 2001).

The future

The two non-philosophical disciplines that stand to benefit the most from philosophical work on action and agency are psychology and law. Psychologists have recently become very interested in our conceptions of agency and free will, and the role these conceptions have in motivating and sustaining moral action. To my mind, the experiments that psychologists perform to reach their conclusions stand to benefit from the conceptual map of the territory that philosophers have developed, and from philosophers' sense of where to expect that subjects in experiments will misunderstand the scenarios used to prompt responses. Criminal law has largely ignored the threat to moral responsibility from both determinism and the sort of indeterminism that is likely to be true, and I think that this is a serious error. Even if one is not convinced by the arguments against moral responsibility, that we are not morally responsible is significantly probable, and should have its repercussions in criminology. Legal studies would also benefit from reflection on exactly which notions of responsibility are sustained by the features of agency that compatibilist accounts have adduced. It is often assumed that such features of agency are sufficient to undergird a notion of responsibility that in turn justifies retributivism, but this is far from obvious.

Few issues in the area of action and agency are currently neglected, but the field would profit from more work on developing new compatibilist strategies, in exploring further possibilities for agent-causal and event-causal libertarianism, in thinking about whether features of agency such as rational deliberation are compatible with a belief in determinism, or a belief in the type of indeterminism that is most likely to be true. Further psychological investigation into the role of assumptions about free will or its absence would be valuable, as would research into the place of the desert-entailing reactive attitudes in our social lives. Advance in our understanding of these issues over the past two decades has been impressive, and there is no indication that that progress is slowing.

References

Barth, Karl (1936-1969). *Church Dogmatics* Edinburgh, T. & T. Clark.

Clarke, Randolph (2003). *Libertarian Theories of Free Will* (Oxford: Oxford University Press).

Ekstrom, Laura W. (2000). *Free Will: A Philosophical Study* (Boulder: Westview).

Emmons, Nathaniel (1860/1987). *The Works of Nathaniel Emmons, D. D.*, ed. Jacob Ide, D.D., Boston: Congregational Board of Publication, 1860; reprinted New York and London:Garland Publishing Company, 1987.

Fischer, John Martin, and Mark Ravizza (1998). *Responsibility and Control: A Theory of Moral Responsibility*, (New York: Cambridge University Press).

Frankfurt, Harry G. (1971). "Freedom of the Will and the Concept of a Person," *Journal of Philosophy* 68, pp. 5-20.

Ginet, Carl (1996). "In Defense of the Principle of Alternative Possibilities: Why I Don't Find Frankfurt's Arguments Convincing," *Philosophical Perspectives* 10, pp. 403-17.

Honderich, Ted (1988). *A Theory of Determinism* (Oxford: Oxford University Press).

Kane, Robert (1985). *Free Will and Values*, (Albany: SUNY Press).

Kane, Robert (1996). *The Significance of Free Will* (New York: Oxford University Press).

Hume, David. (1739/1978) *A Treatise of Human Nature*, Oxford, Oxford University Press.

Mele, Alfred (2006). *Free Will and Luck*, (Oxford: Oxford University Press).

O'Connor, Timothy (2000). *Persons and Causes*, (Oxford: Oxford University Press).

Pereboom, Derk (1995). "Determinism *Al Dente*," *Nous* 29, pp. 21-45.

Pereboom, Derk (2000). "Alternative Possibilities and Causal Histories, *Philosophical Perspectives* 14, 2000.

Pereboom, Derk (2001). *Living Without Free Will* (Cambridge: Cambridge University Press).

Pereboom. Derk (2003). "Source Incompatibilism and Alternative Possibilities," in *Freedom, Responsibility, and Agency: Essays on the Importance of Alternative Possibilities*, Michael McKenna and David Widerker, eds., Aldershot: Ashgate, pp. 185-99.

Pereboom, Derk (2004). "Is Our Conception of Agent Causation Incoherent?" *Philosophical Topics*. 32, pp. 275-86.

Pereboom. Derk (2005a). "Defending Hard Incompatibilism," *Midwest Studies in Philosophy* 29, pp. 228-47.

Pereboom. Derk (2005b). "Free Will, Evil, and Divine Providence," *God and the Ethics of Belief: New Essays in Philosophy of Religion*, Andrew Chignell and Andrew Dole, eds., Cambridge: Cambridge University Press, 2005, pp. 77-98.

Schleiermacher, Friedrich (1821-2/1831/1928). *The Christian Faith*, Philadelphia: Fortress.

Schoeman, Ferdinand D. (1979). "On Incapacitating the Dangerous," *American Philosophical Quarterly* 16.

Smilansky, Saul (2000). *Free Will and Illusion* (Oxford: Oxford University Press).

Spinoza, Baruch (1677/1985). *Ethics*, in *The Collected Works of Spinoza*, ed. and tr. Edwin Curley, Volume 1, (Princeton: Princeton University Press).

Strawson, Galen (1986). *Freedom and Belief* (Oxford: Oxford University Press).

Strawson, Peter F. (1962). "Freedom and Resentment," *Proceedings of the British Academy* 48 (1962), pp. 1-25.

Wallace, R. Jay (1994). *Responsibility and the Moral Sentiments*, (Cambridge, Harvard University Press).

Waller, Bruce (1990). *Freedom Without Responsibility*, (Philadelphia: Temple University Press).

Widerker, David (1995). "Libertarianism and Frankfurt's Attack on the Principle of Alternative Possibilities," *The Philosophical Review* 104, pp. 247-61.

18
Thomas Pink

Professor of Philosophy

King's College, London

Action Theory

1. Why were you initially drawn to theorizing about action and agency?

At school I had been encouraged towards a career as an academic historian. But while at university at Cambridge I rebelled, and looked for another subject as far removed from history as I could find. I discovered the work of Frank Ramsey and, especially, his paper 'Truth and probability', as well as the work on radical interpretation of Donald Davidson and David Lewis. With the example of young philosophers at my university some years ahead of me, especially Anthony Appiah, then a college research fellow, and encouraged by the work on probability and belief of my postgraduate supervisor, Hugh Mellor, I chose to research on decision and game theory. How far could decision theory provide a descriptive psychology of motivation and action within the framework of a wider functionalist theory of the mind?

That, at any rate, was my doctoral thesis. But dissatisfaction with this project led me to spend four years as a banker in London and America - when I began to change my ideas. Rediscovering interest in my subject, and with the support of the economist Frank Hahn, himself deeply interested in the philosophical foundations of rational choice theory, I returned to a research fellowship at Cambridge, but began to work in quite a new direction, one which brought to bear my early interest in history.

The change had come from reading medieval ethical and psychological theory, especially the work of Aquinas. It soon became obvious that medieval theories of action were radically different from anything in modern philosophy. At the heart of this difference lay the medieval theory of the will - of our decision-making capacity. This theory deployed a conception of decisions that is deeply intuitive. Do we not think that taking decisions is something we do, over which we have control as we have over any action; that it is directly up to us what we decide just as much as it is up to us whether we act as decided? In which case human action involves a special kind of action – a mental action-generating action, by which we can determine in advance which further actions we perform. By virtue of being actions that have further actions, the actions decided upon, as their objects and effects, decisions constitute a form, if you like, of second order agency (see Pink 1996 pp15-18). Moreover this second order agency seems to be of great importance. Our freedom seems to depend on our having control of this second order form of agency in particular, so that freedom of action depends on a freedom specifically of the will. For do we not naturally think that it is up to us what we do only because we have the ability to decide for ourselves what we do, and it is up to us what we decide? These intuitions, that intentional action can occur as an action of the will, and that it must be able to do so for freedom to be possible, were shared by all medieval theorists of action.

But these same intuitions were to be comprehensively and very innovatively rejected in the seventeenth century by the originating genius of modern English-language action theory, Thomas Hobbes. Central to Hobbes's theory of action is the idea of voluntariness – for Hobbes and for me, a technical notion. Voluntariness, for our purposes, is acting as one wills and because one so wills. To do A voluntarily is to do A on the basis of a will or pro attitude towards doing A. According to Hobbes, intentional action just is voluntary action. To do A intentionally, as a means to some end, is to do A on the basis of some decision or desire to do A. And freedom, for Hobbes, comes to a complex form of voluntariness: to have the freedom to do A or not is just to have the capacity to do A or not as one wills.

Hobbes's conclusion was that, contrary to what medieval scholasticism had supposed, there could be no agency or freedom of the will itself. For the will itself, he claimed, is not voluntary.

> I acknowledge this liberty, that I can do if I will, but to say, I can will if I will, I take to be an absurd speech.
> Hobbes 1656 p29

We do not and cannot take decisions to do A on the basis of decisions specifically so to decide.

This dispute between Hobbes and the scholastics fascinated me. What was at issue?

Some modern philosophers of action and freedom have tended to agree with Hobbes outright. We find this view in A. J. Ayer or in Donald Davidson. More recently others have agreed with Hobbes's conceptions of agency and freedom, but have tried to make room for a freedom and action of the will by trying to do what Hobbes refused to do – which is to voluntarize, at least to some degree, the will itself. Voluntariness is supposed to come in higher order form, so that, to some degree, we can will as we will to. This approach is familiar from the work of Harry Frankfurt and his followers (see especially Frankfurt 1971). We find the same variety of approaches within rational choice theory. In rational choice theory to do something voluntarily, on the basis of a pro attitude towards doing it, is treated as utility maximization – as doing what maximizes the agent's expected utility. Now orthodox decision theory continues to suppose that it is the voluntary actions decided upon by which we maximize utility. But some revisionists, such as David Lewis, suggest that since decisions are actions, we maximize utility in and through our decisions themselves (see Lewis 1984). Or perhaps, as David Gauthier has explored (in Gauthier 1990), we maximize utility in respect of plans - combinations of decisions and actions decided upon.

But it seemed to me that though decisions are indeed actions, these attempts to voluntarize decision making were misconceived. First because Hobbes seemed to be quite right: the will is not voluntary. This is because the point of decision-making is not to secure good outcomes to be attained in and through taking the decision, but to apply reason as it governs and is concerned with the voluntary actions decided upon. The point of taking a decision about whether to do A or B is to ensure that whichever of these we do is the right action. Which is why the justifications we consider when we take our decision are justifications for doing A and for doing B. So our decision-making is responsive not to the desirability of the decision itself, but rather to that of the action decided upon. Whereas if decision making had been voluntary, something doable just on the basis of deciding so to decide, we could take whatever decisions we preferred to take. We need simply decide on whatever decisions seemed to us the most desirable, and then take those decisions voluntarily, just on the basis of our decision to take them, whether or not this desirability had anything to do with justifications for subsequently acting as decided.

Secondly, if (as is far from obvious) freedom or self-determination does come to no more than voluntariness – acting as one wills – why is anything added to our freedom by the complication of introducing such voluntariness in higher order form? On the Hobbesean theory, the exercise of freedom – our action being determined by us – is ultimately explained in terms of our action being determined not by us, but by a motivation within us that is not itself our doing. And unless we are to be involved in a vicious regress, the appeal to voluntariness in higher order form cannot materially affect this picture. If the Hobbesean view of freedom seems profoundly unsatisfying, because it replaces determination of our action by us with determination of our action by something not our doing and distinct from us, adding higher levels to this view will not remedy the problem.

Medieval action theory was fully aware that decisions are not just further cases of action in voluntary or quasi-voluntary form. Instead of appealing to voluntariness to explain agency, a model of agency that applies unobviously to the will itself, medieval action theory appealed to practical reason. Intentional action was supposed to consist in a mode of exercising rationality – not theoretically, as in the formation of belief, but in a manner that applied reason in its practical or action-governing form. And this mode of exercising rationality, and hence intentional action itself, was to be found in the exercise of the will (for an historical account of this *practical reason-based* conception of human action, see Pink 2004c).

Precisely because the exercise of the will was not understood in terms of voluntariness, nor was the exercise of freedom. Rather the exercise of freedom was linked to intentional action conceived as the application of rationality in practical form; but it was also understood as going beyond any such exercise of a capacity for reason. For the exercise of rationality need not involve any ability to act otherwise – as in cases where acting otherwise would not be to act rationally. Whereas human freedom was generally seen as involving by its very nature an ability to do things or not – its being up to us what we decide and do.

This clash between medieval and modern action theory leaves certain fundamental questions that I think any theory of action must clear-headedly address. What is the relation between three things which might turn out to be quite different: the application of reason in its practical or action-governing form; the exercise of freedom; and voluntariness or the performance of action in voluntary form, on the basis of pro attitudes to its performance? And which of these three does intentional action itself consist in? It is these questions which lie at the centre of my current work on action theory.

2. What other sub-disciplines in philosophy and non-disciplines stand to benefit the most from philosophical work on the nature of action and agency, and how might such engagement be accomplished?

Elizabeth Anscombe said that progress in moral philosophy would depend on progress in moral psychology, and on this she was certainly right. Central especially to the development of ethics must be a better understanding of the ethical significance of action. And that requires, especially, a better understanding of the nature of action itself.

In my view, debates about the moral significance of action are especially closely tied to debates about ethical normativity, and in particular to debates about the nature of moral obligation. These debates go back to the natural law ethics of medieval philosophy, which Hobbes in the seventeenth century was as anxious to discredit as he was anxious to discredit medieval theories of action.

But what is natural law? A system of law, as the medievals understood it, involves a set of binding or obligatory demands on how we act, a set of directives that those governed by it are responsible for following. So action is connected through the idea of law to two other notions: the idea of an obligation, and the idea of responsibility. As law-governed, human action is something that can be bound by obligations; and we have a responsibility for how we act.

Some systems of law are human creations, legislated over time by human custom, or enacted through formal statutes by legislative bodies. This is law in its positive or posited form; and in relation to positive law we speak of specifically legal obligations and of a specifically legal responsibility. The idea of a natural law is the idea of a similar structure of directives on how we act being provided, not by any contingent or positive legislation, but by practical reason itself – by reason in a form that is action-governing. Here the law is natural, because it addresses us not by virtue of our citizenship within any specific human community, but by virtue of our nature as adult humans, which is to be capable of responding to reason and rational justifications in their various forms. Since this non-positive or natural law is supposed to be prior to any positive law, and to constitute the directives, not of any state but of morality itself, we should think of our obligation and responsibility to this law not as merely legal, but as moral. Hence with the natural law is associated a moral obligation and a moral responsibility.

This conception of action as governed by law gives rise to a set of questions that link action theory with jurisprudence and ethics. Are there forms of obligation and responsibility that are specifically for how we act; and if there are, what is it about action that ties it to obligation and to responsibility in these forms? And here we find the questions about action that we have already raised arising again in ethics – this time not as questions about the nature of action itself, but rather as questions about the basis of the relation between action and law in its various forms. Does the connection between obligation and responsibility on the one hand and agency on the other come through voluntariness – through action's being something subject to the will and done on the basis of a decision to do it; or does it come through action's constituting a mode of exercising freedom; or is it simply that in performing action we are exercising a capacity for rationality?

On the one hand we have what I term *ethical rationalism* (see Pink 2007 and Pink forthcoming (a)). Ethical rationalism is the currently influential view of T.M. Scanlon. It assumes that the ethical significance of action lies just in its constituting a mode of exercising rationality. Our moral responsibility for how we act is just a general responsibility for responding to reason. In other words moral responsibility reduces to no more than a general rational appraisability, and our responsibility for how we act is no different in kind from any responsibility we might have for rationally appraisable wants and emotions, no matter how intuitively passive these wants and emotions might be (see Scanlon 1998, p22).

Then we have the view of Hume, which is that the ethical significance of action has nothing at all to do with reason, since when we act no capacity for rationality whatsoever is being exercised. Instead actions are ethically significant merely as signs of admirable virtues of character that are continuous with talents and non-moral abilities.

And then we have views which accept that there is a distinctively moral responsibility for how we act, based on something equally distinctive about the nature of action itself. These views then differ about what the relevant distinctive feature of action might be, and in ways that reflect differences about the nature of action itself.

Post-Hobbesean action theory has characteristically understood action in terms of voluntariness. It is not surprising, then, that within English-language philosophy, it should also often have been via the notion of voluntariness that moral obligation and responsibility have been linked to action. Obligation is conceived as a standard that we must be able to meet or breach at will, on the basis of deciding to do so. And this condition on obligation has in turn often been explained by a connection between obligation and sanction. Obligations are distinguished, or so it is supposed, by being standards that are justifiably to be enforced through sanctions. But, as Herbert Hart argued (see Hart 1968), to be fairly applied sanctions must be avoidable on the basis of a will to do so; in which case, sanctions can only be fairly attached to the voluntary. So obligation, whether moral or legal, is properly a standard on the voluntary; and our responsibility, whether moral or legal, is for what we have the capacity to do or refrain from voluntarily. And the arguments of Frankfurt for basing moral responsibility on voluntariness rather than freedom (see Frankfurt 1969) have proved very congenial to this more general approach to obligation and responsibility.

3. What will be your own most important contributions to theorizing about action and agency, and why?

I will be publishing two linked volumes – *The Ethics of Action: Self-Determination* (already complete and soon to be forthcoming from Oxford University Press) and *The Ethics of Action: Normativity*. Together these will address the central question of whether action, its exercise or its omission, has any distinctive ethical significance; and whether there are distinct kinds of normativity, and distinct forms of rationality, that relate to action in fundamentally different ways.

The first volume, *Self-Determination*, will develop a variety of claims already made in my *Free Will: A Very Short Introduction*. The book will examine the nature of action itself, and whether action involves any distinctive capacity for self-determination. I shall be arguing that medieval theories of intentional action as consisting in a distinctive mode of exercising rationality are correct. Intentional action should be understood in practical reason-based terms. It follows, I shall argue, that action in voluntary form is only one possible form taken by human action, which can also occur, in decision-making and intention-formation, in a form that is by its very nature non-voluntary. Hence we must reject the attempts by Frankfurt and his followers to appeal to voluntariness to understand the self-determination that we exercise in and through our action and that bases our moral responsibility for how we act. Rather self-determination takes the form of freedom; and freedom, its being up to us how we act, consists in a power that can as easily be exercised non-voluntarily as voluntarily. The association between self-determination and voluntariness that has marked English-language philosophy is in fact the product of a deep illusion about the nature of action itself.

The second volume on *Normativity* will develop a theory of moral normativity that is also being published in an ongoing series of articles on moral obligation and moral rationality (see Pink 2004b, Pink 2007 and Pink forthcoming (a)). In line with these articles I shall argue that practical reason involves a plurality of irreducibly distinct kinds of justificatory force the natures of which are to be explained in terms of the distinct kinds of capacity that they address and to which they apply. Human action itself involves a variety of capacities that are ethically significant, each of them addressed by a correspondingly distinctive kind of justificatory force. Two capacities are of particular significance – the capacity for freedom, which is governed by a force of moral obligation; and the capacity for self-realization in relation to arts or skills, which is addressed by a force of merit.

The competing theories of moral normativity provided by past philosophers can be seen as reflecting various levels of sensitivity to the existence of these various kinds of justificatory force.

For example, Scanlonian ethical rationalism effectively denies any such variety of justificatory force within practical reason and any such variety in action's ethical significance. Normative standards and our responsibility for meeting them reduce to a uniform 'reasonableness'. By contrast, Hume's theory of moral normativity is almost exclusively sensitive to the force of merit, wrongly detaching this justificatory force from the surrounding structure of practical reason altogether. Whereas medieval natural law theory was importantly sensitive to the justificatory force of moral obligation and to the power of freedom that we exercise in and through how we act.

The aim of these books is to reconnect moral theory and the theory of action, and to do so by providing a richer understanding of the nature and ethical significance of action itself as well as of the structure of the practical reason that governs how we act.

4. What is one important open problem in philosophical theorizing about action and agency, and what are the prospects for progress?

The free will problem is clearly open if any philosophical problem is. One bar to progress, in my view, is the assumption that the free will problem is essentially a conceptual problem about what it is to have a capacity to act otherwise.

Freedom seems to be a kind of power which we possess over our action. For freedom, if it exists, is a capacity to determine for ourselves how we act. And that is exactly what a power is - a capacity to determine or at least influence what happens. Causation too seems to involve a power. For causes have the capacity to determine or at least influence the occurrence of their effects; which is why we naturally think of causation as involving a power exercised by causes over effects. The free will problem then is about the compatibility of one kind of power, that of prior causes over how we act, with that other power which is our own freedom or control over our action. Does the exercise of one power, freedom, preclude its prior determination by the other, by causation, as incompatibilists suppose; or can the exercise of freedom perfectly well be causally predetermined, as compatibilists maintain?

How is such a problem to be solved? Is it, at least in part, by reference to experience? Certainly we rely on experience rather than purely conceptual inquiry to inform us of what causal powers exist within the world, and which causal powers defeat or preclude the operation of which other causal powers. Perhaps then the free will problem needs to be explored, at least in part, by reference to our experience and to how experience might present powers such as freedom and causation to us.

But – to develop an argument given in greater depth in Pink forthcoming (b) - this is not how the free will problem has been treated within English-language philosophy. To begin, with the 20th century analytic tradition inherited a broadly Humean view of experience – one which ruled out any direct experiential representation of power. At best experience would only represent regularities – such as that fire burns wood – that might be linked to power in its causal form, but not the power itself; and forms of power unassociated with any such kind of regularity, such as the power of freedom under an incompatibilist conception of it, could not be represented in experience at all, even indirectly. Added to this was a view of philosophy as consisting in some form of conceptual or semantic analysis, to be carried out by reflection on sentence meanings. On these views of experience and of the nature of philosophy itself, what freedom involves and, in particular, its relation to causal determinism, can only be a conceptual question, to be resolved by appeal to some form of semantic analysis of the assertion that someone 'can act otherwise'. On this view, whether compatibilism or incompatibilism is true has nothing to do with experience but is determined just by concepts and their contents. If freedom is incompatible with prior causal determination, this must be something that follows, by logic, from platitudes about freedom or the capacity to act otherwise common to all competent users of the concept. Thus Peter van Inwagen has devised a Consequence Argument which is intended to show that incompatibilism is conceptually true in just this way (see van Inwagen 1983, p. 16) - though unfortunately without managing to convince many compatibilists that incompatibilism is indeed a conceptual truth. And, in a similar way, skeptics about the very existence of incompatibilist freedom such as Galen Strawson have also sought to establish victory by conceptual means, seeking to prove that the very idea of freedom in incompatibilist form involves some deep inconsistency.

The *Ethics of Action: Self-Determination* will address the free will problem by beginning an examination of the nature and the phenomenology of power. It will argue that our natural libertarianism – our belief both that incompatibilism is true, and that we do possess freedom in incompatibilist form - is in fact not based on conceptual considerations at all, but rather on experience and the way that experience presents our powers and capacities to us; and that so based it involves no conceptual incoherence. But then nor is there any conceptual incoherence in the opposing compatibilist belief that freedom of action is consistent with causal determinism. The free will problem cannot be resolved by purely conceptual means.

If further progress is to be made with the free will problem, the theory of freedom must be relinked to empirical psychology in its widest sense, and in particular to the theory and study of consciousness and what is represented to us about our own selves and capacities in conscious experience. My *The Ethics of Action: Self-Determination* will attempt to provide a basis for understanding and further investigating the free will problem in these terms.

References

Frankfurt, Harry, "Alternate possibilities and moral responsibility" (1969) in *The Importance of What We Care About* (Cambridge: Cambridge University Press, 1988), pp. 1-10.

Frankfurt, Harry, "Freedom of the will and the concept of a person" (1971) in *The Importance of What We Care About* (Cambridge: Cambridge University Press, 1988), pp. 11-25.

Gauthier, David, "Deterrence, maximization and rationality," in *Moral Dealing* (Ithaca and London: Cornell University Press, 1990), pp.298-321.

Hart, Herbert, *Punishment and Responsibility*, (Oxford: Oxford University Press, 1968).

Hobbes, Thomas, *The Questions Concerning Liberty, Necessity and Chance, clearly stated between Dr Bramhall Bishop of Derry, and Thomas Hobbes of Malmesbury* London (1656).

Lewis, David, "Devil's bargains and the real world," in David Maclean, ed., *The Security Gamble*. (Totowa, NJ: Rowman and Allenheld, 1984), pp.141-54.

Pink, Thomas, *The Psychology of Freedom* (Cambridge: Cambridge University Press, 1996).

Pink, Thomas, *Free Will: A Very Short Introduction* (Oxford: Oxford University Press, 2004a).

Pink, Thomas, "Moral obligation," in Anthony O'Hear, ed., *Modern Moral Philosophy* (Cambridge: Cambridge University Press, 2004b), pp. 159-87.

Pink, Thomas, "Suarez, Hobbes and the scholastic tradition in action theor," in Thomas Pink and Martin Stone, eds., *The Will and Human Action: from Antiquity to the Present Day* (London: Routledge, 2004c).

Pink, Thomas, "Normativity and reason," *Journal of Moral Philosophy* 4 (2007), pp. 406-31.

Pink, Thomas, "Reason, voluntariness and moral responsibility," in Lucy O'Brien and Matthew Soteriou, eds., *Mental Actions* (Oxford: Oxford University Press, forthcoming (a)).

Pink, Thomas, "Free will and consciousness," in T. Bayne, A. Cleeremans, and P. Wilken, eds., *The Oxford Companion to Consciousness* (Oxford: Oxford University Press, forthcoming (b)).

Pink, Thomas, *The Ethics of Action: Self-Determination* (Oxford: Oxford University Press, forthcoming (c)).

Pink, Thomas, *The Ethics of Action: Normativity* (Oxford: Oxford University Press, forthcoming (d)).

Scanlon, T.M., *What We Owe To Each Other* (Cambridge, MA: Harvard University Press, 1998).

Van Inwagen, Peter, *An Essay on Free Will* (Oxford: Clarendon Press, 1983)

19
Joëlle Proust

CNRS Director of Research, Institut Jean-Nicod
Ecole Normale Supérieure et Ecole des Hautes Etudes en Sciences Sociales, France

My answers to five questions on agency
1. Why were you initially drawn to theorizing about action and agency?

I had been introduced to the domain by John Searle's seminar on the philosophy of action, whose contents inspired his 1983 book entitled *Intentionality*. John is an impressive lecturer and on-line thinker; his seminar was, in two respects, deeply innovative. First, John claimed that action itself (rather than the beliefs and desires that might contribute to causing it) has a general structure common to all the Intentional states. Second, he introduced the famous notion of an intention-in-action, thus allowing to analyze as intentional all the spontaneous, embodied ways in which actions are performed. The combination of these two remarkable features of Searle's theory opened up brand new ways of thinking about embodied intentions, and would prove very useful for describing psychological and neurological evidence. My personal involvement in the philosophy of action, however, did not emerge until ten years later, when I set out to explore schizophrenic perturbations of agency awareness.

At the beginning of the nineties, I was conducting research on such general philosophical topics as intentionality, consciousness and concept acquisition, as a member of an interdisciplinary CNRS unit, CREA, where rich interactions between philosophers of mind and language, logicians, anthropologists, experimental psychologists, and psychiatrists were a regular feature. Given my interest in consciousness, I engaged in a collaborative research project with a French psychiatrist, Dr. Henri Grivois, a specialist in the early episodes of psychosis. According to him, patients generally have, at the onset of their illness, a sudden impression of enjoying a deeply felt, reciprocal bond with others, which Grivois named "concernment." Subjects seem to think that people (and objects) convey messages to or about themselves. After a few hours or days, patients come to believe that they have a specific role to play in the community or even in the world at large – thus arriving at an experience of "centrality." The second group of features in Grivois' clinical description relates to a perturbed agency. Patients have the impression that others are all doing the same thing, and are mainly imitating them; they however are the ones who imitate others - either in gestures (echopraxia) or in words (echolalia). They also frequently emulate others' goals. These two group of features, concernment and mimetic behaviors, Grivois speculated, are functionally related. Patients might feel concernment and centrality because of their mimetic disposition.

As a philosopher interested in consciousness, I found that Grivois' theory was quite intriguing. It helped one to approach consciousness from a fresh perspective, based on the direct functional requirements of agency. Dan Dennett, in his *Consciousness Explained*, defends a 'Multiple Drafts model' of consciousness that also tries to assimilate scientific evidence. On his view, information entering the nervous system in a massively parallel way, is locally 'edited' by the brain, with different quasi-narratives emerging at different time scales. Dan was then mainly interested in visual perception and memory; an efficient general rebuttal of the 'Cartesian theater' view of consciousness, his model does not say much about the specific roles of conscious states in action. In a footnote (p.112), however, Dennett briefly reports a 1963 experiment by T.I. Nielsen having to do with agency awareness. A subject is tricked into believing that he is looking at his own gloved hand when drawing a figure: the perceptual 'reafference' for his action – what he actually looks at - is sometimes his, sometimes a hand that performs a different movement. Placed in this condition, a subject who is visually monitoring his drawing hand feels it being *pulled* in the direction of the observed movement each time the observed movement conflicts with his actual performance. In Dennett's terms, this particular brain 'editing' or 'inference' solves a conflict between vision and proprioception of one's actions. How can an inference be experienced as a pull?

The parallel of this case with the feeling of 'concernment' of Grivois' patients in their first psychotic episode is striking. In both cases, subjects have a proprioceptive feeling 'telling them' that something has interfered with their will. In both cases, some kind of conflict is involved between what the subjects predict and what they observe about the consequences of their acting. Grivois' observations contained the seeds of a view, developed since then, that a non-matching comparator might trigger the psychotic sense of extraneity – of a foreign interference - for one's actions and thoughts. An important difference between the two cases, however, is the following: where Nielsen's subjects felt a strong pull to the direction of the (seen) movement, patients with psychosis would feel a diminished sense of agency for their own actions. Where Nielsen's subjects were exposed to an occurrent (accurate) non-matching signal thanks to a functional comparator, patients were exposed either to a permanent (inaccurate) non-matching signal, or to no signal at all, because of a faulty comparator.

This parallel, among other considerations, motivated us to start testing experimentally the 'motor' hypothesis in patients with schizophrenic delusions, with the collaboration of Marc Jeannerod, a neuroscientist of action. If we put a deluded patient in an experimental situation such as Nielsen's, will he be able to tell whether the currently observed hand is his own? We predicted that patients should be impaired, relative to non-deluded patients and normal controls, in recognizing their own actions. Our predictions turned out to be correct (Daprati et al., 1997). Similar conclusions were reached by Chris Frith and his colleagues, using different experimental paradigms and stimuli. Now, the important question is: what philosophical benefit can be drawn from this empirical research?

2. What do you consider to be your own most important contribution(s) to theorizing about action and agency, and why?

The most direct effect of interdisciplinary influences on my philosophical work was to press me into articulating a metaphysics of action that could reflect the functional aspects that psychologists and neuroscientists have been uncovering. In part what clinical evidence taught us was that the senses of bodily and of mental agency are simultaneously perturbed in deluded subjects: their actions seem to them to be externally controlled, and their thoughts to be inserted. This suggests that an adequate theory of action should apply to both object- and self-directed kinds of action. Clearly, action is a dynamic phenomenon through which an agent uses representations to control her physical and social environments or her own thought processes. To reflect this dynamic property of actions, a proper definition needs to express the teleological structure of the causal-representational process through which a particular goal (and a trajectory to reach it) is selected among a range of actions in the agent's repertoire. How are we to accommodate these various functional requirements in defining an empirically sound concept of action?

A first revision is now well-accepted. Beliefs, desires and intentions, with a propositional content, as ordinarily conceived, do not deal easily with the specific ways chosen to perform an action. If one grants that agents have preferential ways to produce outcomes, intentions in action must be able to have *nonconceptual*, that is, protopropositional kinds of content. These contents specify the spatial and temporal dynamics, rhythm, proprioceptive markers, and other phenomenological properties that have to be present for the action to be successful (Proust, 2003). Given that these nonconceptual contents drive motor activity, they are usually called "motor representations" - a term used by neuroscientists to refer to neural activations in the motor area. Motor representations, however, only apply to bodily action. When applied to thought processes, other types of nonconceptual content, with their own dynamic features, are used to select and monitor mental actions; these 'epistemic feelings' are particularly interesting to study, as they form a primary basis for self-knowledge. (Proust, 2007, 2008). A second step was to examine the requirements for the representation of an intention to acquire *executive force*. Not every candidate intention to act is executed; intentions can also be simulated, evaluated and abandoned. How should one distinguish the executive from the simply motivational and epistemic activity evoked by an intention to act? A volitional definition of action was developed in Proust (2005) to spell out this difference.

This definition has a teleological structure, which in the case of action is roughly expressed by the law of action-effect: Actions are behaviors that tend to be executed in a context, and they tend to be executed in this context because they have had a beneficial effect for the agent in this context. Behaviors that have had detrimental consequences in this context tend not to be reproduced. This general teleological structure needs to be complemented, however, in order to (1) express the dispositional range of accessible actions for an agent at t; (2) explain why unsuccessful or inadequately targeted actions may occur; and (3) explain how action patterns can, on a particular occasion, be adjusted and modified to respond to the constraints of a new context. The mathematics of adaptive control systems is helpful in satisfying these requirements with full generality. Regulation laws state which outcomes are associated with specific commands in specific contexts. Feedback laws state which portion of the regulation space is accessible at a given time to an organism with a given learning history. Regulation and feedback laws have been shown to necessarily involve *representations of the action space* (Proust, 2006a). It is indeed a theorem of control theory that the best regulator of a system is one which is a model of that system. In an optimal control system, in other words, the regulator's actions are, as Conant and Ashby write, "merely the system's actions as seen through a specific mapping."[1] In other words, any regulation involves a prior simulation. Action needs to be accounted for in a way that combines such dynamical and representational properties. The concept of volition to act, which I articulated in 2005, attempted to provide such an account. A volition is a dynamic executive event, that decomposes into the following three interconnected properties:

1. A regulation space is available to the agent at the relevant time, t, in which there is at least one trajectory that leads from the current position to a target;

2. There is a salient target at t;

3. A prevailing reward associated with the salient target selects and activates a suitable command at t.

Note that these three conditions correspond respectively to procedural-epistemic, contextual and motivational conditions. They have to apply jointly for a volition to occur (they are necessary and sufficient conditions for a representation of the goal to be endowed with executive force). On this view, a volition does not constitute a self-contained mental action that would prepare bodily action. A volition to bring about G is the representational-executive contribution that normally generates the effects typical of G (whether mental or bodily). Note also that volitions for bodily as well as for mental actions are made accessible by the system's prior history. As in any teleological-etiological definition, such history explains why volitions exist, and how the parameters involved in the three conditions are properly calibrated, or, in certain biased cases, distorted. The particular history profile of an agent is thus able to

---

[1] Conant & Ashby, 1970

explain how she can mistakenly represent that a certain kind of control will bring about a given outcome.

In a (non-dynamic) semantic analysis of volition, a volition is defined as an effort to bring about some change *in virtue of this effort*. One of the benefits of articulating the control structure above is that the *reflexivity* of volitions, intentions, and reasons to act can now be understood as an architectural feature derived from the control structure. As we have seen, control systems are essentially causal-representational loops. In each loop, a given command causally determines, in virtue of its content, a corresponding episode of monitoring, which in turn triggers, in virtue of its content, a new command: reinforcing the former command, or prompting revisions to it. The property of mutual causal influence between these two complementary levels is called "causal contiguity". (Mellor, 1991) Now, an important semantic fact is that *any* causally contiguous representational structure necessarily generates both *representational promiscuity* and a basic, nonconceptual form of *reflexivity*. (Proust, 2007).

There is representational promiscuity because command and monitoring need to compare observed feedback with expected feedback; they need to have a common representation of the goal, and of the route that leads to it. There is reflexivity because monitoring always refers to the specific command that prompts it. Both representational promiscuity and reflexivity have been noticed by classical analyses of action. If you intend to act, your intention also constitutes the satisfaction condition of the completed action: this representational promiscuity indeed depends on the causal/semantic relationship between a command and monitoring episodes. They only differ in that the first states what is to be obtained, while the second reports on what does/does not obtain (a difference in direction of fit,[2] with the same basic content). In every cognitive control structure, representational promiscuity must be present. Monitoring *evaluates* the execution of the command, while the command *directs* or organizes upcoming monitoring. In contrast with beliefs, desires, and intentions, volitions thus involve two directions of fit, based on the same representational schema (as suggested by the idea of comparing what you have with what you want.)

---

[2] A belief is true when it fits the world: it has a mind-to-world direction of fit. Reciprocally, a desire, an intention, or a volition are satisfied if the world adjusts to them: they have a world-to-mind direction of fit. See Austin, 1962.

Let us now examine how volitions to act have reflexivity as a consequence of representational promiscuity. Reflexivity is necessarily generated in a causally contiguous representational loop for two reasons. Resulting as it does from a causally contiguous command episode, every monitoring episode *carries information* about the previous command that caused it. Furthermore, some representational element in monitoring must have the function of carrying this information. It is crucial indeed that the command level identifies the output of a monitoring episode as a response to its own query, which requires in turn that the content of monitoring is structured by the command that causes it. The representational element having the function of a *de se* marker, however, does not need to involve a self-concept (Proust, 2003). This result will not be surprising to those philosophers who, like John Perry, claim that "basic self-knowledge is intrinsically selfless" (1986, 2000). As Perry has shown, it is possible to have information concerning something without representing it explicitly in the thought content. In that case, reflexivity is mentally represented by an "unarticulated" constituent. Recanati (2007) argues that cases of identification-free reflexivity (those that are immune to error of identification) depend on the mode of thinking (like perceiving or intending) rather than on the content of thought. On my own view, the "reflexive" modes are those that involve causal contiguity between two representational events: a (context-sensitive) command episode and a (circumstance-sensitive) evaluation episode (i.e. monitoring).

Obviously, these philosophical observations are relevant to understanding the schizophrenic delusions described above. Adopting a control view of action in fact allows us to adopt a new perspective both on agency and on agency awareness. Recently, philosophers have tried to explain the asymmetry between a preserved sense of ownership (of bodily experience) and a perturbed sense of agency in patients with schizophrenic delusions of control. On the present view, there are as many forms of reflexivity and possible disturbances as there are control loops. Functional considerations suggest that there are at least four such levels, which are respectively *motor* (intentions in action/volitions to move), *self-world* (prior intention/volition to obtain that P- a given change in the world), *self-self* (prior intention/volition to obtain a mental property by affecting oneself), and *self-other* regulations (prior intention/volition to obtain that P in virtue of our common effort). Abnormal phenomenology results from reflexive blindness generated in one or the other of these loops. Reflexive blindness, however, belongs to monitoring, rather than control. It does not affect to the same degree the capacity to act. I tried to explain this interesting dissociation in schizophrenia in Proust (2006b).

3. What other sub-disciplines in philosophy and non- disciplines stand to benefit the most from philosophical work on the nature of action and agency, and how might such engagement be accomplished?

To understand how an empirically adequate conception of action can gain higher relevance to other fields, one obviously needs to have some idea of the features of the philosophical theory that will fulfill this promise. As I have said above, my own view is that the most empirically adequate way of capturing the conceptual structure of action is to see it as the most accomplished form of adaptive control to date. Adaptive control is itself an adaptation whose vehicle is constituted by embodied neural systems. The kind of adaptive control a being possesses determines, by and large, the framework within which his/her perception, emotion and memory will play their respective roles. If one adopts this view, the four most directly affected fields are, in science, mathematics, evolutionary biology, and the cognitive sciences (including cognitive psychopathology), and, in philosophy, epistemology.

Why *mathematics*? Mathematics is close to philosophy in that it aims to capture necessary relations between propositions. Dynamic system theories, such as the viability theory, starting from the hypothesis that dynamic systems are associated with changing environments, allow us to understand and describe the constraints to which agency needs to respond. In particular, viability theory (Aubin, 1991) allows the modeling of rational decisions in uncertain contexts in a way that radically minimizes the number of parameters that need to be represented for a preference to emerge. If the metaphysical assumption that agents are a subclass of adaptive control systems is correct, mathematicians, philosophers and cognitive psychologists will have to work together in order to come up with specific classes of control models of action that meet the crucial constraint of parametric reduction.

Evolutionary Biology studies the interaction between evolutionary history, adaptations, and selection pressures, and, in particular, the evolution of mental capacities across phylogenetic trees. It can be fertilized by philosophical work on agency, as is shown by the impact on the field of Sterelny's (2003) book. Much more needs to be done, however, to grasp the evolution of forms of action in non-human animals and the role which the linguistic expression of goals and values can play in controlled agency.

The Cognitive Sciences, and in particular Cognitive Psychopathology and Neuropsychology, have already drawn inspiration from the philosophy of action, by using, sometimes uncritically, concepts able to describe behavioral evidence (for example, the notion of an intention-in-action has been widely used by neuroscientists.) We have seen, furthermore, how philosophy and psychiatry have influenced each other in determining the dimensions of self-awareness involved in agency, and worked jointly with cognitive scientists on accounts of psychiatric disorders.

Epistemology, however, strikes me as the philosophical subdomain that has the most to gain from current research on mental agency. In order to fully understand the concept of entitlement or prima facie justification, in which a subject feels entitled to form a belief without being able to explicitly articulate the reasons that he has to form that belief or the norm that he is applying, one needs to explain philosophically how this implicit knowledge has been formed and what content it has. Current work on mental action, and, in particular, on the control structure that it involves (in metacognitive judgments such as: *I need to stop/pursue this line of reasoning,* or in an attempt to retrieve an item from memory) is able to shed light on this issue. (Proust, 2008)

4. What do you regard as the most neglected issues in contemporary work on action and agency that deserve more attention?

Relying as they mostly do on folk-psychological intuitions, analytic philosophers tend to conflate two dimensions of agency: the motivational and the executive. Distinguishing volition from intention is meant to provide the required distinction: you can desire A, know how to get A by doing P, intend to do P to get A, while failing to attempt to do P. Conversely, you may execute P without having a reason, or a motivation to do so. As psychologists such as Theodule Ribot have shown us, there can be neuropsychological disturbances of volition that do not affect motivation, and conversely (see the imitation syndrome, described in Lhermitte, 1986).

A movement that is voluntarily performed feels distinctively "effortful", and the effects of a willful movement have a distinctive temporal signature as compared with effects passively observed (Haggard, 2003). Volition itself, however, has no specific phenomenology; Malebranche correctly stressed that agents start moving their body (or mentally focusing, in mental action) to attain their goals, without knowing how they do it. My own account as summarized above only offers a teleological explanation for the switch from 'epistemic-motivational' to 'active'; this type of definition identifies a selected function without offering a detailed metaphysical solution. The puzzle that a teleological explanation solves is that agents cannot be said to voluntarily switch into the active condition. In some sense, willing is something that happens to you, which does not mean that you cannot select from among desires those that you want to influence your future willing episodes. It strikes me, however, that the issue deserves to be dealt with in more detail, by studying the properties of dynamic systems, or otherwise.

5. What are the most important open problems in philosophical theorizing about action and agency, and what are the prospects for progress?

Philosophers enjoy doing mostly what they know how to do; as a result, agency has up to now mainly been studied in philosophy through attitudes and their propositional contents. The domain of emotion, however, has proved difficult to approach in these terms; similarly, the domain of action resists a simple belief-desire analysis. In spite of these well-known problems, most analytic philosophers stick to their guns. Why should they have to understand brain activity to theorize about agency, or about consciousness? The less science, the more philosophy (the saying goes!) Is not a proper distinction between a personal level (what I feel and can report about my states of awareness) and subpersonal levels (what happens in my brain that causally explains how I feel, report, and do things) able to justify us in *not* bothering to collect scientific evidence?

The problem with this general strategy is that the distinction that it presupposes is highly variable, self-interpretive and theory-laden. As Dennett took pains to show, the limit between subpersonal and personal facts may change with time scales, attentional demands and health. There is no firm ground in the personal that is not constrained by a myriad of subpersonal representations, which philosophers cannot afford to entirely ignore, in particular if they recognize the existence of nonconceptual forms of mental content. The mental cannot reside in a supposedly 'final' narrative layer, as articulated in language. It seems difficult, in short, to deny that neuroscience, experimental psychology, neuropsychology and cognitive psychopathology deliver facts and evidence that any conceptual view of consciousness or agency needs to take into account if it is to be empirically adequate.

This does not mean, however, that philosophers need to summarize endless facts about the way the brain sends action commands and monitors them. What is rather needed is a precise analysis of the dynamic properties of agentive systems, ultimately leading to a general theory of the non-conceptual and conceptual conditions of action selection and recognition. On my view, the prospects for philosophical progress on this issue presently call for the collaborative insights of mathematicians and computer scientists, on the one hand, and philosophers and psychologists, on the other hand.

Acknowledgment

I express all my thanks to my colleague Dick Carter for his comments and his linguistic help.

References

Aubin, J.P. 1991. *Viability theory.* Boston, Basel : Birkhauser.

Austin, J.L. 1962. *How to do things with Words: The William James Lectures delivered at Harvard University in 1955.* Ed. J. O. Urmson. Oxford: Clarendon.

Conant, R. C., and Ashby, W. R. 1970. Every good regulator of a system must be a model of that system, *International Journal of Systems Science*, 1: 89-97.

Daprati, E., Franck, N., Georgieff, N., Proust, J., Pacherie, E., Dalery, J. & Jeannerod, M. 1997. Looking for the agent, an investigation into self-consciousness and consciousness of the action in schizophrenic patients, *Cognition.* Vol. 65, 71- 86.

Dennett, D. 1991. *Consciousness Explained.* Boston, Little, Brown & Company.

Frith C.D. 1992. *The Cognitive Neuropsychology of Schizophrenia*, Hillsdale, Lawrence Erlbaum Associates.

Grivois, H. 1998. Coordination et subjectivité dans la psychose naissante. In H. Grivois et J. Proust (eds.), *Subjectivité et conscience d'agir, approches clinique et cognitive de la psychose*, Paris, Presses Universitaires de France, 1998, 35-73.

Haggard, P. 2003. Conscious awareness of intention and of action, in J. Roessler & N.Eilan (eds.), *Agency and self-awareness: issues in philosophy and psychology*, Oxford, Oxford University Press, 111-127

Lhermitte, F., Pillon, B., Serdaru, M. 1986. Human Autonomy and the Frontal Lobes. Part I: Imitation and Utilization Behaviour, *Annals of Neurology, 19, 4,* 326-334.

Mellor, H. 1991. I and now, in: *Matters of Metaphysics*, Cambridge, Cambridge University Press, 17-29.

Nielsen, T.I. 1963. Volition: A new experimental approach, *Scandinavian Journal of Psychology*, 4, 225-230.

Proust, J. 2000. Awareness of Agency: Three Levels of Analysis, in T. Metzinger (ed.), *The Neural Correlates of Consciousness*, Cambridge, MIT Press, 307-324.

Proust, J. 2001. A plea for mental acts, *Synthese*, 129, 105-128.

Proust, J. 2003_a. Action, in B. Smith (ed.), *John Searle,* Cambridge, Mass.: Cambridge University Press, 102-127.

Proust, J. 2003_b. Thinking of oneself as the same, *Consciousness and Cognition*, 12, 4, 495-509.

Proust, J. 2005. *La nature de la volonté*, Paris, Folio-Gallimard.

Proust, J. 2006_a. Agency in schizophrenics from a control theory viewpoint, in W. Prinz & N. Sebanz (eds.), *Disorders of volition*, Cambridge, MIT Press, 87-118.

Proust, J. 2006_b. Rationality and metacognition in non-human animals, in S. Hurley & M. Nudds (eds.), *Rational Animals?*, Oxford, Oxford University Press, 247-274.

Proust, J. 2007. Metacognition and metarepresentation : is a self-directed theory of mind a precondition for metacognition ? *Synthese,* 159, 271-295.

Proust, J. 2008 (in print). Is there a sense of agency for thought? In L. O'Brien ed. , *Mental action*, Oxford, Oxford University Press.

Searle, J.R. 1983. *Intentionality, an Essay in the Philosophy of Mind,* Cambridge, Cambridge University Press.

Sterelny, K. 2003. *Thought in a Hostile World, The evolution of Human Cognition*, Oxford: Blackwell.

20
Abraham Roth

Associate Professor of Philosophy
Ohio State University, USA

It would be hard to find anyone working in action theory proper who was not at least initially drawn to the field by the debates between causalists and anti-causalists over the nature of action and its explanation in terms of reasons. Anti-causalists saw agency as a fundamentally goal directed matter, and saw reasons explanation as teleological or purposive. Causalists acknowledged that reasons explanation is purposive. But they also saw action as fitting into a natural event-causal order, and defended an understanding of reasons explanation that involved causation by psychological attitudes: a desire that specifies some aim of the agent, and an instrumental belief about how the action might achieve it. Together, the belief/desire pairs rationalize or make sense of the action; but this intelligibility amounts to an explanation of the action, according to the causalist, only if the attitudes in question cause it.[1]

Anti-causalists like Anscombe[2] emphasized the notion of intention, and causalists like Davidson initially did not. I think that one of the fruitful outcomes of this debate is that the engagement with anti-casualists led causalists to develop a robust conception of the psychological attitude of intention.[3] Intention differs fundamentally from other attitudes, such as desire, in that it involves a

---

[1] Donald Davidson's influential papers are collected in *Essays on Actions and Events*, Oxford: Clarendon (1980).

[2] The classic work is G.E.M. Anscombe, *Intention,* Oxford: Blackwell (1957); 2nd ed. Ithaca, Cornell University Press (1963). For a more recent discussion, see George Wilson, *The Intentionality of Human Action*, Stanford, CA: Stanford University Press (1989). This sophisticated contribution weds, in what some might describe as an unholy union, an Anscombian anti-causalism with a very Davidsonian concern with logical form.

[3] Gilbert Harman, "Practical Reasoning", *Review of Metaphysics 79* (1976),431-463, and *Change in View,* Cambridge: MIT Press (1986); Michael Bratman, *Intentions, Plans, and Practical Reason*, Cambridge, MA: Harvard

special sort of commitment to action. This makes a difference for practical reasoning and rationality. Intention leads to means-end reasoning, and is subject to demands for consistency in a way that desire is not.

This important work on intention focused almost exclusively on individual agency. But often individuals act together. More recently, there has been growing interest in the question of how to extend work on individual agency to address issues that arise in shared agency. And in this regard, I think that the notions of intention and commitment are particularly useful.

Early discussion of collective action favored a reductive/individualistic approach, guided in part by the desire to avoid metaphysical excess (e.g. positing group minds and group mental states).[4] This sort of approach was subject to forceful critique by Searle.[5] But Searle's rejection of reductive individualism did not amount to any literal endorsement of groups with minds of their own. Instead, Searle posited that individuals could exhibit, alongside of ordinary individual intentional states, a basic or primitive form of collective intentionality. But Searle insisted that this collective intentionality could be had by a single individual independently of what is going on around her (indeed, it could be exhibited by an isolated brain in a vat), and no recipe was offered of how individuals with such primitive we-intentional attitudes were to be related in order to count as acting together.

Bratman points to an important way in which individuals are related to one another in collective action: each participant's plans for realizing the collective goal are compatible, or mesh, with the plans of every other participant.[6] More generally, a practical intersubjectivity holds between them; the relevant intentions of each participant in collective action are subject to consistency and coherence with those of every other participant.[7] Using the resources

---

University Press (1986). Some anticipation might be found in H.P. Grice, "Intention and Uncertainty", *Proceedings of the British Academy* 57 (1971).

[4] For important statements, see R. Tuomela, "Actions by Collectives", *Philosophical Perspectives* 3, 471-96 (1989), and R. Tuomela and K. Miller, "We-Intentions", *Philosophical Studies* 53, 367-89 (1988).

[5] J. Searle, "Collective Intentions and Actions", in *Intentions in Communication*, P. Cohen, J. Morgan and M. Pollack, eds., Cambridge, MA: MIT Press (1990).

[6] M. Bratman, *Faces of Intention: Selected Essays on Intention and Agency*, Cambridge: Cambridge Univ. Press, (1999).

[7] Abraham Roth, "Practical Intersubjectivity", in *Socializing Metaphysics – the Nature of Social Reality*, F. Schmitt, ed., Lanham MD: Rowman &

of his planning theory of intention, Bratman posits an interlocking structure of individual intentions at the core of collective action. The aim of Bratman's sophisticated and influential form of individualism is to tap into the norms of individual intention-based commitment in order to account for the practical intersubjectivity associated with shared agency.

Another important feature of collective action has been identified by Margaret Gilbert.[8] These are the mutual obligations or "contralateral commitments" each individual has to other participants to do his or her share of the activity.[9] Gilbert's joint commitment thesis is that these commitments are constitutive of collective or shared action. One might agree with Gilbert that contralateral commitments are essential to collective action, but reject her claim that they are primitive. I think that an intention-based account of contralateral commitments can be illuminating. But if we're to take this path, the structure of intentions identified by Bratman will not help. Indeed, we'll have to depart from individualism and countenance the possibility of different individuals acting directly or immediately on one another's intentions, much in the way that one can act directly on one's own intentions.[10] I think that this is the only way we can hope to generalize the idea of an intention-based commitment into something that holds *between individuals* and thereby account for the contralateral commitments between participants of collective action.

Underlying the distinctive commitment in individual intention is an authority to settle what it is that one will do in the future, and a corresponding entitlement later to any practical warrant or justification that might derive from the practical reasoning and judgment that went into forming the intention in the first place. One of the outstanding problems in the theory of shared agency, as I see it, is understanding the corresponding normative structure in the interpersonal cases: if I'm acting directly on your intention, what is the nature of your authority to issue such an intention for me? And how am I, in acting on your intention, entitled to your

---

Littlefield (2003).

[8] M. Gilbert, "Walking Together: A Paradigmatic Social Phenomenon", *Midwest Studies in Philosophy 15:* 1-14 (1990); *Sociality and Responsibility*, Lanham, Md: Rowman & Littlefield (2000).

[9] Gilbert's term is *obligation*, but this is misleading in that it suggests that the phenomenon is moral, something Gilbert (rightly) denies.

[10] Abraham Roth, "Shared Agency and Contralateral Commitments", *Philosophical Review* 113 v.3 (2004), 359-410.

practical judgment, and to whatever warrant you may accrue from thinking the matter through? The issues here are related to those arising in recent discussion of the epistemology of testimony, especially concerning the nature of a non-evidential form of justification or warrant for believing what one is told.[11] I think that both the epistemology of testimony and the theory of collective agency stand to benefit from an interchange of ideas on these issues.

The general strategy here is to understand aspects of collective action, including the normative phenomena of mutual obligation and practical intersubjectivity, in terms of the rational norms of commitment associated with intention. But is there really such a thing as a rationality of intention-based commitment? Are the corresponding rational requirements genuinely normative? That is, do they have a legitimate claim to be action guiding? Consider one such requirement, the so-called instrumental principle. Roughly put, it states that when one intends some end, one should intend the necessary means. [12] One worry with this principle is that it might sanction an illegitimate bootstrapping of reasons. Suppose that one has no good reason to A – perhaps A-ing is the case familiar from the literature (one hopes not from real life!) of counting the blades of grass in the neighborhood. If one nevertheless goes on so to intend, then whatever reason we have to conform to the instrumental principle would seem to give one a reason to intend the necessary means, such as keeping a log to avoid losing one's place and double counting blades of grass. But this seems absurd; there is no reason to keep this log.

In an important series of papers, John Broome has raised this sort of bootstrapping challenge for many rational principles, not just those concerning intention-based commitment.[13] He has, more-

---

[11] See for example, Tyler Burge, "Content Preservation", *Philosophical Review 102* (1993), 457-88, and Richard Moran, "Getting Told and Being Believed", *Philosopher's Imprint*, Ann Arbor, MI: Scholarly Publishing Office, University of Michigan, University Library, vol. 5, no. 5, pp. 1-29, (2005), http://hdl.handle.net/2027/spo.3521354.0005.005

[12] The status of this principle has been made prominent in recent discussion by the influential work by C. Korsgaard, e.g. in "The Normativity of Instrumental Reason", in G. Cullity & B. Gaut eds., *Ethics and Practical Reason*, Oxford: Oxford University Press (1997).

[13] J. Broome, "Normative Requirements", *Ratio* 12, (1999) 398-419; "Are Intentions Reasons?", in *Practical Rationality and Preference*, C. Morris & A. Ripstein, eds., Cambridge, Cambridge Univ. Press (2001); "Reasons", in *Reason and Value*, R. J. Wallace, P. Pettit, S. Scheffler, M. Smith, eds., Oxford: Oxford University Press. Broome credits Bratman with the original insight to

over, suggested ways to formulate principles to avoid bootstrapping. On Broome's reading of the instrumental principle, when one has the intention to A, one has conclusive reason *either* to intend the necessary means *or* to give up the intention. While one has reason to satisfy the principle, this by itself will not allow for the "detachment" that would allow one to draw a conclusion about *which* disjunct one has a reason to adopt. In the above example, satisfying the instrumental principle would involve either drawing up a log for counting the grass, or giving up the intention. We cannot detach the former and conclude that one has reason to draw up the log, and so the problematic bootstrapping is avoided.

Broome's proposals have inspired some challenging criticism.[14] But one issue closer to our concerns here has not received attention. This is the matter of whether Broome's so called "widescope" formulations of rational requirements can capture the commitment that is distinctive of intention. The intention to A hardly amounts to any commitment to A-ing if the normative or rational impact of intention could, for all that's been said, just as easily be to drop the intention as it is to intend the necessary means. The project, then, would be to add further principles governing intentions to try to capture this commitment. But the question remains of whether this can be done in a way that does not introduce just the sort of bootstrapping that the proposal originally was meant to eliminate.

The challenge of bootstrapping has led some to be skeptical about understanding rationality in terms of the sorts of principles that I think are fundamental to intention based commitment. I'm more sanguine about the prospects for a solution here, although it might require us to rethink whether bootstrapping is as problematic as it may appear.

But, finally, even if skeptical challenges about the normativity of intention-based commitment can be faced down, there remains the further question of whether these requirements can be applied or developed in an interpersonal context for an account of shared agency. An immediate obstacle is an internalist intuition about rationality defended by some[15] to the effect that whether an individual counts as rational or not supervenes upon the individual

---

the bootstrapping worry. See also T. Scanlon, "Reasons: A Puzzling Duality?" in Wallace et. al. for important discussion of a related concern.

[14] N. Kolodny, "Why Be Rational?", *Mind* 114, (2005).

[15] E.g., R. Wedgewood, "Internalism Explained," *Philosophy and Phenomenological Research* 65 (2002), 349-369.

subject's mind (and not, for example on what other individuals believe or intend). This supervenience claim would appear to rule out the sort of rational requirements that ground the possibility of acting directly on the intentions of others. This might then speak in favor of an individualistic approach to understanding collective action, such as that of Bratman. But we should not treat internalism and the corresponding supervenience claim as sacrosanct. They rely, after all, on intuitions about control and responsibility that might be resisted. Such intuitions, especially if gleaned from solipsistic scenarios highly abstracted from ordinary situations (e.g. evil demons or brains in vats), should not be regarded as a neutral criterion against which we might assess rational requirements that might be proposed in the debate between individualistic and non-individualistic accounts of shared agency.

21

Galen Strawson

Professor of Philosophy
University of Reading, UK

---

1. Why were you initially drawn to theorizing about action and agency?

I switched to philosophy after the start of my last year at Cambridge University and took the Final ('Part 2') philosophy exams in May 1973 after less than six months study of the subject. I then did many other things—including working on a building site and as a television researcher, living in Paris, and getting married—that did not include philosophy, so that when I began graduate work at Oxford in October 1974 I still knew very little. Things were not much changed in the spring of 1975 when, sitting in a "carrel" in the library of Wolfson College, Oxford, reading Jonathan Bennett's book *Kant's Dialectic* (before having read Kant himself), I came to the section on the problem of free will, of freedom of action. It was quite new to me and I was gripped. I went on to read Kant and my father's paper, "Freedom and Resentment," which I admired but found unsatisfactory. One day's exposure was enough to guarantee that the question of free will became the topic of my BPhil thesis (1977), my DPhil thesis ("Freedom and Belief and Belief in Freedom," 1983), my first book (*Freedom and Belief*, 1986) and several subsequent articles.

I don't know why I was so strongly drawn to the topic. I was amazed by the inexorability of the proof that free will as ordinarily and loosely understood, "strong" free will, as I will call it (free will of the sort that grounds "ultimate moral responsibility," free will that makes punishment and reward fully morally justifiable without any trace of any appeal to pragmatic or consequentialist considerations), is impossible. I was absorbed by the fact that one could prove the impossibility of something one could not help believing in, something that was in addition (or seemed to be) of the very greatest importance in human life. It seems to me that there's nothing quite like this anywhere else in philosophy. Skeptical conclusions can be startling in philosophy, conclusions to the effect that we can't know something we thought we knew. But the conclusion that strong free will is impossible is not a skeptical conclusion. It's nothing like the conclusion that we can't know whether or not an "external" world exists in the way we think it does. The conclusion of the argument against free will is a knowledge claim: it's the positive metaphysical conclusion that we can know for sure that strong free will is impossible.

2. What do you consider to be your own most important contribution(s) to theorizing about action and agency, and why?

I have argued that strong free will or "ultimate responsibility" is impossible whether determinism is true or false. I think it's useful to have a clear statement of the point, and this is one of the things I have tried to do. In its simplest form, the argument runs as follows. "(1) You do what you do because of the way you are. (2) So in order to be ultimately responsible for what you do you need to be ultimately responsible for what you are—at least in certain crucial mental respects. (3) But you can't be *ultimately* responsible for what you are in any respect at all. (4) So you can't be ultimately responsible for what you do." It is, no doubt, an obvious point—at least after reflecting on why (3) is true—but it needs to be kept in play and regularly re-examined.[1] Many people continue to think that strong free will might be possible if determinism were false, and it is important to make it clear that this is not so.

I've also argued that the basic set of possible metaphysical positions about free will is well known, and that we need to go beyond it and focus on the "cognitive phenomenology" of freedom, which is

> concerned with our beliefs, feelings, attitudes, practices, and ways of conceiving or thinking about the world, in so far as these involve the notion of freedom ..., with the experience we have of being free agents,

---

[1] For a brief statement, see Sommers & Strawson (2003).

and of being truly responsible for what we do in such a way that we can be truly deserving of (moral) praise and blame. It considers the causes, the character, and the consequences of this experience. Why concentrate in this way on the experience of being free, rather than the thing itself? Because the best way to try to achieve a comprehensive understanding of the free will debate, and of the reason why it is interminable, is to study the thing that keeps it going—our experience of freedom. Because this experience is something real, complex, and important, even if free will itself is not real. (Strawson 1986, p. 1)

3. What other sub-disciplines in philosophy and non-disciplines stand to benefit the most from philosophical work on the nature of action and agency, and how might such engagement be accomplished?

The philosophy of action stands at the center of a great nexus of interrelated concerns including ethics, the general study of reasons, psychophysiology, cognitive science, the study of the human being as an essentially embodied and world-embedded creature, cultural anthropology, and questions to do with the nature of the self. This is because action stands at the centre of human life. As philosophy, the theory of action has its own distinctive *a priori* concerns, but work in experimental psychology is no less important to it when it is taken in its full extent. That said, I can't see that any new special work is needed when it comes to interdisciplinary engagement. The key connections are I think well in place and locked in.

So far as the problem of free will is concerned, I think that there's some very interesting social-psychological work still to be done on phenomenological matters, on the experience of free will and the extent to which it may vary across persons and cultures. I think it will be rather difficult to do this research well. It will prove to be a delicate matter. Contradictory results will be obtained and experimental protocols will have to be very carefully and sensitively designed. With time, though, I think clear results will emerge.

4. What do you regard as the most neglected issues in contemporary work on action and agency that deserve more attention?

Although I don't think it still suffers from serious neglect, I'm inclined to repeat the point that we need a more fully articulated phenomenology of free will.[2] I think it will come, for the interest of the area has recently been increasingly recognized, and the challenge it presents is being taken up.[3] It's important to stress the point that a phenomenology of free will is a cognitive phenomenology, because the word 'phenomenology' has recently and unhelpfully come to be associated principally with sensory experience rather than with experience taken as a whole, i.e. experience in all its conceptually informed (conceptually structured, conceptually penetrated) complexity, and the experience of free will is of course a conceptually informed experience *par excellence*.[4] Note that cognitive phenomenology as I understand it needn't be thought of as being concerned only with such conscious occurrent phenomena; any element of a creature's general conceptual set or outlook (a dispositional matter) is a proper object of study for cognitive phenomenology, as I understand it, just so long as it *informs* or *conditions* the character of its experience at some time, or is poised to do so.

On a second and separate matter, I think that more attention ought to be paid to the phenomenon of *mental* action and behavior. There was a time when the distinction between *overt* and *covert* behavior (including action)—between behavior that was publicly observable and behavior that wasn't—was a standard one. Even the arch-behaviorist Gilbert Ryle found it natural to include such things as "dwelling in imagination on possible disasters" under the heading of behavior (1949, p. 129). In the past fifty years or so, however, this distinction has been eroded to the point where most think that 'behavior' (and 'action') simply means something that is by definition overt or publicly observable,

---

[2] Strictly speaking 'phenomenology' is the *study of* the character of experience (it is an 'ology'). But it has also recently come to be used to denote the object of that study, i.e. the character of experience itself.

[3] I have in mind recent work by, among others, Richard Holton, Joshua Knobe, Eddy Nahmias, Shaun Nichols, Tamler Sommers, Steven Stich.

[4] This is not to say that there aren't primitive forms or bases of such experience to be found in creatures that are, relative to ourselves, conceptually impoverished.

and many have been misled, and have in particular failed to think things through with full generality, as a result of this error. It's not as if behavior is thought to require large-scale bodily motion in all cases; the motionlessness of the lioness before she springs is generally allowed to be an instance of behavior. As for public observability: no one sensible denies that a piece of mental action or behavior that has no overt expression involves neuronal changes that are in principle fully publicly observable. For all that, many people still balk at the idea of mental action. They need to shake off a habitual association between the notions of action and behavior and public observability (one of its causes is the great hangover of twentieth-century analytic philosophy—the radical confusion of epistemology with metaphysics).[5] Imagine that one is listening to the radio, motionless in bed, and a voice says:

Take the number 7—square it—add 1—divide by 2—multiply by 3—add 6—take the square root—take the square root again—subtract 3—multiply by infinity—subtract 1—take the square root.

One can leave out the last two steps if one wishes.

5. What are the most important open problems in philosophical theorizing about action and agency, and what are the prospects for progress?

I have no clear sense of particular pressing open questions. Once again, I think that the cognitive phenomenology of free will deserves further close attention, and a more scientific treatment (so far as this is possible). For the rest I feel what I have always felt. The theory of action is quite fearsomely difficult, but there is a clear sense in which it does not raise any overwhelming philosophical problems. We know what is going on when it comes to action. We know the basic facts. The problem is that it's quite extraordinarily hard to describe the whole phenomenon precisely. The difficulty is to find a way of putting things—a terminology—that allows one to make all the needed distinctions without being led into confusion or falsehood. The task is in this sense simply a task of *description*.

---

[5] I discuss this point about mental action and behavior in 'Behavior', chapter 10 of *Mental Reality* (1994), along with a question that arises before we ask which instances of behavior count as instances of action: the question of which bodily movements or changes count as instances of behavior.

To say that this is the task is not to say that it is not a philosophically important task—it is very important. It is just that the philosophical achievement will simply be the evolution and comprehensive deployment of a fully adequate terminology. It will be an enormous achievement, if anyone ever manages it, but it will not involve radical new insights or reveal anything we did not know.

References

Bennett, J. (1974) *Kant's dialectic*. Cambridge: Cambridge University Press.

Ryle, G. (1949) *The concept of mind*. Chicago: University of Chicago Press.

Sommers, T. & Strawson, G. (2003) 'You Cannot Make Yourself The Way You Are' The Believer March pp 78-87.

Strawson, G. (1986) *Freedom and belief*. Oxford: Oxford University Press.

Strawson, G. (1994) Mental reality. Cambridge, MA: MIT Press.

21. Galen Strawson

22
Raimo Tuomela

Professor of Philosophy

University of Helsinki, Finland

The editors of this volume presented the following questions for the participants to answer:

1. Why were you initially drawn to theorizing about action and agency?

2. What do you consider to be your most important contributions to theorizing about action and agency, and why?

3. What other sub-disciplines in philosophy and non-philosophical disciplines stand to benefit the most from philosophical work on the nature of action and agency, and how might such engagement be accomplished?

4. What do you regard as the most neglected issues in contemporary work on action and agency that deserve more attention?

5. What are the most important open problems in philosophical action and agency, and what are the prospects for progress?

I have decided to concentrate on answering the second of the above questions and will give only short answers to the other ones.

(1) As to the first question, as a university student my major was originally psychology, although I also studied philosophy (especially philosophy and methodology of science) and several other subjects, such as mathematics and sociology. My main interests in psychology were theoretical and social psychology. I wrote two doctoral dissertations, one at the University of Helsinki and the

other one in the logic and methodology program at Stanford University. Both dissertations were in philosophy of science. Later philosophical action theory became my central interest. Having published an extensive monograph on the causal theory of action in 1977 it occurred to me that some of my more formal treatments could be analogically used to clarify and philosophize about multi-agent action. This led me to studying social action and after several books and numerous papers to studying human sociality in general.

(2) Proceeding to the second question, I now present my theoretical approach to sociality in a somewhat simplified way that should be understandable also to non-specialists. After my lengthy presentation I will briefly answer the other questions that the editors put to the authors.

Humans are social beings living and adapted to living in groups, indeed, to functioning in several different groups during their lives. My general underlying assumption, indeed a commonplace fact, which gives ontological grounding for the motivation of human sociality is this: Human beings need, and tend to desire, to live in *orderly* groups for enhancing the *well-being* of their members. This need, involving as an obvious consequence also the need to be recognized and respected by others, motivates people to seek institutional and other collectively satisfactory solutions to collective action dilemmas, viz., dilemmas where individual and collective interests are in conflict. While all humans may be taken to have the mentioned need, not all of them do obey the created social order, viz., social rules and norms (including fairness norms), precisely because of their opposing, often selfish desires and perhaps their desires to distinguish themselves and be different from others. Yet, orderly group life on a local, as well as on a global, level is a must in a world of growing dependence between peoples and, indeed, despite some free-riding and non-cooperation, human groups tend to succeed in maintaining social order. I claim below that this is due not so much to altruism towards others or their other prosocial motivation as to their group-based motivation and commitments, viz., the authoritative reasons their memberships in their social groups give them for their action that promotes the group's interests. They thus typically are disposed to think in terms of "we", their group, and to act for the benefit of the group, where the group's views and attitudes gives them a reason to act so.

Building on the above motivational idea, I will argue that "we-

thinking"—collective intentionality in its full, "we-mode" sense—
forms the core of human sociality and indeed takes better into
account the above main motivational idea than individualistic
thinking or "I-mode" thinking and acting, and in game-theoretical
context it is also capable of resolving collective action dilemmas
that standard game theory cannot resolve.[1]

The we-mode approach is based on the intuitive idea that the
acting agent in central group contexts is the group viewed as an
agent, and the individual agent is not the primary actor but rather
a representative acting for the group. To go into some detail, according
to the intuitive view, the group can be regarded as an
agent from a conceptual and justificatory point of view, but ontologically
it only exists as a social system, not as an agent, and it
can only function via its members' functioning appropriately. The
ontological and causal work is done by the members' actions and
joint actions and what these produce. My conceptually and psychologically
holistic starting point is simply that there is a group
(an instrumentally viewed agent) that is the intentional—but not
the ontological—subject of attitudes and actions. The group is
assumed to commit itself to a group "ethos" (certain constitutive
goals, beliefs, standards, norms, etc.) and to act accordingly. This
intuitive picture can be explicated for the group-member level
and seen to involve three central ideas to be called "authoritative
group reason," the "Collectivity Condition," and "collective
commitment" (see below.) Let me emphasize that, in contrast, in
the I-mode case the individual is the sole acting agent. This is
a crucial difference, which my we-mode approach tries to make
sufficiently clear and ontologically palatable.

Translated into the group-member level the above holistic view
gives this. The group members function as group members as if
they were cogs in a machine, viz. the group agent capable of action.
Because of this, the group's ethos, as a central "jointness"
element assumed to be (extensively) accepted by the group members,
gives them their central reason for acting as a group member.
The reason is an authoritative one when the group members
themselves have participated in the creation of the ethos by their
collective acceptance.[2] Similarly, because of being members of a

---

[1] For the we-mode approach, see Tuomela (1984), (1995), (2000), and (2007). This paper summarizes the main ideas included in the we-mode approach. For lack of space, the reader is referred especially to my 2007 book for detailed analyses and arguments.

[2] See Tuomela (2007), chapter 6, for a discussion and rebuttal of the kind

group agent, the group members will "stand or fall together" or "be in the same boat" when acting as group members. This is explicated by the Collectivity Condition, the satisfaction of which will come about though the members' collective commitment to the ethos.

The we-mode group's commitment to its ethos amounts to the members' collective commitment to it. Here the conceptual starting point is the group's accepting an ethos (that could be a goal) with commitment to its satisfaction and maintenance. On the group-member level, this amounts to the group members' performative collective acceptance (indeed, collective construction) of an ethos (e.g. a goal) as the group's ethos (goal) to which they collectively commit themselves, where collective commitment accordingly is "reasoned" by the group commitment and where collective commitment also involves the members being directly socially committed to each other to function as group members, typically to further and maintain the ethos.[3] We-mode thinking, feeling, and acting accordingly presupposes reflexive collective acceptance ("construction") of the group's ethos and often also of some other, nonconstitutive content as the object of the group's attitudes.[4] The collectively accepted contents must be taken to be for the benefit and use of the group. The group members here also construct themselves as their group, viewing the group as an entity. The members here are "in the same boat"—explicated by the (strong) Collectivity Condition below. In all, the members are taken to view and "construct" their (we-mode) group as an entity guiding their lives when their group membership is salient and it also requires them to function as ethos-obeying and ethos-furthering group members and as "one agent."

In a nutshell, the we-mode is taken to involve the notion of a social group in a strong sense involving the features of an *(authoritative) group reason*, *collective commitment* of the members

---

of bootstrapping looming here.

[3] Cf. the somewhat different account by Gilbert in her 1989 book and later works. Her approach otherwise bears similarities to mine, although she seems to regard collective agents as literally ontologically existing..

[4] The members' collective acceptance of a "content," roughly, amounts to coming to hold a relevant "group-reasoned" joint intention or belief (or the like) with that content and being collectively committed to the content as well as acting appropriately to the held joint attitude. We-mode collective acceptance of this kind clearly differs from the members' private, I-mode acceptance (where the three central features of the we-mode, involved also here, are missing.)

to the group's reason-giving ethos (reflecting, as we may say, the group's commitment to its ethos), and the resulting group uniformity making the *Collectivity Condition* satisfied on the member level.

To elaborate on the above, a we-mode group may accept leaders authorized to have the power to give orders and directives, thus reasons to act, to the members. A group reason is a reason based on what the group believes, intends, wants, and conceptually constructs (accepts) for itself, etc., and these group attitudes are basically understood in terms of what the group members jointly believe, intend, want, and collectively construct for the group. The conceptual direction in the we-mode is *top down*, viz. group level to member level, whereas in the I-mode the conceptual direction is *bottom up*, viz. from the member level to the group level.[5]

In the I-mode case some people can agree to build a bridge together but still function as private persons in the sense that their private desires and beliefs are decisive—while they can accept, e.g., compromises, etc. Individual rationality basically guides their activities although also moral considerations may get involved. Their "collective commitment" is different from the we-mode case, as it is not necessarily based on functioning for the benefit of the group but rather at least normally in part for their private individual benefit. While group-based reasons, goals, utilities, beliefs, norms, etc., are essentially involved in the we-mode group, reasons cannot be in the same strong sense involved in the I-mode case but only in a weaker sense based on private acceptance.

Acting as a group member in a we-mode group is based on what the group decides, orders, or requires (etc.) and the group members give some of their "natural" authority to the group. The group members form (we-mode) attitudes for their group by collective acceptance. Examples are given by "We will build a bridge together as a group" (group intention), "We believe that stars determine our fate," or "We believe that Euros are our money" (group beliefs). Such attitudes can serve as group reasons. Thus, that the group believes or intends—or, equivalently, given the strong "we," that we believe or intend something—can serve as

---

[5] The ontological direction in the we-mode is only partially top down, as there are no group agents in a literal ontological sense although groups can ontologically be viewed as social systems in a sense not reducible to the individual or even to the "jointness" level.

a group member's reason to act in appropriate ways amounting to his part of the group's action. For example, in the case of the joint action of painting a house the chain of justification is from a group's intention to paint the house to the members' joint intention to see to it that the house gets painted by them *in toto*. The joint intention normally justifies each member's intention to perform his part and also his performing it.[6]

An important divide here is between a group thinking and acting as one agent (we-mode group) versus some agents acting and interacting, perhaps in concert, in pursuit of their (possibly shared) private goals (I-mode group). Group reasons (we-mode reasons) and private or I-mode reasons for acting and having attitudes thus are different in kind, and the group level (containing group reasons) is not reducible to and might not be even supervenient on the private, I-mode level. Only the we-mode can properly account for the generality that the group level involves relative to group members (think of fluctuating membership, the historical dimension of the group, the stability that e.g. helps to make group responsibility possible) and the kind of (partial) depersonalization that group life involves.

As to collective commitment, in order for a group member to act as a group member, she must be required to be committed (bound, typically voluntarily) to performing actions that further the group's ethos and other matters that the group is pursuing. Indeed, the members should be (and a "sufficient" number of them must be) collectively committed, viz., committed as group members, to participating in group activities. This can be justified in terms of its being an entailment of group membership and the assumption that the group is relevantly committed.[7] The group's commitment to a goal, for instance, translates into the members' collective commitment to it, and this entails that they are together committed in a group-derived sense to the goal and, especially, to its satisfaction. It is also entailed that they are normatively, in a group-involving sense committed to each other to performing their parts of the members' attempts to achieve the goal for the group. This can be called directed group-social commitment. The

---

[6] A more detailed account of the justificatory inferences is given in Tuomela (2007), Chapter 4.

[7] That the group is so committed can come about in various ways, e.g. through its leaders' effecting it or the group members previous or current (and sufficiently extensive) collective acceptance, or by means of e.g. some previously agreed upon institutional mechanism.

collective commitment here thus is essentially a group-involving idea, and it also entails that a group member in general cannot give up her commitment without the group's consent.[8]

Consider the example where the members' group reason, a group goal, in a we-mode group is represented by "G is our (group's) goal." This involves the members' having and sharing goal G as their group's goal and their being collectively committed to it. The group goal is one that they have jointly chosen for their group, or one that the leaders (operative members) have decided upon, or perhaps a goal that the group has accepted and codified to be its goal a long time, say a century, ago but accepted as a goal by the present members. Their being collectively committed to G amounts, roughly, to saying that ideally each member has bound herself to the members' seeing to it jointly that G will be satisfied, given normal conditions, and that each member is prepared to do his share of the group's achieving G and being committed to the others to do his share.

Two basic features that distinguish collective commitment from collective or "aggregated" private commitments in the I-mode case are these:

1. We-mode collective commitment is derived from a group reason (recall the top-down feature of the we-mode)

2. Qua being based on the group's commitment a member cannot give it up without other group members' consent. This is because it is a ground principle that both on conceptual and functional grounds all the group members ought to be collectively committed when the group is committed to some content p (based on its intending to bring about p or to uphold p, depending on the case).

Commitment here needs to be normative only in a "technical" sense relating to the case of an agent's having intentionally adopted a goal. The members accordingly are weakly normatively committed in the meant technical sense to doing whatever they reasonably can to achieve the goal. These features can be partly clarified in terms of the kind of practical reasoning the members are supposed to be disposed to perform in the present case.[9]

---

[8] See e.g. Gilbert (1989), Tuomela (2002, 2007).
[9] See e.g. the schemas (W1) and (W2) and other schemas in Tuomela (1995) and (2000).

Also, in the case of I-mode groups, the members, functioning on their private reasons, can, of course, jointly paint a house, sharing an intention. They can also have representatives or delegates for them. In this case a group member in principle is fully in charge of whatever she takes part in, although she and the others can still agree to delegate group tasks to some members. Group reasons in a weak sense (directly based on the members' private reasons in contrast to the we-mode case based on the group's beliefs or goals or normative commitments, etc.) may contingently be involved. When they are, we are dealing with I-mode collective intentionality, viz. the *pro-group I-mode*.

It is often useful to view a group as an agent capable of acting as a unit. Thus a group can be taken to accept views, form intentions, act, and be responsible. However, it is not an extra agent over and above the group members. When a group acts, its members must act as group members. One can thus redescribe the group's functioning and acting at the group member level, in terms of the group members' functioning in appropriate ways as group members. This is basically we-mode activity. It follows from the idea of a group acting or functioning as one agent that the members ought to function in line with this. They can be said to be necessarily "in the same boat" or "stand or fall together." Here the (strong) *Collectivity Condition* is satisfied. Formulated for the special case of goal satisfaction it necessarily connects the members as follows: Necessarily (as based on the group members' reflexive construction of a goal as its goal), the goal is satisfied for a member if and only if it is satisfied for all (other) members.[10] Thus, if you and I have the goal to go to Alfonzo's for lunch, this goal as a jointly accepted we-mode goal is satisfied for me only if we both go to Alfonzo's (and similarly for you).

In the pro-group I-mode case with privately shared goals a weak collectivity condition will be satisfied. For example, some persons may share a (private) goal or intention where the goal or intention requires all the participants' contribution. When the goal is satisfied for them, it is satisfied on contingent grounds—in contrast to the quasi-conceptual grounds (viz., on the basis of the participants' collective construction) in the we-mode case. However, in some other I-mode cases the participants might just make an agreement to achieve a goal together (e.g., go to the movies

---

[10] See Tuomela (2002), chapters 5 and 6 for the reflexive nature of collective acceptance in our construction sense.

together). Then we are dealing with a collectivity condition which comes relatively close to the we-mode collectivity condition. For here the goal is simultaneously satisfied (or respectively fails to be satisfied) for the participants due to their private promises and they are only privately but not collectively committed to what has been promised. Here also "forgroupness" (the full group reason aspect) is missing and the (strong) Collectivity Condition fails to be satisfied (as agreement-making as such does not make for the reflexive construction of the goal as the group's goal).

Most joint action types, like lifting a table or singing a song together can be performed in the I-mode and in the we-mode, although each token of table lifting is either an I-mode action or a we-mode action (but not both). In the case of I-mode joint action the participants can be assumed normally to intend roughly in the way "I intend that we do something X (e.g. lift a table) together and I will perform a relevant part of this jointly performed action X." Here doing X together amounts to each participant doing his part because of his private goal (e.g., to get the table jointly lifted and to participate in the joint lifting of the table) as a private person but with the understanding of the dependencies in question. The participants still need not construct the situation as their group (in the entitative sense) doing something but rather as their doing it together. In the we-mode the participants see themselves as a group that is acting as a unit, trying to see to it that a certain jointly intended outcome will be realized. They participate for a group reason (e.g. the group intention) that recommends or demands a certain action for the benefit of the group. They are collectively committed to the action—because of their joint intention based on or derived from the group reason, viz. the group's having the intended goal. In the I-mode case the participants are not similarly collectively committed and do not mutually view and collectively construct themselves as acting as a group or as one agent. Rather they view themselves as an "aggregate" of interdependent individuals and intend to achieve a certain result on the basis of their private personal (and, e.g., promise-based) commitments to the joint task at hand. In the pro-group I-mode case they intend the result to be at least in part for the use of their group, too, and thus function on the basis of a *weak group reason*.

One may ask which of the modes works better in actual life and what kinds of arguments one can present for and against the we-mode and, respectively, the I-mode. Here I will be particularly interested in comparing how the we-mode fares in comparison with the pro-group I-mode concerning the group's functionality.

I will now summarize some of the main differences (mainly conceptual ones) between the we-mode and the pro-group I-mode in the form of a table.

	WE-MODE	I-MODE
(1) conceptual and justificatory direction "top down"	yes	no
(2) collectively constructed group and group goal, etc.	yes	no
(3) strong collectivity condition	yes	no
(4) strong collective commitment	yes	no
(5) strong authoritative group reason	yes	no
(6) members' group-based goals, beliefs, etc are based and supervenient on their private goals, beliefs, etc.	no	yes
(7) group responsibility (qua a group)	yes	no
(8) members' presupposed right and responsibility to monitor and sanction ethos-opposing actions and to help others when needed	yes	no

To summarize my answer to the editors' second question, my most central contribution to action theory in my view is the development of a conceptual framework of collective and especially "jointness" concepts. It concerns e.g. joint intention and action, mutual and joint belief, joint attitudes in general, and in the case of groups (instrumentally) viewed as collective agents, their analogous attitudes—group intentions and actions, group beliefs, etc. Especially, I have emphasized and analyzed the difference between we-mode concepts through the explication of various aspects of functioning as a full-blown group member and I-mode concepts concerned with functioning as a private person, be that concerned with group (or collective) contexts or not. Accordingly, I have distinguished between two kinds of collective intentionality, we-mode and (pro-group) I-mode collective intentionality. Spelling out all this in detail and showing the relationships between we-mode and progroup I-mode collective intentionality and also showing that in some contexts the we-mode wins over the pro-group I-mode (in several senses of "winning over") was the main topic of my recent

2007 book. Focusing on the we-mode has made it clear that we can see sociality and social life in a new light: the we-mode is the core notion in the construction of society and sociality in general.

(3) As to the editors' third question, I venture to make the following conjectural remarks and claims from the point of view of my theorizing. In the case of collective social action, research in action theory itself (including of course single-agent action theory) will derive benefits from the we-mode approach, also in the case of the study of single-agent action. More interestingly, philosophy of mind will also benefit—especially if we-mode mental states turn out to be real, as I have argued.

There is also an impact on political philosophy and political science will benefit, too. The we-mode approach has theoretical connections to communitarianism and republicanism and this indicates how the detailed analyses of the we-mode approach can be of help here.

The we-mode approach has consequences for collective decision-making: e.g., accounting for how groups can arrive at goals, values, beliefs, and other group attitudes. For instance, the role of Arrow's impossibility result must be rethought when the group's point of view and its non-individualistic decision mechanism is adopted and the idea of acting as a proper group member is taken seriously.

Also moral philosophy will be affected. Especially the following topics are to be emphasized: group and collective responsibility, acting as a group member, performing one's part of a joint project, e.g., such as achieving the common good, cooperation, treating someone as a means versus as an end in itself (typically a we-mode notion). Furthermore, the we-mode also connects to mutual recognition, mutual respect of rights, trust, and helping as moral ideas.

As to collective action theory, free-riderism differs in we-mode and I-mode groups due to the nature of these groups. Cooperation problems such as collective action dilemmas (more precisely, games of common interest with interdependence) in a sense disappear when viewed from the group's perspective with the group as the main active agent—although an agent that does not strictly speaking ontologically exist as an agent and that can act only vicariously in virtue of its members' actions.

The we-mode approach has applications to cultural evolution (e.g. in terms of group selection that uses we-mode group notions) and to social psychology (e.g. making more precise certain aspects of the social identity theory).

Economics and its rational choice approach is known to be highly individualistic and to involve too few central social elements in its—also otherwise impoverished—conceptual framework. For instance, economics seems capable of giving only rather thin individualistic accounts of cooperation and of social institutions. The we-mode approach can help here.[11]

(4) As to the fourth question, in the case of collective social action, serious applications to political philosophy and moral philosophy are to be expected. See the above comments to the third question.

(5) As to the fifth question about the most important open problems in philosophical action and agency, and the prospects for progress, I again refer to my answer to the third question.

References

Gilbert, M. 1989. *On Social Facts*. London: Routledge.

Tuomela, R. 1977. *Human Action and Its Explanation*. Dordrecht: Reidel.

Tuomela, R. 1984. *A Theory of Social Action*. Dordrecht: Reidel.

Tuomela, R. 1995. *The Importance of Us: A Philosophical Study of Basic Social Notions*. Stanford UP, Stanford.

Tuomela, R. 2000. *Cooperation: A Philosophical Study*. Kluwer, Dordrecht.

Tuomela, R. 2002. *The Philosophy of Social Practices: A Collective Acceptance View*. Cambridge UP, Cambridge.

Tuomela, R. 2007. *The Philosophy of Sociality: The Shared Point of View*, Oxford UP, New York

---

[11] My conjectural claims given as answers to the third question have to some extent been substantiated in my 2007 book.

23
Manuel Vargas

Associate Professor of Philosophy

University of San Fransisco, USA

---

1. Why were you initially drawn to theorizing about action and agency?

In terms of my own first-personal narrative, the most obvious proximal cause of my theorizing about agency was a graduate seminar on free will taught by Peter van Inwagen. It was my first semester of graduate school, and van Inwagen's forceful presentation of incompatibilism made a big impression on me. I left that course thinking incompatibilism was both obvious and irrefutable. The only problem was that I didn't stay at Notre Dame. I transferred to Stanford in the following year, where I discovered the truth of a remark John Fischer once made: *Indiana is for Incompatibilists and California is for Compatibilists.* Some of the folks there who most influenced me, especially Michael Bratman and Ken Taylor, are thoroughgoing compatibilists. I was really struck by the fact that both of these smart, thoughtful guys seemed genuinely puzzled by the impulse to incompatibilism. I wasn't entirely ready to give up on my incompatibilism (which was by then shifting from libertarianism to hard incompatibilism), but I felt a need to be able to find some way to reconcile it with an appreciation for the appeal that compatibilism clearly seemed to have for some otherwise compelling philosophers. And, so my interest in thinking about free agency and free action began to take root.

So, that's the intellectualized part of the story. But there is also the fact of my local conditions when all of this was going on. For good or ill, I kept taking seminars where the problem of free will would crop up in the course of things. Out of sheer laziness (or, as I like to think about it, out of a dimly sensed need to conserve my energies for later), I kept seizing on the topic as a subject matter for seminar papers, whether the course was on Hume, Aristotle,

Nietzsche, philosophy of mind, or philosophy action. Thus, when it came time to write a dissertation, free will seemed like an obvious choice. It was certainly going to require less preparation than any other topic, I (perhaps falsely) thought. So there I went— and here I am.

Having given this first-personal narrative, I feel compelled to flag that I'm actually somewhat suspicious about the status of these kinds of reports. To be sure, accounts like the one I just gave is the sort of response we expect to questions that demand an explanation of what we have done or been drawn to do. But, these first-personal narratives —narratives emphasizing reasons and context-specific practical deliberation— seem susceptible to undermining by a range of alternative explanations. We might, for example, imagine that some day we will be able to give a neurochemical story about why I did what I did. Or, we'll be able to point to a sociological story that explains what I did. Or, we could go in for an old-fashioned deflationary story in terms of unobvious psychological forces of dubious rationality. And, at least on the surface of it, all of these explanations seem to threaten the kind of explanation I initially offered of my attraction to philosophical issues of agency. This isn't to say that I think such explanations have no place, or that action explanations can be reduced or eliminated. I think it is a very difficult matter to say what the relationship is between these various forms of explanation are for human action, and whether one or another should or could rightly displace the sort of first-personal narrative that serves as our default explanatory position. I mention it, though, because these matters reach to the heart of philosophy of action. Indeed, in some ways it illustrates how the subject matter is ubiquitous and foundational.

2. What do you consider to be your own most important contribution(s) to theorizing about action and agency, and why?

By my lights, estimations of importance of contribution are most fruitfully made by other people near the end of one's career, when further disavowals and obfuscation by the author become difficult (or ideally, impossible). So, I fervently hope that this is a wildly inappropriate time for assessments of my work.

That said, I have no reason to believe that I've made any particularly important contribution to this literature, even by my own lights. Don't get me wrong— I certainly *hope* to make some contribution over the next few decades. And, I am delighted to be included in this volume, as it is chock full of people I greatly admire and from whom I have learned so much. However, I am no peer to the members of this distinguished lineup, so I imagine my inclusion in this volume reflects some optimism about my potential for future contribution more than the judgment that I have already provided a substantive contribution.

Nevertheless, I do have something to say about one way of conceiving of the nature of contributions to philosophy, and how such contributions might be measured. My preferred way of thinking about the nature of philosophical contributions is in terms of an answer to this question: To what extent did the purported contribution help us make progress in understanding the subject matter? Given this metric, there are many ways an account could make a contribution. One way is simple enough—just *be right*. That's a pretty rare thing in philosophy, though. A second way to contribute to progress in understanding an issue is by raising problems, identifying puzzles, or pointing to matters that merit attention. A third kind of progress is neither a matter of being right nor a matter of asking useful questions. Instead, it is a kind of progress that is usually only achieved by being interestingly wrong. It is a familiar enough achievement to make a philosophical contribution by developing an underappreciated possibility and getting other philosophers to respond to it. Of course, the usual result is that we discard the proposal when we understand why that possibility is not the right one. In doing this, though, we can accomplish two things. First, we constrain the scope of remaining viable possibilities. Second, we can trigger new innovations or open up new possibilities that were previously invisible to us. So, I believe that both of these possibilities provide an underappreciated route by which a philosopher can make a contribution to understanding some subject matter.

One consequence of this picture is that is that it is misguided to conceive of philosophical progress (and philosophical success or failure) in the paradigmatic case as the achievement or failure of some lone, heroic figure. Instead, I think we are better off thinking about these things in terms of the success or failure of a collective, knowledge-seeking enterprise that (hopefully) makes progress on the backs of our collective work and interaction. So, even if no one individual has got the right account of intentional action, free will, or what have you, we might still be collectively making progress towards achieving the True Account. I do not wish to deny that there might well be individuals who have made considerably greater contributions in the course of things. But, it is important to remember that those contributions are also collective, requiring large networks of education and idea dissemination, as well as a cultural context that facilitates and takes seriously the kind of inquiry that yields some philosophical achievement.

It is also worth noting that even in the case of an individual, it is quite likely that we'll miss the mark in our assessments of his or her work. Here's why: we don't normally track actual contributions in the sense I have suggested. It could turn out that whatever contribution a given philosopher makes is not appreciated for the role it *in fact* plays in our collective project of truth seeking. Being demonstrably wrong about some matter, and forcing the literature to point it out (or inspiring someone with the right professional visibility to highlight his or her avoidance of the error) can permit us to collectively move on to some other matter. In doing so, it can sometimes be the crucial thing needed to move us closer to the right account. Note, however, that it is also exactly the sort of thing we tend to ignore or fail to recognize in our assessments of philosophical contributions. In philosophy, instructive failure is oftentimes more fruitful than (let's admit it, a usually short lived) "success." Yet, we rarely celebrate such failure and we virtually never measure accomplishment by it. Moreover, even when we attend to useful failures, the utility of the failure is not always obvious to us. So, although I think there is a reasonable metric for thinking about what constitutes a greater and lesser contribution to philosophy, I'm also skeptical about whether we're very often in a position to accurately evaluate the matter.

In the spirit of answering the likely intent of the question, though, I will say something that more directly addresses the substance of the question. If I were to guess about what other philosophers are likely to cite as my contributions to the field thus far, I'd point to two things. One concerns my approach to the problem of free will and moral responsibility, something I call *moderate revisionism* (Fischer, Kane, Pereboom, & Vargas, 2007; Vargas, 2004; Vargas, 2005a). This approach is a response to the thought that our commonsense conceptions of free will and moral responsibility cannot be made consistent with an independently plausible, broadly naturalistic picture of the world. (See my answer to the above question about why I got bugged by this issue.) Moderate revisionism is a way of responding to the problem of reconciling our self-image with a naturalistic picture of the world, which I take to be independently plausible. The answer I have been developing is one that abandons some particularly problematic elements of commonsense, and attempts to show how we can re-anchor our understanding of free will and moral responsibility in things that do not depend on our being agents of the sort described by libertarianism.

If this view has any contribution to make, in the sense in which I think of philosophical contributions, it might be the following. First, it helps bring to the foreground the role of intuitions in our theory building in this domain. Consequently, it makes particularly salient the way in which philosophers have tended to build their metaphysical commitments out of commonsense. Secondly, it helps to sharpen questions about the relationship of the normative to the metaphysical. As I see things, anyway, this is a domain in which we can make excellent progress if we put aside our pre-philosophical convictions and instead ask ourselves what conception of agency is required to justify our practices of praise and blame, and what is needed to license the judgments we make of these things.

The second philosophical contribution my work might be taken to have concerns the articulation of a kind of puzzle raised by the relationship of an epistemic requirement on responsibility and the conditions under which we acquire various capacities that are taken to constitute our free and responsible agency. The epistemic requirement is, roughly, the requirement that an agent needs some awareness of likely outcomes of the action in order to be held responsible for it. In "The Trouble With Tracing" (Vargas, 2005b) I argue that either the knowledge condition isn't satisfied when we acquire a significant number of our action-determining capacities and dispositions, or else we have an inadequate account of the knowledge condition.

I am not the only one who has picked up on this puzzle, but I think my discussion of it has provided a useful target for some further philosophical rumination on the matter. It remains to be seen whether the issue has any legs, though. Moreover, I think it is an open question whether or not the inevitable dissolution of the problem moves us closer to the truth about the conditions for moral responsibility.

3. What other sub-disciplines in philosophy and non-disciplines stand to benefit the most from philosophical work on the nature of action and agency, and how might such engagement be accomplished?

Psychologists and neuroscientists interested in agency and action have a good deal to learn from philosophical work on agency. And, there is plenty philosophers of agency can learn by studying work in psychology and neuroscience. Still, even a cursory glance at work by scientists interested in agency too often reveals impoverished conceptual resources when it comes to interpreting their own data or drawing out the philosophical ramification of the work. There are, now, more philosophically minded folks who have started to wade into these matters, but there is a long way to go.

Inside philosophy, it is less clear to me how much philosophers in other subfields might learn from studying the philosophy of action, at least those parts with which my own work is concerned. My doubt is partly driven by the thought that philosophy of agency — a term I use to apply to both philosophy of action as it is traditionally conceived of as well as more general issues of agency that include things like free will, moral responsibility, and autonomy— appropriates so much from neighboring fields. Philosophy of agency integrates issues in metaphysics, philosophy of mind, moral psychology, and ethics. In this, it is like many other fields in philosophy, but more so. That is, philosophy of agency integrates issues from a wider range of fields than most fields in philosophy, and consequently, we are still absorbing much of what we need know. Until we've absorbed a bit more, it isn't clear to me that we're going to be offering much to other areas in philosophy. Naturally, I hope I am wrong. And, I think, there are pockets of philosophy agency where I am clearly wrong. However, within those areas I focus on, where there is some direction of influence running the other way (from philosophy of agency to some other subfield), the influence tends to come from roughly normative aspects of work on agency. And, it seems to me that perhaps the most promising direction from work on agency to normative issues that ought to be pursued by someone— perhaps an ambitious graduate student?— involves connections with political philosophy. There has been some work on notions of autonomy in political liberalism that have grown out of work that was done in the context of work in philosophy of action. And, Sam Scheffler has done interesting work on the way in which conceptions of agency and responsibility interact with various issues in political philosophy. However, my sense is that there is more to be said on these matters.

4. What do you regard as the most neglected issues in contemporary work on action and agency that deserve more attention?

I can't speak with authority about philosophy of agency more generally, but there are several issues connected with work on free will and moral responsibility that seem to me to be neglected. For example, philosophical accounts of moral responsibility are not particular useful at offering guidance in real world circumstances. Whether or not it is a vice that our theories do not ordinarily offer useful guidance in real world contexts, I think such a service would be an undeniable virtue. However, I am inclined to think that there are at least two barriers to the development of action-guiding theories of moral responsibility.

First, we do not have a good grasp of the ways in which situations structure the powers of agents. Philosophers working on agency have tended to think about the powers of agents in atomistic terms. That is, philosophers have tended to think of agents as self-contained things to be understood entirely detached from a context or environment (including psychological and cultural). Such pictures of our agency are, I think, deeply flawed, or at the very least, profoundly misleading. If our powers are partly structured by our environments, until we have a good understanding of the ways in which this interaction between agent and environment occur, we will not be able to provide much guidance in real world cases— precisely because real world cases *are* cases embedded in environments.

A second barrier to the attainment of action-guiding theories is that we lack an epistemology of responsibility in non-ideal circumstances. That is, we do not have a philosophical account of how to make judgments of responsibility given the messiness of real-world circumstances, circumstances where full information about the agency of others and the deliberative circumstances of their choices is impossible to secure. Moreover, growing scientific skepticism about the veracity of even well intentioned first personal reports is surely no help. Given the consequences of moral praise and blame, what is needed is some account of how we might get reasonable evidence about the powers of agents as they are relevant to responsibility, along with some standard of deciding what counts as adequate evidence given our epistemically imperfect circumstances. This is not to say that we do not make such judgments all the time. And, indeed, legal assessments of responsibility have grappled with a version of this problem for a long time. However, it seems to me that in the case of philosophical accounts of moral responsibility we have not even begun to do this work.

Two other problems strike me as deserving of more attention: the epistemic condition on moral responsibility (roughly, the idea that agents have to know something about the consequences of their action in order to be appropriately held responsible) and the relationship of risk to blameworthiness. I do not have any sense of how these matters should be sorted out, but I do think it would be worthwhile for philosophers interested in responsibility to think more about these issues.

5. What are the most important open problems in philosophical theorizing about action and agency, and what are the prospects for progress?

When it comes to important open problems connected to action and agency, we have an embarrassment of riches. Among them, I'd say that some of the most important and difficult problems concern the connection of the normative to the natural, and the matter of how we account for the ontology of the normative dimensions of human agency (including rational, epistemic, and moral aspects). I can imagine some philosophers disputing whether these matters are properly in the domain of philosophy of action, but even if they are not I think they are clearly in the domain of philosophy of agency.

The ubiquity of the problem I mentioned —the intersection of the natural and the normative in human agency— can be seen throughout the existing literature. We see it in attempts to understand the nature of practical reason and the integration of agent-based and world-based inputs to it; we see it in debates about the causal theory of action and the place it gives to reasons in a world of causes; we see it in disputes over the conditions of free will and responsible agency; and, we see it in discussions about the role of knowledge as it conditions and structures various forms of agency.

I am also inclined to think there are a number of open problems connected to the literature of free will that we are just starting to address in a direct and fruitful way. So, for example, I think we are on the verge of small cottage industry surrounding the matter of desert, including whether and how it is relevant to the success or failure of various accounts of free will and moral responsibility. I also think we are finally engaging with some deep and complex methodological issues surrounding how we build accounts of free will and moral responsibility. The matter of intuitions and their relationship to the metaphysics of free will seems to me to me to be a crucial and unresolved issue.

I also believe there is a growing sense that the dominant jargon of the field is oftentimes as much hindrance as help. For example, the fixation on the compatibility-with-determinism debate, and the attendant emphasis on whether one is a compatibilist or incompatibilist can sometimes obscure threats that have little or no direct relationship to determinism. My claim is not that we cannot useful deploy the language of compatibility. Rather, my point is that given the varieties of matters around which compatibility and incompatibility talk arise (including free will, moral responsibility, deliberation, maximally desirable forms of agency, etc.) the language of compatibilism and incompatibilism *simpliciter* has a utility comparable to the distinction between realism and antirealism is in metaphysics, or as internalism and externalism is in moral psychology (which is to say: very little).

I don't have a confident assessment about the near-term prospects for progress on these matters. However, I do remain optimistic about the possibility of our collective progress, over larger lengths of time. Even if the flood of false theories spilling from the lips of philosophers doesn't abate any time soon, identifying *why* they are false is an important kind of progress available to us. And, I think prospects are quite good that we will some day come to understand why nearly all of our going theories, mine included, are on these matters, mightily mistaken. I confess to being cheered by this possibility.

Bibliography

Fischer, J. M., Kane, R., Pereboom, D., & Vargas, M. (2007). *Four Views on Free Will.* Malden, MA: Blackwell.

Vargas, M. (2004). Responsibility and the Aims of Theory: Strawson and Revisionism. *Pacific Philosophical Quarterly,* 85(2), 218-241.

Vargas, M. (2005a). The Revisionist's Guide to Responsibility. *Philosophical Studies,* 125(3), 399-429.

Vargas, M. (2005b). The Trouble With Tracing. *Midwest Studies in Philosophy*, 29(1), 269-291.

24
George Wilson

Professor of Philosophy
University of Southern California, USA

Debates About Causalism in the Theory of Action

What led me into the theory of action was sheer bafflement. Donald Davidson had presented an enormously influential argument about the character of commonsense explanations of action, and I simply couldn't follow it. I say this as encouragement to others who are just now becoming interested in the field but find their interest intermittently laced with bouts of confusion.

To explain what I take to be my chief intervention in action theory, I'm afraid that it is necessary to make a brief excursus into the history of my confusion here. At the time I began working on *The Intentionality of Human Action*,[1] the chief questions in the area concerned the nature of explanations of intentional actions in terms of reasons. Did these reason explanations of why the relevant action had been performed cite the pertinent reasons as causes of the action in question? Or, alternatively, did the agent's reasons for acting explain the action in some different way that did not presuppose a causal link between the reasons and the action they purported to explain? Actually, by the time I was writing, there was a broad consensus that Davidson had settled these questions in his classic "Actions, Reasons, and Causes"[2] and that he had settled them in favor of the causal account. Davidson had offered an argument I will discuss in a moment that seemed to many to have shown that there was no serious alternative to the 'causalist' approach.

---

[1] Revised and Enlarged Edition (Stanford, CA: Stanford University Press, 1989).

[2] Reprinted in *Essays on Actions and Events* (Oxford: Clarendon Press, 1980), pp. 3-19.

Davidson was arguing against a range of writers who took their inspiration from Wittgenstein and held that reason explanations were not causal. Some had argued that there was a conceptual incoherence in the very idea that a reason explanation presented the agent's desires, beliefs, and intentions as causal factors of the action. Each of these authors made some suggestion about the kind of non-causal explanation that reason explanations supposedly involved. In my opinion, Davidson was right on two important scores. The arguments for the conceptual incoherence of causalism were unsound, and, for the most part, the putative 'non-causal' alternatives were either faulty or very hard to grasp. However, Davidson also gave a positive argument for causalism that many people found entirely convincing. Here is a brief version of the argument. Suppose that on a certain occasion an agent has a definite reason R for Φing. Perhaps she wants to Ψ and believes that Φing is an optimal means of Ψing. Suppose also that on the occasion in question the agent actually does Φ. It does not follow from these suppositions that R was the reason why the agent performed her act of Φing. The agent might have Φ'd for some reason other than R or inadvertently Φ'd for no reason at all. Intuitively, R will be a reason why the agent Φ'd on the pertinent occasion only if the agent performed her act *because* she had the reason R. However, the "because" in this last formulation must mark some kind of explanatory connection between R and the act of Φing in question. Davidson reminds us that ordinary causation is an explanatory connection that could satisfy the requirement, and it is utterly unclear what other explanatory connection might yield an intelligible, alternative answer. Therefore, the components of the agent's reasons must be construed as causes of the action that they explain.

However, I was puzzled by Davidson's argument for the following reason. It seemed to me that Elizabeth Anscombe, in her monograph *Intention*,[3] had sketched an apparent alternative to the causalist approach—an alternative that Davidson seemed simply to ignore. Anscombe's discussion is notoriously difficult to interpret, but here are the main components in the alternative line of thought I thought that I discerned. i) She held that when we ask, '*Why* did the agent perform her (intentional) act of Φing?', the 'why'- question we raise has a special and distinctive sense.

---

[3] Anscombe, 2nd edition (Cambridge, MA: Harvard University Press, 2000).

A good part of her monograph attempts to clarify this sense. ii) *One* way of answering the query that is raised by the 'why'- question is to identify the intention that the agent had in Φing. We answer this question at least partially when we respond that the agent Φ'd with the intention of Ψing. iii) The explanatory point of giving an intention that that the agent had in Φing is to identify an aim or objective or goal that the particular act of Φing had for the agent as she performed it. Much as we can explain why an organism produces a certain biological activity by specifying a function that the activity had for the organism, we can explain why an agent performed a certain action by specifying a goal or objective that the action had for the agent. (This comparison is mine and not Anscombe's.) Thus, on my reconstruction of Anscombe, intentional actions are explained in terms of reasons by constructing a distinctive but quite familiar kind of teleological explanation of why the action was performed.

As noted above, Davidson does not explicitly consider the Anscombe alternative. Still, it is clear from his essay that he would not accept that a proposal of this sort yields a *genuine* alternative to his brand of causalism. For instance, he would agree that reason explanations of action are teleological in something like the broad sense that I have just outlined. However, he also clearly supposes that teleological explanations of action are themselves just causal explanations of a certain kind. Very roughly, he believes that, in giving the aim of an action for the agent, we are saying, in effect, that the agent had the relevant aim (where having that aim is an internal state of the agent), and her having that aim was, among other factors, a cause of her action. Whatever one thinks of this contention, it is important to understand that the argumentative ground has shifted. Davidson holds that there is no alternative to the causalist account of reason explanations, but his view is plausible only if he is right that an important class of teleological propositions have the kind of causal analysis that he implicitly favors. This constitutes a rather strong conceptual claim, a claim for which, as far as I can see, he provides no independent argument.

I think that it is possible to elucidate the dialectical misfire in somewhat starker terms, although here my proposals go beyond anything that Anscombe says explicitly.

Consider statements of the form

a) The agent Φ'd with the intention of Ψing,

or alternatively

b) In Φing, the agent intended to Ψ.

As I noted before, Anscombe tells us that such statements generally give the aim or goal or objective of the agent's act of Φing. Indeed, I am inclined to think that the concept of intention in action just is the concept of a certain kind of goal directedness that is manifested in the action itself. I have proposed that a) and b) are tantamount to the claim that

c) The agent's Φ'd, and her act of Φing was directed by her (in a distinctive first person way) at promoting the goal of Ψing.

I add the qualification, "in a distinctive first person way," to mark the point that behavior that is intended to Ψ is something more than simply behavior that is directed at a goal. The behavior in intentional action is under the guidance of the agent, and that guidance is exercised in an epistemically privileged fashion. I believe that this qualification is important, but it is also hard to clarify, especially in a limited space. The issue here is closely tied to Anscombe's well-known but controversial thesis that agents have 'knowledge without observation' of their own intentional actions. In guiding their intentional movements, agents have knowledge of both the goal of their behavior and of its evolving trajectory in the situation–knowledge that is not derived significantly from observation of the behavior itself or of the immediate environment in which it occurs. In any case, it was my view, inspired by Anscombe, that it is just this notion of the agent's epistemically privileged guidance of her behavior toward an objective that grounds reason explanations of action and, moreover, that this characteristic teleological connection is not reducible to the type of causalist analysis that Davidson envisages. In my opinion, the nature of reason explanations of action turns in the end on questions about the *nature* of human or personal agency in its broadest and most basic instantiations.

Davidson did not directly address this Anscombe inspired alternative, and, it is my impression that his position and hers simply failed to engage one another in the implicit debate between them. Nevertheless, it is patent that Davidson rejected any line of thought of the type that I have sketched, although it is surprising to notice that this rejection is framed quite obliquely and is presented almost as a passing thought. For example, he notoriously asserts in "Actions, Reasons, and Causes, "The expression 'the intention with which James went to church' has the outward form of a description, but in fact it is syncategorematic and cannot be taken to refer to an entity, state, disposition, or event."[4] The reference to syncategorematicity is pretty gnomic in this context, but Davidson means that the apparent reference to something called "intention" in statements of form a) is only apparent and that a) and b) can and should be parsed in causalist terms. Roughly, for Davidson, a) means that the act of Φing was caused in the right way by the agent's relevant desire and instrumental belief. It is caused, in Davidson's phrase, by the agent's 'primary reason' for Φing. In a later work like "Intending," Davidson modified his causalist account of intention in action to allow for present directed intention to function as a crucial causal factor in his analysis. But, his overall causalist perspective remained unchanged. However, no reason whatsoever had been given for expecting that the project of giving a causalist analysis of agent teleology will succeed.

In *The Intentionality of Human Action*, I went on to argue at length that the project will inevitably be unsuccessful. More recently, Scott Sehon, in his recent book *Teleological Realism*,[5] adds a range of important considerations to the case against the reductive project of causalism. Both of us have emphasized that states of wanting, desiring, and associated beliefs can cause all sorts of involuntary behavior, including behavior which might even promote, by sheer happenstance, the agent's desired ends. For this reason, causalist accounts do nothing to capture the specific point that, in intentional action, it is the agent herself who guides and controls the behavior toward the anticipated goal. (This is the problem of deviant causal chains.) In his essay, "What Happens When Someone Acts?" David Velleman offers a nice statement of the larger problem that confronts causalism. He says, "In a full-blooded action, an intention is formed by the agent himself, but not by his reasons for acting. Reasons affect his intention by influencing him to form it, but they thus affect his intention by affecting him first. And the agent moves his limbs in execution of his intention; his intention doesn't move his limbs by itself."[6] Now Velleman is himself an idiosyncratic causalist, and, as he goes on in his article to explain, he thinks that these worries can be

---

[4] p. 8.

[5] (Cambridge, MA: MIT Press), 2005.

[6] *The Possibility of Practical Reason* (Oxford: Oxford University Press, 2000). p 148. Velleman may mean to be stating a problem somewhat different than the one I have in mind, but his words capture my concern well.

dispelled. Obviously, I am much less sanguine. At the same time, there are, as I will explain in the last part of this article, a number of additional facets of understanding action that I did not adequately address.

In the intervening years, philosophers sympathetic to Davidson have developed arguments in support of a causalist approach and have constructed more elaborate and sophisticated causalist accounts of acting with a certain intention and of the reason explanations that are grounded upon this relation. Al Mele has been especially persistent and resourceful in defending such a causalist theory of action.[7] Unsurprisingly, my position on these matters at least has not budged, but I also have come to doubt that the relevant debates will reach an uncontroversial resolution. There will always be ways of trying to patch up defective versions of the causalist's analytic program.

In these remarks, I have focused rather narrowly on the specifics of a fundamental disagreement between Davidson and Anscombe about the explanatory force of reason explanations of action. Perhaps it is worth mentioning that I have long thought that the sort of primitive teleology that I discern in these explanations has a potentially attractive metaphysical feature. Let us go back briefly to explanations of biological states and processes in terms of their functions. Thus, for example, when we wonder why a spider intermittently emits a certain kind of protein loaded substance, we may, on one interpretation of the question, be asking about the function that these emissions have for the spider. The function here is roughly this. Spiders require a regular supply of material for spinning webs, and the protein substance provides them with the material that they need. They regularly employ the substance to satisfy that need. Naturally, there is also some kind of biochemical explanation of the causes of these emissions in the spider, and we expect there to be some broad alignment between the causal story and the function explanation. Nevertheless, we don't expect that these two kinds of explanation of the protein substance emissions are somehow in competition with one another. Explanations of both kinds are about the same kind of biological process, but each kind of explanation answers a significantly different 'why'-question about the process. There is no reason to imagine that, say, the causal explanation is in rivalry with the function expla-

---

[7] See especially, *Springs of Action* (New York, Oxford University Press, 1992)

nation, and there is no imminent danger that one will exclude the correctness of the other.

I suggested that the situation might be much the same in connection with teleological reason explanations of actions. No doubt there *are* causal explanations of the behavior that constitutes action. Neurophysiological studies of voluntary movement are one important source of causal accounts at a certain level of physical analysis, and there is no reason, in principal, why those accounts cannot be made indefinitely detailed and complete. Now explanations of actions in terms of the goals toward which they have been directed by the agent are not the same as function explanation of event types in biology, and the differences between the two sorts of teleological explanations engender complications in the issues at this point. Nevertheless, it has seemed credible to me and to others that reason explanations of intentional action and neurophysiological causal explanations of the same behavior need not stand in any exclusionary relation to one another. To repeat, I proposed that the explanations were dealing with the same events (the agent's behavior) but answered quite different questions about them.

On the other hand, if reason explanations *do* purport to give causal explanations of the actions in terms of the psychological states like desires, beliefs, and intentions, then there is a more serious problem about whether our commonsense framework for understanding agency might not simply be a kind of primitive rival to the more sophisticated causal analyses produced by the neural sciences. Probably, most philosophers have believed that the danger of a rivalry between the two accounts will be best deflected by some kind of identification of the psychological with the physical. Maybe this is so, but at least forty years of discussion has shown how difficult it is to frame a plausible version of the sort of substantive identification that would be needed, and philosophers have discovered how difficult it is to defend any particular version when it is have been stated in adequate detail. It has long seemed to me to be an attractive feature of my view that it avoided any direct commitment to such a program of psychophysical identifications.

Jaegwon Kim's well-known paper, "Mechanism, Purpose, and Explanatory Exclusion"[8] remains the classic dissection of the problems that arise concerning alternative explanations of the same

---

[8] *Philosophical Perspectives* 3 (1989), pp. 77-108.

phenomena. Sehon's *Teleological Realism* is an important recent discussion of these complicated topics, mixing metaphysics and methodology in an extremely illuminating fashion. Perhaps, it is worth mentioning two broad areas that deserve further investigation in this connection. First, many have supposed that the invocation of teleological explanations that are not reducible to causal explanations of a suitable type must represent a violation of a 'naturalistic' perspective on the world. But I have argued at some length that a significant range of explanations in the special physical sciences are not causal explanations either, at least not in the standard understanding of the concept. For instance, we can explain the wobbling behavior of a top loaded metal strut as the loaded system achieves stability by appealing to the equilibrium positions available to the loaded system and the fact that the settling into stability must satisfy a Law of Least Work. Second, the concept (or concepts) of 'causation' has long been a subject of philosophical inquiry, but it is my impression that there is still a good deal of sorting out that needs to be achieved. Inquiry in this domain is currently continuing in a lively and productive way.

Having said all this, I now think that many of my questions about reason explanations were framed too narrowly around a rather thin conception of explaining why an agent acted. What I have in mind is this. It is possible to know a reason for which an agent acted without understanding very much at all about why that reason was the reason for which he acted. Maybe I know that James went to church with the intention of pleasing his mother while feeling utterly perplexed as to why it was so important to him then to please his mother or about why he chose church attendance as a means of pleasing her. I can know this reason for which he acted while feeling that the action to be explained is still largely unintelligible to me. (Perhaps I have background knowledge that James dislikes his atheistic mother.) In some cases, I recognize that the agent Φed in order to Ψ, but I also know that he had a range of other options. He might have decided not to Ψ at all, or he might have selected a means other than Φing as a better route to his objective. Moreover, questions like this about why the agent Φed often have relatively clear answers that closer inquiry into the agent's situation will supply. Someone may explain to me why it was so important to him at the time that he should Ψ. Or they may explain why he preferred Φing as a way to Ψ over any other option that seemed open to him the relevant occasion. Or they may explain why, although his preferences didn't really favor

Φing, he could be weak or compulsive about Φing nonetheless.

In "Actions, Reasons, and Causes," Davidson was chiefly concerned with simple explanations of intentional action that were grounded upon the agent's primary reasons for acting, and I, in fact, followed him in this focus. Call these *"minimal* explanations" of a reason for which the agent acted. My present point is to emphasize that reason explanations of why an agent acts are often substantially more than minimal and that the range of explanatory strategies that are invoked in an extended elucidation is rather large and diverse. It seems to me that both the rudimentary causalism in Davidson's early work and the teleological alternative that I defended don't tell us much of anything about the character of the thicker dimensions of these more than minimal reason explanations. Are some or all of these more than minimal explanations teleological explanations of some kind? Or are they merely causal explanations that trace the chain of causes further down the causal chain? Or neither? Or both together? I think it would take a fair amount of further work to give any of these philosophical alternatives a usefully debatable sense.

In focusing too narrowly on the minimal reasons for which an agent acted, I was focusing on a basic, ubiquitous mode of agency, but it is not the sort of 'full-blooded' agency that Velleman evokes in the passage that I quoted above. If someone tosses a ball at my face, and I spontaneously catch it to protect myself, then I have acted with an obvious intention and there is thus an obvious reason why I acted. This action, however, was performed in the absence of any significant reflection on what I was to do. More full-blooded and interesting forms of behavior do arise out of more or less complicated kinds of practical reflection, and a reasonably enlightening explanation of why an agent acted seeks to reveal some of the determinative role of the practical reflection upon which the action depended. An agent engages in a piece of practical reasoning with the intention of settling upon a goal or objective which he will seek, in ensuing activity, to pursue. Of course, this stretch of practical reasoning will not, as a rule, be consciously rehearsed, but its structure and content will significantly define what a corresponding reason explanation of the action might purport to capture for us.

These considerations show, in my opinion, that practical reasoning to a chosen goal is an irreducibly teleological activity. Nevertheless, even if I am right about this point, it doesn't help much with the problem I am trying to raise at this juncture. The goal directed aspect of practical reasoning tells one very little about the structure and content of the implicit processing of practical considerations that a richer explanation of the action ought to illuminate. Various philosophers besides Velleman–Harry Frankfurt, Michael Bratman, Gary Watson, for example–have stressed the importance of more full-blooded modes of agency. I agree that these modes correspond to further dimensions of our more than minimal attempts to specify the reasons *why* an agent acted as he did. Corresponding to thinner and more full-blooded conceptions of agency, there are also thinner and more full-blooded explanations of the same deliberated action. I concentrated on the thinner forms of explanation, and consequently there are dimensions of our understanding of actions that my earlier account of reason explanation did not effectively engage. The contemporary literature on full-blooded agency and on practical reason has not particularly turned its attention to the implications of this research for the older debates about the nature of rationalizing explanations of action. However, as that omission comes to be rectified, then, I believe, the traditional questions will be transformed. The questions that will face us will undoubtedly be varied and messy, but there will be the possibility of genuine movement on some old questions that have tended to grow ossified and less fruitful in recent years.

About the Editors

Jesús H. Aguilar earned his Ph.D. in Philosophy from McGill University. He is an Assistant Professor of Philosophy at Rochester Institute of Technology. His research interests are in philosophy of action, philosophy of mind, philosophy of art, and Latin-American philosophy. He has published in *Dialectica*, *Philosophia*, *Human Studies*, *Variaciones Borges*, *Ergo*, and elsewhere.

Andrei A. Buckareff earned his Ph.D. in Philosophy from the University of Rochester. He is an Assistant Professor of Philosophy at Marist College. His research focuses on philosophy of action and related issues in epistemology, metaphysics, philosophy of mind, and philosophy of religion. He has published articles in *Canadian Journal of Philosophy*, *Dialogue*, *Journal of Philosophical Research*, *Philosophia*, *Philosophical Studies*, *Religious Studies*, and elsewhere.

About Philosophy of Action: 5 Questions

Broadly characterized, the philosophy of action encompasses a host of problems about the nature and scope of human action and agency, including, but not limited to, intention and intentional action, the ontology of action, reason-explanations of action, motivation and practical reason, free will and moral responsibility, mental agency, social action, controlling attitudes, *akrasia* and *enkrasia*, and many other issues. *Philosophy of Action: 5 Questions* is a collection of short interviews based on 5 questions presented to some of the most influential and prominent scholars in this philosophical field. We hear their views on philosophy of action, its aim, scope, use, the future, and how their work fits in these respects.

Index

agency, iii, iv, 1–3, 5–7, 9–14, 17–23, 25, 26, 28–30, 36, 37, 40, 45, 50–54, 59, 64, 67, 68, 70, 87–90, 98, 117, 119, 121–125, 127, 142, 156–165, 167, 170, 172–176, 178–180, 184, 194–196, 198–201, 203, 218, 219, 222–224, 226, 233–235, 239–244, 247–250, 261, 272–274, 277–281, 286, 289, 291, 292
agent-causation, 7, 15
Anscombe, Elizabeth, 1, 19, 23, 225, 247, 284–286, 288
Appiah, Kwame Anthony, 221
Aquinas, St. Thomas, 221
Aristotle, 66, 68, 129, 151, 183, 193, 273
Arminius, Jacobus, 203
attitudes, iii, 3, 9, 29, 48, 64, 84, 88, 104, 106–110, 176, 216–218, 225, 242, 247, 248, 254, 262–266, 270, 271
Audi, Robert, 183, 184
Austin, J. L., 101, 102, 114, 149, 153, 243
autonomy, 113, 114, 176, 180, 196, 202, 244, 278
Ayer, A. J., 99, 114, 223

Barth, Karl, 203, 218

belief, 3, 11, 18–20, 28, 45, 48, 49, 52, 59, 60, 62, 63, 68, 75, 76, 80, 87, 88, 106, 108, 109, 117, 126, 129, 130, 139, 143, 158–160, 200, 215, 217, 218, 220, 221, 224, 230, 241, 242, 247, 253, 259, 270, 287
Bennett, Jonathan, 141, 253, 259
Boethius, 155
Borges, Jorge Luis, 70
Bramhall, Bishop John, 100, 231
Bratman, Michael, 31, 248, 249, 252, 273, 292
Broome, John, 20, 250, 251
Burge, Tyler, 111, 115

Castañeda, Hector-Neri, 20
causal deviance, 8, 11, 12, 157
causal theory of action, 14, 262, 280
cause, 7, 8, 28, 39, 42, 47, 51, 55, 61, 102, 112, 120–124, 142, 144, 145, 147, 152, 175, 177, 185, 187–189, 193, 198, 204, 213, 214, 247, 273, 285, 287
chance, 60, 63, 100, 142, 150, 151, 231
Chisholm, Roderick, 8, 45–47, 53, 179

choice, 18, 19, 26, 27, 41, 47–56, 70, 105, 110, 141, 142, 176, 177, 180, 195, 196, 202, 211, 212, 221, 223, 272, 274
cognitive science, 28, 68, 138, 139, 255
compatibilism, 36, 63, 104, 106–108, 113, 116, 137, 163, 171, 180, 181, 203–205, 215, 230, 273, 281
consciousness, 1, 62, 87, 88, 98, 101, 102, 111, 112, 115, 116, 142–145, 147, 152–154, 185, 190, 193, 199, 230, 232–234, 242–244
control, 3, 5–7, 9, 10, 13, 25, 27, 33–35, 39–41, 48, 51, 53, 54, 66, 71–73, 89, 90, 94–97, 104, 107, 146–151, 153, 156, 157, 159, 163, 167, 175, 179, 180, 183, 184, 196, 198–202, 207–210, 213, 219, 222, 229, 235, 237–241, 244
counterfactuals, 32, 41, 92, 138, 172

Dancy, Jonathan, 49
Davidson, Donald, 2, 6, 7, 19, 20, 60, 67, 87, 119–121, 123, 127, 183, 184, 193, 221, 223, 247, 283–288, 291
decision, 18, 19, 25, 130, 139, 141, 142, 146, 147, 151, 152, 155, 158, 163, 164, 176, 185–190, 203, 212–214, 221–223, 226, 228, 271
deliberation, 25, 89, 141, 142, 146–148, 150, 151, 163, 174, 176, 196, 207–210, 218, 274, 281
Dennett, Daniel, 42, 115, 144, 153, 154, 179, 234, 242, 243
Descartes, René, 66, 102, 145
desire, 19, 20, 28, 48, 49, 55, 62, 66, 68, 82, 87–90, 93, 94, 96, 104, 105, 109, 113, 126, 129, 130, 133, 143, 159, 160, 163, 175, 184, 200, 201, 206–211, 222, 241, 242, 247, 248, 262, 287
determinism, 6, 7, 27, 29, 32–34, 39–42, 50, 54, 56, 57, 59, 60, 64, 67, 70, 71, 74, 77, 79, 81, 82, 99–117, 139, 142, 146, 148, 150, 155, 156, 162, 164, 167–176, 179–181, 197, 198, 203–205, 207, 210, 213, 216, 218, 219, 230, 254, 281
dispositions, 202, 277
doing, 19, 26, 62, 69, 71–76, 78–80, 89, 120–124, 126, 132–134, 148, 149, 151, 156, 157, 163, 172, 178, 186, 192, 206, 222–224, 234, 241, 242, 267, 269, 275, 276

emotion, 61–63, 66–68, 91–94, 96, 135, 240, 242
ethics, 10, 13, 28, 36, 60, 65, 66, 68, 76, 117, 160,

176, 181, 183, 191, 193, 200, 220, 225–227, 230, 232, 255, 278
evil, 31, 69, 81, 181, 182, 204, 220

Fischer, John Martin, 39, 54, 56, 57, 63, 70, 115, 147, 148, 153, 171, 175, 179, 180, 206, 219, 273, 276, 281
foreknowledge, divine, 33, 34, 41, 42, 168
Frankfurt Counterexamples, 32–34, 41, 42, 54–57, 71, 73, 75, 76, 148, 149, 154, 171–173, 211, 227
Frankfurt, Harry, 31, 32, 56, 148, 149, 154, 171–173, 179, 182, 206, 219, 220, 223, 227, 228, 231, 292
free action, 27, 37, 47, 59, 167, 172, 192, 193, 197, 273
free will, iii, 6, 7, 25–28, 31, 36–38, 45, 59–61, 63–67, 76, 81, 84, 85, 87, 98, 104, 115–117, 137–139, 153–155, 161–164, 166–173, 175–181, 184–186, 188, 189, 191–193, 196, 199, 202, 203, 205, 211, 215, 218–220, 227, 229–232, 253–257, 273–281
Frith, Chris, 235, 243

Gauthier, David, 223, 231
Gilbert, Margaret, 21, 249, 272

Ginet, Carl, 41, 115, 149, 154, 170, 172, 179, 211, 219
guidance, 33–35, 39, 147, 148, 175, 279, 286

Haji, Ishtiyaque, 175, 180
Hampshire, Stuart, 99, 115
hard determinism, 59
hard incompatibilism, 205, 212, 215–217, 220, 273
Harman, Gilbert, 20
Hart, Herbert L., 227, 231
Hobbes, Thomas, 100, 222, 223, 225, 231
Honderich, Ted, 115, 180, 215, 219
Hornsby, Jennifer, 127
Hume, David, 60, 66, 99, 129, 135, 197, 198, 206, 219, 226, 228, 273

identification, 110, 120, 239, 289
incompatibilism, 6, 42, 104, 106–109, 113, 116, 137, 173, 180, 205, 210–212, 215–217, 219, 220, 230, 273, 281
indeterminism, 7, 27, 60, 146, 148–152, 218
intending, 6, 20, 22, 147, 152, 157, 163, 239, 267, 287
intention, iii, 14, 19, 20, 22, 28, 36, 50, 52, 53, 56, 98, 106, 131, 142–145, 156, 158, 160, 186–191, 200, 201, 228, 233, 236, 238, 239, 241, 244, 247–251, 265, 266, 268–270, 284–288, 290, 291

intentional action, iii, 7, 8, 11, 14, 22, 129–131, 133, 136, 138, 142, 152, 192, 202, 222, 224, 225, 227, 275, 286, 287, 289, 291
intentionality, 87–89, 98, 138, 157, 199, 233, 244, 248, 263, 268, 270, 283, 287
irrationality (see also 'rationality' and 'weakness of will'), 69, 79, 80, 183, 184, 193

James, William, 4, 66, 243
Jeannerod, Marc, 235, 243
justification, 18, 68, 98, 101, 104, 107, 111, 113, 215, 216, 241, 249, 250, 266

Kane, Robert, 41, 48, 64, 65, 107, 116, 150, 154, 172, 180, 211, 212, 219, 276, 281
Kant, Immanuel, 59, 60, 68, 109, 113, 164, 253, 259
Kenny, Anthony, 109, 116
Kierkegaard, Soren, 129
Kim, Jaegwon, 289
Kolodny, Niko, 20

laws of nature, 27, 36, 70, 71, 165, 168, 171, 174, 197, 198, 210
Lewis, David, 8, 171, 180, 221, 223, 231
libertarianism, 45, 46, 50, 57, 63, 182, 212–215, 218, 220, 230, 273, 277

Libet, Benjamin, 102, 158, 185–191, 193, 194, 199
Locke, John, 32
Lowe, E. J., 109, 114, 117, 150, 154
luck, 129, 154, 162, 163, 184, 192, 193, 213, 219

Malle, Bertram, 129, 130, 138
Marx, Karl, 129
McKenna, Michael, 42, 148, 154, 180–182, 211, 220
Mele, Alfred, 28, 130, 138, 148, 150, 154, 172, 177, 181, 193, 194, 201, 213, 219, 288
mental action and agency, iii, 9, 11, 50, 51, 161, 222, 235, 237, 241, 242, 256
mental causation, 126, 142, 143, 145, 147, 152, 153, 159, 199
Mill, John Stewart, 59
motives, 66, 90, 204

Nagel, Thomas, 25, 26
necessity, 61, 68, 72, 114, 231
neuroscience, 22, 23, 37, 39, 64, 76, 103, 114, 115, 154, 177, 185, 191, 192, 199, 243, 278
Nielsen, T.I., 234, 235, 244
Nietzsche, Friedrich, 129, 135, 274

O'Connor, Timothy, 51–53, 181, 202, 213, 219
omniscience, divine, 31, 37

Peacocke, Christopher, 8
Pears, David, 184
Pereboom, Derk, 42, 55, 56, 117, 167, 173, 181,

213, 214, 216, 218–220, 276, 281
Perry, John, 239
physicalism, 10, 102, 112, 199
planning, 19–23, 25, 186, 249
Plato, 151, 183
possibility, 6, 8, 11, 12, 21, 33, 37, 41, 50, 54, 55, 57, 79, 90, 96, 106, 113, 124, 143, 151, 152, 184, 190, 198, 212, 249, 252, 275, 281, 292
power, 5, 47, 48, 52, 53, 71, 72, 105, 116, 142, 147, 186, 195, 202, 213, 228–230
practical reason(ing), iii, 9, 11, 20, 60, 63, 68–70, 77, 79, 81, 82, 84, 95, 96, 98, 160, 216, 217, 224, 225, 227–229, 248, 249, 267, 280, 291, 292
Prior, Arthur, 141, 154
psychology, iii, 12, 23, 28, 55, 64, 76, 77, 125, 126, 129, 130, 138, 145, 158, 183–185, 191–193, 199, 218, 221, 225, 230, 231, 243, 244, 255, 261, 271, 278, 281
Putnam, Hilary, 111, 117

rationality, 18, 20, 22, 23, 61, 62, 66, 68–70, 77, 79–81, 84, 87, 93, 154, 224, 226–228, 231, 244, 248, 250, 251, 265, 274
Ravizza, Mark, 33, 35, 39, 147, 153, 175, 179, 180, 206, 219
Raz, Joseph, 20
reactive attitudes, 29, 216–218
reduction, 7, 10, 144, 145, 160, 196, 240
Reid, Thomas, 47
responsibility, moral, iii, 2–4, 10, 12, 22, 25, 28–42, 54, 57, 63, 69, 70, 72, 82, 90, 99, 100, 106, 110, 138, 139, 149, 154, 156, 164, 167–169, 171–179, 192, 197, 205, 206, 208–213, 215, 216, 218, 226–228, 231, 253, 276–281
revisionism, 276, 281
Rorty, Amelie, 184
Roskies, Adina, 36, 39, 138, 139
Ryle, Gilbert, 256, 259

Scanlon, T.M., 25, 178, 181, 226, 232
Scheffler, Samuel, 278
Schleiermacher, Friedrich, 203, 205, 220
Schlick, Moritz, 104, 117
Schoeman, Ferdinand, 182, 216, 220
Searle, John, 102, 143–145, 151–154, 233, 244, 248
Sehon, Scott, 287, 290
self, 1, 4, 11, 17, 20–23, 26, 35, 46, 47, 55, 61, 62, 77, 96, 103, 113, 114, 124, 165, 179, 183, 184, 194, 195, 211, 216, 224, 227, 228, 230, 232, 235, 237, 239, 241–244, 255, 276, 279

self-knowledge, 19, 236, 239
Sellars, Wilfred, 165, 181
semi-compatibilism, 63, 108, 171
Smilansky, Saul, 215, 220
Solomon, Robert, 66
Spinoza, Benedict, 135, 205, 215, 220
Strawson, Galen, 117, 215, 220, 230, 259
Strawson, P. F., 42, 101, 106, 176, 216, 220

Taylor, Richard, 50
teleological explanation, 48, 50, 51, 242, 285
trying, 6, 54, 113, 122, 147, 150, 157, 178, 223, 269, 288, 291

van Inwagen, Peter, 34, 43, 50, 71, 117, 170, 172, 181, 197, 230, 232, 273
Velleman, J. David, 19, 20, 287, 291, 292
volition, 157, 158, 163, 164, 193, 204, 237–239, 241, 242, 244

Wallace, R. Jay, 42, 178, 182, 207, 220
Waller, Bruce, 215, 220
wants, 150, 206, 209, 226, 265, 284
Watson, Gary, 67, 176, 179, 182, 292
weakness of will (akrasia), iii, 60, 77, 90, 94, 160, 183, 184
Wegner, Daniel, 23, 143, 154, 185, 186, 194, 199
Widerker, David, 41, 148, 154, 172, 180–182, 211, 220
will, iii, iv, 6–8, 10, 12, 14, 15, 18–23, 25–28, 30, 31, 36–38, 41, 43, 45, 51, 52, 55–57, 59–61, 63–67, 69, 73–77, 80, 81, 83–85, 87, 88, 90–94, 96–98, 100, 102, 104, 115–117, 120, 121, 123, 125–127, 132, 135–139, 147, 153–155, 157, 158, 160–164, 166–173, 175–181, 183–194, 196–203, 205–207, 210, 211, 213, 215, 218–220, 222–224, 226–232, 234, 235, 238–240, 249, 251, 253–258, 261, 262, 264, 265, 267–271, 273–281, 283, 284, 287–292
Wittgenstein, Ludwig, 2, 129, 284

www.ingramcontent.com/pod-product-compliance
Lightning Source LLC
Chambersburg PA
CBHW021136230426
43667CB00005B/138